EUROPE, DEMOCRACY AND THE DISSOLUTION OF BRITAIN

Europe, Democracy and the Dissolution of Britain

An Essay on the Issue of Europe in UK Public Discourse

P. W. PRESTON

Dartmouth

Aldershot . Brookfield USA . Singapore . Sydney

© P. W. Preston, 1994

Published by
Dartmouth Publishing Company Limited
Gower House
Croft Road
Aldershot
Hants GU11 3HR
England

Dartmouth Publishing Company
Old Post Road
Brookfield
Vermont 05036
USA

British Library Cataloguing in Publication Data
Preston, P. W.
  Europe, Democracy and the Dissolution of
  Britain: Essay on the Issue of Europe in
  UK Public Discourse
  I. Title
  341.2422

Library of Congress Cataloging-in-Publication Data
Preston, P.W. (Peter Wallace), 1949-
    Europe, democracy, and the dissolution of Britain : an essay on
  the issue of Europe in UK public discourse / Peter W. Preston.
      p.   cm.
    Includes bibliographical references and index.
    ISBN 1-85521-519-5 : $57.95 (U.S. : est.)
    1. European federation–Public opinion. 2. Public opinion–Great
  Britain. 3. Great Britain–Politics and government–1979- 4. Great
  Britain–Foreign relations–1945-
  JN15.P685   1994
  940.55'9–dc20   94-11915
                                                              CIP

Printed in Great Britain by Ipswich Book Co. Ltd., Ipswich, Suffolk
ISBN 1 85521 519 5

Contents

Preface

As the Berlin Wall fell in the autumn of 1989 Europe witnessed the opening moves in an extraordinary sequence of changes to long familiar political patterns, and it is now clear that the entire post-Second World War political settlement in Europe has been overthrown. A confused period of reorganization has begun. In this new situation the drive for European unification will shape the politics of the UK throughout the 1990s. The challenges will involve not merely the detail of policy making at governmental level, the stuff of routine political conflict, but also the ways in which we think of ourselves as political and social agents. It is likely that the decade will see the first stages in a process which will entail the progressive reconstruction not only of familiar political debates but also our sense of ourselves as Britons.

The political classes of the UK have preferred to ignore the challenges posed by the developing reconstruction of Europe, and with it, Britain, and public discourse has been narrowly national and economistic. In the 1980s the general political stance of the Conservatives has been one of 'dual parasitism': economically on the EC understood as a free trade area, and politically on the USA via the special relationship within NATO. In the post-1989 period their stance in regard to European union has been one of 'dilute and delay' in the hope of remaking the EC as a loose free trade area. The Labour Party's deeply conservative labourist ethos has remained intact and with it their ingrained little Englander suspicion of Europe, and the system has continued to marginalize the contribution of other political parties. These essentially defensive stances are unlikely to prove adequate to the challenges of the 1990s.

In the end, however, it must be acknowledged that all these changes are driven by shifting patterns of structural power within the global system, and the 1990s are likely to see changes within UK economic, political, social and cultural patterns as the movement towards a united Europe continues. The key concerns for the UK polity during this period of complex change will be with the related tasks of Europeanization, modernization and democratization as the polity strives to catch-up and join-in with the patterns of life of mainland European Community partners.

This essay discusses the political-cultural structures of the UK with particular reference to the responses made by major political groups to the business of complex change in Europe, and more especially the pressure for European Community integration. The approach taken in the text is hermeneutic-critical and focuses on those historically occasioned cultural discourses whereby the people of the UK have variously understood themselves as political/social agents, and with reference to an ideal-typical model of social-democratic Europe considers the possibility that the externally generated pressures for change inside the UK might just prove overwhelming. In such an event the patterns of renewal would be likely to be far-reaching, and the possibility would emerge of the UK polity joining the European political-institutional and cultural mainstream.

I should note, finally, that I have called this piece of work an essay to indicate that the text is rather more speculative than the conventions of academic discourse usually allow, and I hope that readers will excuse those intellectual infelicities occasioned by my having taken the liberty of skating over some areas of pretty thin ice. The justification so far as I am concerned is threefold: firstly, against those who would disingenuously stress continuity we need to fix in place an appreciation of the scale of the changes of the period 1989-91; secondly, the issues addressed are likely to be central to political discourse through the 1990s; and thirdly, we might reasonably expect these matters to be dealt with more effectively when they are fully acknowledged in the public sphere.

Acknowledgements

This essay has taken shape over the last few years. The initial conversations in respect of the basic themes of the argument took place whilst I was Humboldt Fellow at the Sociology of Development Research Center of the University of Bielefeld, Germany, where I was the academic guest of Professor Hans-Dieter Evers. I am happy to record my thanks to Professor Evers and his colleagues, and to the officials of the Humboldt Foundation, for making my stay in Germany both useful and thoroughly enjoyable. Thereafter, the first draft was made in the small Yorkshire village of Melbourne, where my parents and neighbours helped me rediscover something of my 'roots', and the definitive text was prepared at the Department of Government of the University of Strathclyde, Scotland. An early synopsis of the text was read by David Judge who offered encouragement, and Dave Marsh kindly scanned the completed manuscript and offered useful comments, as did my four anonymous readers - my thanks to them. The final preparation of the manuscript has been accomplished in the early part of my Canon Fellowship at the Institute of Comparative Culture, Sophia University, Japan, and I am happy to record my thanks to my academic host Professor John Clammer, and to the officials of the Canon Foundation in Europe, for affording me the opportunity to work in Japan. The responsibility for the text is, of course, mine.

1 The pressures for change

Over the period 1989-1991 it became clear that the UK was bound up in a pattern of complex political-economic and cultural change that was remaking Europe. The early signals of these epochal movements were the visits to Germany made by George Bush and Mikhail Gorbachev in early 1989, with one marking a major realignment within the old alliance pattern of the West and the other the beginning of the end of the entire post-Second World War settlement. A few months later in Berlin matters were clarified not merely for the astonished and delighted immediate participants, those who danced on the wall in front of the Brandenburg Gate, but beyond that, thanks to the television networks, for a world audience. At that moment the political, cultural and intellectual world that we Europeans had inhabited for some forty-odd years changed beneath our feet. Of course in itself the opening of the inner-German border would not have had such a dramatic impact, but this event was the breach which opened up a flood of changes as a series of structural pressures came together, and came to a head.

Within the sphere of the Atlantic Alliance fissures had been opening up over the later years of the Reagan presidency, and the issue that finally occasioned a reconfiguration of established relationships was the Nato decision to look for a new short range nuclear weapons system to be based in Germany. As debate continued within the Nato alliance open conflict broke out between the British and the German governments: Mrs Thatcher insisted that the new weapons be deployed, and the government of Chancellor Kohl refused. At a meeting between George Bush and Helmut Kohl, in May 1989 at Mainz, the Americans deferred to the wishes of the

German government. At that point a major shift had been accomplished in the order of precedence within the Atlantic Alliance with the German government superseding the British. A circumstance that reflected changes in the relative economic power of the participants; with the USA now clearly entering a phase of long-term relative decline, Germany increasingly the dominant power in Europe, and the UK no longer able to persuade anyone that decline had not been the order of the day for decades.

Over roughly the same time period, from the mid-1980s to the latter years of the decade, discussions about the nature of the European Community had begun to take on a slightly new tone. In 1985 the Single European Act had been agreed at the Luxembourg Summit and this committed the community members to completing the single market by 1992. The whole matter had been presented initially in fairly straightforward business-economics terms; however as the detail of market-unification was pursued it became apparent that a much wider harmonization was implied in the commitments made in the act. By 1989 the original European Community ideal of federation was poised ready to be reanimated if circumstances allowed.

At this point it was evident that long established relationships, political-economic and diplomatic, within the West generally, and in Europe, were undergoing significant change. In the early months of 1989 recognition of these matters was relatively muted. Expectations seem to have been of change that was essentially more of the same, as the old familiar participants/issues repositioned themselves in a continuing game. However, to the changes within the Atlantic Alliance, and the slowly evolving dynamic of the European Community, a new element was added: Mikhail Gorbachev.

The reform processes within the USSR and the eastern block which centred on the notions of perestroika and glasnost constituted the third element in the growing pressure for extensive systemic change in Europe. It may well be the case that the results of Gorbachev's reform processes within the USSR were mixed, but it is clear beyond doubt that the opening to the West made by Gorbachev irrevocably changed relationships between East and West, and the post-Second World War system of blocks began to be dismantled. Of course there were further and yet more dramatic changes to come.

In November 1989 the pressures that were to sweep away the post-war settlement finally burst through the dam of received structures. On November 9, at the end of a confused press conference, the collapsing regime of the German Democratic Republic announced that the inner-German border was to be opened on the following weekend. We then had the pictures of Berliners dancing on the wall in front of the Brandenburg Gate: the unimaginable had happened, and during the autumn of 1989 a series of revolutions rippled through eastern Europe ending in spectacular and bloody fashion with Romania's Christmas revolution. The full extent of these changes was finally made clear via the August coup in Moscow and the December 1991 resignation of Gorbachev as the USSR dissolved itself into a clutch of new nationstates and a residual, and somewhat unstable looking, Commonwealth of Independent States.

This overt sequence of events overthrew the received wisdom and political certainties of forty years, and when it was complete all the participants were faced with the task of reading and reacting to the phase of complex change now so evidently underway. In the case of Western Europe it is clear that the sequence of changes of 1989-91 have received a rapid, coherent and dramatic response. This has taken the central form of a re-affirmation of the ideal of European unity which animated the founding of the European Community. In the wake of the events of 1989 the pressures for systemic change within Europe found expression in the programme for a federal European Community which moved beyond the Single Market, and which received explicit and troubled delineation at the Maastricht Summit of December 1991.

In the UK the reaction of the state-regime was one of dismay as their Atlanticist sense of their role in the world and their domestic legitimating ideology were undermined to be replaced by notions of European union. After an interregnum which lasted from April 1989 to December 1991, during which period the UK state clearly had no idea how to react, a new posture began to be discerned and at Maastricht it arguably found its first formulation. This was essentially a posture of 'dilute and delay', in the hope of arriving at what in effect would be a loose free trade area, as the programme of European union clearly threatened the position of the UK ruling groups who would be faced with democratizing an essentially pre-democratic oligarchic polity.

In this essay I discuss the political-cultural structures of the UK with particular reference to the responses made by major political groups to the business of complex change in Europe, and in particular to the programme for European Community integration. The analysis focuses on those historically occasioned readings of our circumstances with reference to which we in the United Kingdom have variously understood ourselves as political/social agents. In the text the opening trio of chapters consider the received political-cultural structures of the UK polity.

In chapter two I look at the way in which present day institutional, party-political, and ideational structures were established through the period of the development of capitalism in the UK. Certain basic elements of UK institutional arrangements trace back to the settlements made in the seventeenth century, and party political formations, along with much of our contemporary vocabulary of political thought, date from the late nineteenth century and the early years of this century. The upshot I take to be a patrician pre-democratic state coupled to an invented empire-nationalism of Britain, which finds formal expression, institutional and ideological, in the system of parliamentary liberal-democracy.

In chapter three the business of liberal-individualism, taken as one of the central features of UK political culture, is pursued and its expression in both formal and informal political discourse is noted. The argument is advanced that such individualism is theoretically incoherent and acts to lock the UK population into an emotivist culture.

A further discussion of received cultural structures is made in chapter four when postmodernist celebrations of the individual construction of life-styles via consumption in the market place are discussed. Against the proponents of postmodernist market-seduction the text advances the view that it would be better to speak in terms of a demobilized population routinely excluded from power in a system which both requires deference and permits protest.

In chapters five and six, attention turns from structures to agents: the major political parties and the configurations of economic and political forces which they represent. Thus chapter five considers the role of the Conservative Party in articulating the material interests of the right. The episode of the New Right is considered and with reference to current debates it is proposed that their 1980s political project can best be characterized as one of dual parasitism: politically on the USA, and economically on the European Community (understood by them as a free trade area). The problem for the UK right is that present changes in Europe, and the programme for a united European Community, threaten directly their political grip on the UK and thus their externally-focused economic interests. The only available strategy, and the one that seems to have been adopted post-Thatcher, is to dilute and delay moves towards a more unified Europe in the hope of arriving at what in effect would be merely a free-trade area. Relatedly, for the centre/left discussed in chapter six, the problem centrally involves both institutional reforms and the effective articulation of arguments relevant to the 1990s. In the case of the Labour Party, if we understand them to have been effectively coopted years ago by the established power holders agreeing to modest programmes of ameliorist welfare, then the problem is precisely that of suddenly having to deal with the possibility of reaffirming that modernist project to which their late nineteenth century style mass manual working class socialism nominally commits them. Most commentators seem to be of the opinion that the labour movement is deeply conservative. The scale of the organisational and intellectual changes needed is large and the difficulties of securing such changes cannot be underestimated. Similarly, for the other parts of the centre/left the problem is of effectively articulating a view in the context of a system that acts to marginalize their contribution.

In chapters seven and eight the text looks at contemporary structural change and agent responses, and considers the construction of new discourses adequate to emergent structures in Europe. Focusing directly on the dynamics of complex change in Europe and the reactions of groups within the UK polity, chapter seven analyses present debate in terms of its characteristic economism, nationalism, and short-sightedness. These responses amount to little more than strategies of denial and they are unlikely to suffice. Against the modesty of available reactions the text argues that present patterns of change in Europe are likely to override received UK structures and discourses and that groups within the UK simply have to fashion prospective responses. In chapter eight I offer a sketch of an analysis of complex change cast in terms of the core European social theoretic tradition. In broad terms this would involve detailing change in patterns of power, production and knowledge. Finally, in chapter nine, I present a summary review of the argument of the essay.

In conception this text is both interpretive and critical. It aims to deal with the political-cultural structures of the UK polity with particular reference to what seems to me to be an overwhelming likelihood of extensive and far-reaching changes being occasioned by the present dynamics of complex change in Europe. The specific machineries of interpretation derive largely from the humanist marxian tradition, and the lessons in respect of analysing complex change which flow from the post-Second World War career of Third World development theory. Relatedly the ethic affirmed in the essay is informed by the modernist project of the rational pursuit of formal and substantive democracy, and in discussing the situation of the UK the critical referent is an ideal-type compounded of this notion of democracy plus the practical example of northwestern European social-democracy. Reaffirming the modernist project opens up many prospects. In terms of the politics of the UK it gives us a route to the future: a chance to catch up and join in with the rest of Europe, which in many respects is developmentally far in advance of the UK.

2 The political-cultural systems of the UK

Introduction

There has been much work published recently which deals with the historical occasion of the establishment of the modern UK. Familiar structural features are traced back to particular historical episodes of conflict between classes within the context of the developing world capitalist system. I want to take note of this work so as to get some idea of how familiar political structures including institutions, parties, and sets of ideas, have been put in place. The theorists whom I have in mind would be the historians of 'British marxist history', and the political theorists and commentators associated with New Left Review.

The former group would include Christopher Hill, Edward Thompson, Rodney Hilton and Eric Hobsbawm, and Harvey Kaye[1] takes them to comprise a distinctive tradition within the broad field of marxist historiography in that they have: (i) tried to move away from an economistic notion of class, and from economic determinism; (ii) had a common historical problem in the issue of the overall rise of capitalism (that is, social change broadly); (iii) focused on the detail of the interaction of groups over time, a 'class struggle' focus; (iv) looked at the history of ordinary people, that is, 'history-from-below'; and (v) fed their work into UK political discourse. Amongst the later group I would mention Perry Anderson and Tom Nairn, whose work moves in similar areas of concern

---

[1] H. Kaye *The British Marxist Historians*, Cambridge, Polity, 1984

yet which has a more directly politically engaged character. In terms of the intentions of the theorists the shift is from scholarship towards political commentary[2]. There have been sharp exchanges between the two groups, in particular Thompson and Nairn/Anderson, but I see them as involved in rather different tasks. In this essay I am concerned with present changes in UK political thinking, and it is therefore the style of political commentary of Nairn/Anderson which will come to the fore.

Overall this chapter addresses two broad concerns: (i) the historical occasion and general character of the UK polity in the shift to the modern world; and (ii) the character of the extant traditions of political discourse lodged within this polity, both official ideologies and their reflection in common discourse.

The historical occasion and general character of the UK polity in the shift to the modern world

The broad intellectual and political contexts within which the arguments of Nairn and Anderson were first deployed have recently been reviewed by Anderson[3], who notes the influence of what was then the newly discovered work of Gramsci, and the desire of contributors to New Left Review to offer similarly general and politically critical discussions of the situation of the UK. Anderson notes that this work has continued in various ways over the last twenty-odd years, with Nairn looking to the rise and nature of nationstatehood in the shift to the modern world, and Anderson himself turning to the comparative and historical analysis of the European state-system. I will pursue these matters in the company of Nairn.

Nairn's strategy is intellectually reflexive, which is to say that he examines the sets of ideas through which we read the world as he presents the reading of the world which he supports. Thus in regard to the relationship of the material-economic dynamic of the modern world and the political/ideological structures of states and nations he first notes, following debates with Ernest Gellner[4], that the drive to the modern world demanded the political form of the sovereign state (a bounded juridical unit competitively interacting with other such units) which in turn demanded an appropriately mobilized population. Put crudely, the shift from politically

---

[2] Within the hermeneutic-critical tradition upon which I draw it is appropriate to consider both the conception of enquiry affirmed in the work of an author and the intentions to which the work is addressed. In this sort of fashion it is possible to speak of social theorizing comprising a loosely related diversity of discrete modes of social theoretic engagement. In this sense the work of Thompson et al on the one hand, and Nairn/Anderson on the other, represent different modes of engagement. See P.W. Preston *New Trends in Development Theory*, London, Routledge, 1985

[3] On this see the Foreword to P. Anderson *English Questions*, London, Verso, 1992

[4] E. Gellner *Thought and Change*, London, Weidenfeld, 1964; E. Gellner *Nations and Nationalism*, Oxford, Blackwell, 1983

decentralized agrarian feudalism to industrial capitalism required states which in turn required nations, and in the eighteenth century ruling groups promptly invented them. The result, in Nairn's view, is that through the eighteenth and nineteenth centuries Europeans came to inhabit worlds, real and cognitive, of interacting bounded nationstates, each with its nationalism. However, in the case of the UK the shift from agrarian feudalism to industrial capitalism was initiated prior to the episode of the eighteenth century Enlightenment with its republican democratic ideas. It is wrong, argues Nairn, to read the early developmental history of the UK in terms of democracy, nation, modernity and so on, when these ideas only entered political discourse after the UK's development trajectory had been given its preliminary expression. Overall, Nairn's argument, recently restated in his magisterial text *The Enchanted Glass*[5], is that the modern UK polity has moved through three phases, which together underpin its present form.

The phase of parliamentary absolutism

Phase one sees the establishment of parliamentary absolutism in the English Revolution of 1640-88 with freedom for the propertied as the system shifts economically from agrarian feudalism to agriculture-based mercantile capitalism. The earliest phase of the development history of the present day UK is, on Nairn's argument, pre-modern. The development project of liberal England in the seventeenth century did not look forward to the modern world as did the American and French Revolutions, rather it looked backwards to the city-state republicanism of Renaissance Venice, or of the seventeenth century Dutch Stadtholderate: oligarchic, hierarchical, and mercantile. Picking up the idea that the English Revolution was essentially pre-modern we find Nairn's characterization, which draws on Christopher Hill, is that although

> in certain ways anticipating subsequent modes of middle-class politicization and struggle, in others the English Revolution and its 1688 state-form remained firmly tied to the epoch of the Renaissance ... England permanently kept its structure of oligarchy...an aristocratic, family-based elite uniting landownership with large scale commerce and managing 'its' society as a cooptive estate[6].

And the political ideas drawn upon also came from this period: political rule 'by an enlightened caste imbued with (and legitimated by) all the wisdom of Classicism'[7].

---

[5] T. Nairn *The Enchanted Glass*, London, Radius, 1988

[6] ibid. pp. 151-2

[7] ibid. p. 152. See also L. Colley *Britons Forging the Nation 1707-1837*, London, Yale, 1992, especially chapter two on the role of merchant groups in forging the structure/discourse of 'Britain'. In particular she points to the popularity of the painter Canaletto who popularized pictures of London-as-Venice (p.62).

It is in this early-modern period so far as Nairn is concerned that the fundamental political-economic structure and political-cultural discourse of the UK was fixed in place. It has proved flexible and successful, and the polity was and remains pre-democratic. Says Nairn: 'It is the distinctive political coordinates of the early-modern that provide a definite historical location explaining both the half-modern and the unmistakably archaic aspects of twentieth century Britain'[8]. In Nairn's view the English Revolution established an oligarchy which deployed a central political myth, that of the crown-in-parliament. It was pre-democratic as the political changes had 'impacted on a world not yet ready, either theoretically or materially, for the lasting successor to Absolutism: popular sovereignty, with its implications of lower-order power and ethnicity, democracy and nationalism'[9]. The political discourse of contemporary Britain reaches back to this period. Nairn argues that the nature of the shift to the modern world accomplished by the UK created 'a pre-democratic class state distinct both from the Absolute Monarchies still dominating Europe and (later) from the lower-class, more emphatically bourgeois and nationalist regimes aimed at by revolutionaries in the spirit of 1776, 1789 and 1848'[10]. Overall what we have is a patrician reform-from-above, and the intellectual vehicle for theorizing this political process was provided by Hobbes and Locke with liberalism[11]: an intellectual tradition which continues to be influential. It is this developmental location that structures the UK and shows how the official ideology - that the UK is really a disguised republic - systematically misrepresents and misleads.

The phase of the invention of Britain

Phase two sees the incorporation of Scotland in 1707 and the invention of British nationalism. Linda Colley presents this structure/discourse of 'Britain' as a project both occasioned by long hostility to the mainland (especially religious conflict and war), and fuelled by the expectations of enhanced material wealth (in particular within the integrated UK market and via overseas trade and empire). After the trauma of the American rebellion the new UK empire was not English, but came to be inclusively

---

8 ibid. p.154

9 ibid. pp.163-4. On the monarchy see Colley *Britons* chapter five, and David Canadine 'The Context Performance and Meaning of Ritual: The British Monarchy and the Invention of Tradition, 1820-1977' in E. Hobsbawm and T. Ranger eds.*The Invention of Tradition*, Cambridge, Cambridge University Press

10 ibid.

11 See C. B. Macpherson *Democratic Theory*, Oxford, Oxford University Press, 1973. The gist of his critical work being that liberal-democracy is an untenable conflation of the traditions of liberalism and democracy. This sort of attempt to 'reach back' beyond liberalism to recover Aristotelian derived ideas of democracy also made by Habermas, Arendt and MacIntyre. Broadly, I follow their lead. A subtle contemporary review is made by R. Plant *Modern Political Thought*, Oxford, Blackwell, 1991

'British'[12]. All of this culminates in the period around the turn of the nineteenth century with the social and economic upheaval of the industrial revolution, the political shock of the republican democratic revolution in France coupled to the ideas of the Enlightenment, and the episode of war and the military defeat of Napoleon. It was the period of the British counter-revolution and with the defeat of Chartism at home, and competitor states in mainland Europe, the British landed ruling class joined with the commercial and industrial groups and consolidated their power.

Benedict Anderson[13], writing on the idea of nation, argues that the UK shifted to a modern-type nationstate comparatively late. The 'nationalism' was always an 'official nationalism', constructed and imposed from above. In the period 1790-1820 the UK political structure, and its discourse of sovereign-in-parliament and so on, were challenged by the thoroughgoing modernism of the French Enlightenment coupled to industrialization and inter-state warfare. Military victory and rapid industrialization presented the ruling oligarchy with a favourable context for modernization. It is this period that sees the invention of British-English nationalism; an invented tradition, a quasi-republic centred on the monarchy. Nairn argues that a crucial aspect of the success of the UK ruling class counter-revolution, in particular in regard to its invention of 'Britain', was the use of the monarchy. The Royal-National 'We' is invented and put in place within the developing political culture. Nairn points out that when the UK eventually responded to eighteenth century modernist republicanism, with its universalist notions of democracy and the celebration of reason (natural and social scientific), it did indeed invent a nationalism, however 'it was forged not only to express the general social conditions of modernity but (uniquely) also for the opposite motive: to pre-empt and politically arrest these conditions'[14].

With the defeat of the Chartist project notions of republican democracy tend to drop out of UK anti-system discourse. The period sees the making of the English working class as Thompson has established[15], but Nairn argues that it is a de-mobilized class. Against Marx and Engels who saw the rise of corresponding societies, unions, and so on, as a shift from political to social protest or revolutionary strategies, Nairn insists that this shift was evidence of political defeat[16], and he notes that 'one is forced to recognise

---

[12] Colley *Britons* chapters one, two and three. And we can note the Scottish Enlightenment theorizes a patrician reform-for-progress that was focused on an agricultural economic base swept away by industrial modernization. On this see D. Daiches et al. eds. *A Hotbed of Genius*, Edinburgh, Edinburgh University Press, 1986. Of course there is a wealth of material on this period and for a hermeneutic type treatment see A. MacIntyre *Whose Justice, Which Rationality?*, London, Duckworth, 1988

[13] B. Anderson *Imagined Communities*, London, Verso, 1983. The expression comes from Hugh Setton-Watson

[14] Nairn *Enchanted Glass* p.135

[15] E . P. Thompson *The Making of the English Working Class*, Harmondsworth, Penguin, 1976

[16] Nairn *Enchanted Glass* pp.203-8

the virtually total triumph of a conservative political order'[17]. In regard to the marxist tradition Nairn argues that Marx was right about capitalism and the dynamic of production but he was wrong about the UK polity fitting that model because, in fact, it was essentially a mercantile capitalist system[18]. Marx underestimated the importance of the political as against economic-social structural. And this is a point Nairn makes in respect of nationalism against Marx in his earlier *The Break up of Britain*[19]: the UK is seen not so much as an industrial-class state rather as a national-developmental one. The Crown served and continues to serve a quite particular form of capitalism: it is essentially driven by the accumulative dynamic of mercantilism rather than industrial production, hence 'the Crown-mystique is the spiritual breath of a specifically anachronistic and parasitical form of capitalist evolution: a form which though rooted in early-modern times was able to endure'[20].

It is this underlying form that enables Monarchism to survive:

> an early or pre-bourgeois revolution which installed Capital and Property in power long before an urban middle class had evolved sufficiently to become a national standard-bearer of modernity. Since capitalism 'triumphed' in that sense too soon, it found itself decisively locked into the early-modern forms of commercial and financial dominance: a chronic pre-modernity from which there was to be no developmental escape...A mercantile city-state economy had turned into super-Venice and even succeeded for a time in heading the mainstream of global development [21].

That essential core ran through the nineteenth century and the southeastern English 'grand bourgeoisie' remained an oligarchy in charge of an outward-looking economic-trading system: 'Its off-shore and commercial nature remained far more important than either its primitive industrialization or its late-Victorian parade of oversees possessions'[22]. This pattern of development has continued down to the present. Against theorists like Sidney Pollard[23] who urge an industrial strategy to counter national decline, Nairn points out that national decline, as diagnosed by Pollard et al, is perfectly compatible with continuing success for the ruling oligarchy. Indeed Pollard et al have a mistaken focus precisely because they take nationstatehood as given, but says Nairn,

> this Crown-and-Capital land is not really a nationstate: it is more accurately described as a Southern-lowland hegemonic bloc uniting an hereditary elite to the central processing unit of commercial and financial capital. For the latter the 'nation'

[17] ibid.

[18] ibid. p.245

[19] T. Nairn *The Break-Up of Britain*, London, New Left Books, 1977

[20] Nairn *Enchanted Glass* p.236

[21] ibid. p.239

[22] ibid.

[23] S. Pollard *The Wasting of the British Economy*, London, Croom Helm, 1982

has always been too small ... Had either nationstate economics or Republican nationalism ever emerged it would, of course, have signified ... the dominance of the North and industrial capital over exchange-value and trade [24].

In all this, Nairn[25] argues, the 'Crown' is the capstone of the system's ideological legitimation in British nationalism. In the UK a mythic past is celebrated to cover an increasingly backward present. Nairn argues that

British history since around 1800 is a slow and staged counter-revolution which for long retained the appearance of liberalism because so much of the political world was worse. As decline and failure have corroded this antique liberality the appearance has been shed, but in the same period the Monarchical glass of national identity has constantly brightened and extended its radiant appeal. Originally ... the myth of Monarchy was employed to build up national-popular identity ... a safely anti-Republican nationalism which would keep the spirit of democracy at bay ... Now the myth is amplified and diffused in order to rally this same identity, to preserve a national self-image (and the old power-reality it serves) against the greater tensions of a polity in disintegration [26].

The Crown overrides 'class' and it stands for a national-community. It always was a myth and now Nairn sees it collapsing[27].

The phase of a pre-democratic system in place

The period of the nineteenth century sees further class-defensive moves on the part of the ruling class with both significant social and political reforms and the promotion of empire-nationalism. As the UK continues to act as the metropolitan centre of a global network, and as its industrial sector reaches its apogee in the period before the First World War, the monarchy-nationalism is popularized. The essential political-economic and political-discourse structures of the UK stay the same, as the outward looking southeastern bourgeoisie continue to prosper whilst the metropolitan unit in total, the British Isles, enters a period of long and continuing decline. In this late nineteenth century period of reform and ruling class readjustment, the present shape of UK political discourse (the ideas, the groupings and the institutional vehicles) was fixed in place.

Nairn argues that the English Revolution put into power a landed-commercial bourgeoisie who understood themselves and their historical project in terms which harked back to Renaissance city-states, and in responding to the multiple-aspected challenges of the late eighteenth and early nineteenth century emergence of the modernist project they fixed in place an outward-looking mercantilist capitalism. Nairn argues that whilst political republicanism was broken along with the Chartists, the new

---

[24] Nairn *Enchanted Glass* p.243

[25] ibid. p.250

[26] ibid. p.215

[27] ibid. pp.371-77

industrial sector took a little longer to deal with. However, the trade-based south did triumph over the production-based north[28]. Nairn argues that the period of the late nineteenth century

> totemization of Queen Victoria coincided exactly with London's definitive take-over of provincial Britain and the fabrication of a High Imperialist variant of 'Greatness'. Until then the situation had been potentially quite different. Largely independent of Southern finance and culture, the lower orders of Britain's uplands and Northern river valleys had at least maintained a self-respecting presence [29].

On the European mainland powerful capitals reflected monarchical absolutism. In the UK there was a stronger provincial economy and society:

> This was true above all of social and political movements. Owing little or nothing to metropolitan influence, the public opinion they generated was usually anti-central, identifying London principally as the centre of Old Corruption and organised resistance to progress - the core of a slow counter-revolution in command of the State but not yet enjoying a hegemony of all social existence...But it was precisely these bourgeois and radical tendencies which were sat upon and suffocated by the great Monarchic revival towards the century's end [30].

London asserted its authority, and this was the authority (somewhat modified through being contested) of the southeastern trading bourgeoisie. British imperialism with its celebration of the monarchy revivified the old pre-modern ruling class, and thus the system survived even as nationstate began its long and continuing decline.

In Nairn's view the institutional and ideological structures of the UK polity were fixed in place by the closing years of the nineteenth century. An essentially pre-democratic liberal oligarchy had successfully absorbed the twin nineteenth century challenges of rapid industrialization and popular calls for democratization. As for the challenge posed by the Labour Party, Nairn argues that it never was democratic in either political-programme aspiration or internal organisation:

> Its key organisational nexus is not undemocratic but anti-democratic: the plebeian obverse of patrician familiarity, vehicled through a pseudo-proletarian rhetoric of 'unity'. What 'unity' in this castrate sense denotes is class solidarity minus formal democracy and individual rights - the totemic or anthropological allegiance of 'class', rather than the political transcendence of genuine class struggle [31].

Nairn takes the real 'working class' to have been formed, as Thompson[32] indicates, in class-struggle to secure republican democracy. However it was

---

[28] Arguments which recall Barrington Moore Jr *The Social Origins of Dictatorship and Democracy*, Boston, Beacon Press 1966

[29] Nairn *Enchanted Glass* p.280

[30] ibid. pp.280-1

[31] ibid. p.290

[32] Thompson *English Working Class*

defeated and thereafter it accommodated to its defeat (and was obliged to by the victors) with a subordination akin to 'social apartheid'[33]. Class antagonism in the UK on the part of the workers is not evidence of 'unconquerable will, but of acceptance'[34]. The institutions of the working class, unions say, were absorbed by the victorious system. Nairn argues that the UK came early to capitalism and it was an early form which as a result of the historical good fortune of rulers was fixed in place. Familiar class consciousness is thus consciousness of defeat: '"Class" is nothing but the ... congealed, scab-like, social memory of democratic defeat and containment, and of the rich culture of consolation evolved for and by the prisoners'[35].

The development experience of the UK

In a more general endpiece, which both attempts to locate various Western nationstates within the historical project of modernity, and to report on how far the overall project has advanced, Nairn suggests that it is arguably far earlier than the centre/left usually thinks. The American and French Revolutions presaged the disappearance of Europe's ancien regimes, but there has been nothing quick about this disappearance. Arno Mayer[36] argues that the First World War was precipitated by this refusal to leave the historical stage, and that the whole period from 1914 through to 1945 is to be seen as the process of the dissolution of Europe's old regimes. Nairn comments that capitalism and its associated bourgeois society 'have made their way into the historical mainstream far more hesitantly, unevenly and incompletely than either the prophets or the historians of the process have imagined'[37], and Nairn, like Mayer, thinks that in reality the old world of late feudalism did not just fade away in the nineteenth century, it responded actively: 'The Habsburgs, Hohenzollerns and Romanovs secured Absolutist domination of the European land-mass until 1917'[38]. When finally they collapsed it was not bourgeois democracy that came into its own, rather the ferocious reaction of European fascism which in turn was defeated only in 1945. It is only since the 1950s that anything like the nineteenth century centre/left theoretical picture of bourgeois capitalist democracy has made it into existence: 'In other words, the European Ancien Regime still isn't ancient, and its only just history'[39]. In this perspective the rather differently derived arguments of Jurgen Habermas, which will figure later in this text,

---

33 Nairn *Enchanted Glass* p.316
34 ibid.
35 ibid. p.321
36 A. Mayer *The Persistence of the Old Regime*, New York, Croom Helm, 1981
37 Nairn *Enchanted Glass* p.373
38 ibid. p.374
39 ibid.p.375

take on a sharper outline as the completion of the modernist project is taken to be a matter outstanding[40].

In the perspective offered by Nairn and Mayer the UK system doesn't look quite so odd. Archaic, yes, but then its immediate global system environs have only just modernized. Where once its patrician-democracy did look preferable to the Absolutisms and reaction of the European mainland, now it looks outmoded and the question is whether it will finally be modernized. Nairn clearly doubts it. A necessary condition of UK modernization is the pursuit of republican democracy, but Nairn thinks maybe the de-industrialization, coupled to labourist incapacity for relevant thinking, has taken things too far, and that the future of the UK will involve the further outward development of the southeastern bourgeoisie via their absorption into a 'larger European entity'[41] and the marginalization of the provinces.

Critical debates in respect of UK structures

There has been much attention paid by centre/left commentators to this matter of the historical occasion and resultant structure of the contemporary UK polity. Only the orthodox are sanguine, and here we find the 'official ideology' which celebrates the evolutionary development of liberal-democracy whilst acknowledging some post-empire problems of adjustment. The centre/left commentators seem to have it in common that they take the development trajectory of the UK to have been blocked or otherwise stymied: in place of a progressive political-economic dynamic they diagnose an ambiguous stasis, an absence of the broad advance anticipated in classic social theory and seemingly evident elsewhere, coupled to areas of apparent regression.

In Nairn's case he takes the UK to be a state-nation (not a nationstate in the modernist expectation) whose political-economy is essentially an outward-looking mercantile capitalism. This political-economic structure was in essentials put in place in the English Revolution, and although reformed in some particulars subsequently it retains to the present this archaic structure. And in turn this archaic political-economy has been legitimated via a quite particular ideology of demobilization, the Royal-British ideology of national-familyhood. The upshot being that political discourse in the UK is blocked from raising the issue of the completion of the modernist project, and this, thinks Nairn, is the precondition of an advance now irrefutably needed as the UK is left behind by the finally established bourgeois democracies of the mainland.

There is also a sub-debate to note here in respect of the Nairn/Anderson thesis which overlapped with wider arguments in regard to the use of structuralism, and which centred on the proper roles of theory and history

---

[40] J. Habermas *The Structural Transformation of the Public Sphere*, Cambridge, Polity, 1989
[41] Nairn *Enchanted Glass* p.391

in marxist analysis. Nairn/Anderson were attacked by Thompson and others and accused of stressing 'state' and 'ideology' in place of the real experience of class, and of relentlessly denigrating the culture of the UK in the light of a largely unacknowledged ideal-typical characterization of the French Revolution[42]. There was also a substantive issue between Nairn/Anderson, who saw the UK as dominated by a southeastern trading/commercial bourgeoisie, and the more orthodox left who stressed both the role of industrialists and the activity of the UK working classes. At this distance in time the debates seem rather over-stated. Nairn/Anderson might be weaker historians than Thompson, and the other British marxist historians, but as Anderson remarks the work of the theorists around New Left Review was an attempt to diagnose the nature of present day problems[43]. One could speak of different intellectual projects. Against the engaged critique of Anderson and Nairn, the historians with their attention to the detail of processes tend to see bad history, and whilst I too think scholarship must eschew deploying recipes Anderson and Nairn are not writing straightforward interpretive-scholarship, they are as Leys says trying to read history so as to illuminate today's political battles[44].

In a very similar fashion an illuminating critical commentary has recently been presented by Ellen Meiskins-Wood[45]. The author argues that historical reflection on these matters is quite often shaped by the 'bourgeois paradigm' which acts to read the French experience into that of everyone else. In a similar vein Colin Mooers speaks of a 'normative theory of bourgeois revolution'[46]. This paradigm affirms a shift from traditional to modern ordered by the conflict of aristocracy and bourgeoisie. Meiskins-Wood takes the view that Anderson-Nairn use this paradigm to argue that British capitalism is an 'early variant' and is now both deformed and developmentally stuck. The criteria for evaluating the British experience is thus a compound of (i) the bourgeois paradigm and (ii) the overall experience of mainland Europe. Against this line of analysis Meiskins-Wood argues after the example of Robert Brenner for the specificity of capitalism as an historically generated pattern of life. On this basis it can be granted that the UK version was indeed early but that, against Anderson and Nairn, it was also thoroughly expressed, and not somehow half-hearted. Yet once again the odd nature of this debate is revealed as Meiskins-Wood argues against the schematic/theoretical models of Anderson and Nairn whilst at the same time offering one of her own that is, moreover, politically much less focused as it reduces to a generalized affirmation of 'democracy'. However, for my purposes what is important is the idea which

---

[42] ibid.pp.378-81

[43] Anderson *English Questions*, see Foreword

[44] C. Leys *Politics in Britain: From Labourism to Thatcherism*, London, Verso, 1989, p.14

[45] E. Meiskens-Wood *The Pristince Culture of Capitalism*, London, Verso, 1991

[46] C. Mooers *The Making of Bourgeois Europe*, London, Verso, 1991

all these theorists share to the effect that UK political-economic structures have developed over the post-Civil War period to underpin a presently impotent political culture. A polity seemingly content with drift and decline.

Ralph Miliband[47] offers a similar characterization, arguing that the UK polity is a capitalist-democracy which allows that individuals and groups can have an impact whilst the system generally acts to demobilize opposition and block open debate. Miliband (like Nairn) cites Harold Laski and Keith Middlemas as two of the very few theorists who have addressed this issue of demobilization, or as Miliband puts it, containment. Miliband diagnoses parliamentarism as the key ruling class strategy of demobilization, and argues that it enshrines the electoral principle and thereby legitimates government and political system and that all political life comes to centre on parliament. The nineteenth century notion of democracy which is a rich and substantive ethic is seized by the parliamentary politicians and made their own, and this empties the ethic of its force. Miliband judges that the Labour Party was ever a parliamentary and constitutional party, and was never a threat to the status quo.

One comment on Miliband, which paradoxically is also true of Nairn, is that his text remains focused on the UK. There is no sense that change in the global system, or a wider European centre/left renaissance, might also evoke change in the UK. However, to be fair, both texts date from the early or mid-1980s and the phenomena of complex change in Europe has only become inescapably central for discussion of the UK post-1989. Nonetheless, other theorists have tried to link the experience of the UK to changes in the wider system: thus Leys[48] follows Nairn in looking at political-economic structure and associated political discourse and speaks, after Gramsci, of 'historical blocks' and the 'general crisis' where the historical block dissolves, and here Leys acknowledges the wider global-system contexts.

Colin Leys identifies two 'general crises' for the system ushered in by the English Revolution. The first was the late nineteenth century response to economic problems, foreign competitors, and the rise of the organised working class; and the upshot is the early twentieth century period of liberal-reform. It also sees the establishment of labourism. Overall, an episode of defensive reform in which the characteristics of the contemporary UK polity were fixed in place. And the second crisis came in the post-Second World War period with the failure of Wilson and then Heath to reform the productive base of the UK economy in the face of the new global patterns of productive activity. Following these failures comes Thatcher, who also fails. As the crisis continues the polity drifts in an authoritarian direction. Again, with Leys we have the theme of long term

---

[47] R.Miliband *Capitalist Democracy in Britain*, Oxford, Oxford University Press, 1982
[48] Leys *Politics in Britain*

decline and the strength/weakness of the system - strong enough to protect its power base against internal reform pressures, but too weak to stem this long term decline within the wider system.

National decline and agents of possible change

In his discussion of Leys-type 'decline arguments'[49], Nairn points out that the southeastern commercial financial and landowning bourgeoisie, the dominant ruling-class fraction, have been successful. Nairn points out that class success is perfectly compatible with national decline and argues that the southern bourgeoisie regard the UK generally as 'provinces' which are available for exploitation but not crucial to their world-system role. In this perspective all those diagnoses of decline which are cast, as in Leys and Pollard, in national terms are rather missing a crucial point: the ruling class is outward-looking and its success within the global system is perfectly compatible with the decline of the 'national unit'.

On this David Marquand[50] argues that in the late nineteenth century the UK political class locked itself into an intellectual-political and institutional posture that ensured relative economic decline. Unlike all other European nationstates the UK never became, or established, the sort of developmental state which was created in western Europe and theorized via social-democracy; instead we find celebrations of the market. At the root of the celebration of the market is the notion of possessive individualism, and the institutional political form of the Westminister model, whereby political life revolves around an essentially liberal minimum state which is organisationally and ideologically incapable of acting as an agent of development. What is needed, for Marquand, is decentralization and democratization as the basis for a dialogic-educative politics. But, Nairn might ask, how do we get to such a desirable situation? The ruling class is not declining, it adjusts, and the already secondary do the declining.

Pollard, with Keith Smith[51], sees relative decline and addresses it in national terms. Pollard identifies the post-Second World War period as one of precipitate decline and the root cause is identified as comprising a mix of City of London dominance of the economy (and this includes a 'contempt for production') and a ludicrous neo-classical economics which is accepted in the City and the Whitehall state-machine, and which routinely gets the story wrong. Pollard's diagnosis of neglect of production points to a developmental strategy. But, again, how are we to get to this position?

Clearly Nairn's arguments make problems for other centre/left critics of extant circumstances: thus Marquand's arguments for a 'new centre politics'

---

[49]There is of course a very large literature on 'UK decline', and this essay is a particular contribution to it, however for the more familiar material see A. Gamble *Britain in Decline: Economic Policy, Political Strategy and the British State*, Macmillan 1990

[50] D. Marquand *The Unprincipled Society*, London, Fontana, 1988

[51] K. Smith *The British Economic Crisis*, Harmondsworth, Penguin, 1987

look unhelpful; and Pollard/Smith with their arguments for a 'new improved labourism' look similarly rather besides the point. Likewise, Paul Hirst's[52] arguments for corporatism. It is not recipes that are needed but changes in power structures. At which point it might be noted that Nairn's arguments in regard to structurally occasioned stasis/decline recall quite strongly material related to the development experience of Third World countries, and the lessons of forty-years of development theorizing suggest that 'exhortation plus recipes' are no-use. Rather it is the dynamics of structural change that have to be illuminated and the possibilities for progressive agent response identified. Following Nairn, one can ask where are the sources of power which might change the present system-configuration?

There are really two points here: the first concerns the narrow issue of how to go about taking power from the extant ruling class so as to usher in a group with a developmentalist strategy (and here the issues of labourist incompetence and democratic deficits crop up); and the second relates to the way in which theorists focus on the UK-as-bounded-unit. It is not very sensible to read the UK political-economy, and hence political discourse, in those terms. Recalling Susan Strange's[53] text on international political-economy, we have to look at the position of the UK within the wider system of which it is an integral part. It seems to me that we must shift from seeing the UK as a bounded-unit interacting with other bounded-units, liberal-individualism writ large, and instead see the UK state as reading/controlling trans-state system flows so as to maximize the advantages, external and UK-internal, of the group in control. On the arguments of all the noted commentators the UK ruling class never has been focused on UK development in the past so why should it suddenly start now?

Nairn does begin to look for progressive agents. If the system is in decline then maybe Britain will 'break-up': the southeastern ruling group will go its own way, leaving the discarded provinces free to pick-up the modernist project once again. Christopher Harvie has recently argued that Scotish cultural traditions of community fit easily into the political model of a 'Europe of the regions'[54], but the southern ruling group shows no signs of giving up Scotland; indeed there are negative arguments for keeping control[55]. Relatedly, we could ask if it is possible to envision any reanimation of the modernist project being initiated by the Labour Party, but I rather think that Nairn has written them off. It is difficult to imagine such a commitment from the Labour Party, and as they continue to exhaust

---

[52] P. Hirst *After Thatcher*, London, Collins, 1989

[53] S. Strange *States and Markets*, London, Pinter, 1988

[54] C.Harvie *Cultural Weapons: Scotland and survival in a new Europe*, Edinburgh, Polygon, 1992

[55] Thus Chomsky argues that the USA fears the power of the 'good example' in Latin America and prefers dictators to nationalist-progressives. See N. Chomsky *Deterring Democracy*, London, Vintage, 1992

even as they incapacitate all centre/left political space it seems to me that we have to ask whether the project can be animated from the outside. And here it might be that the dynamics of European change will advance the modernist project. On this Will Hutton[56] has regularly identified mainland European social/Christian democracy as a 'Third Way' between Anglo-American liberal free-markets and the old eastern European command economies.

It seems to me that we should stop looking for agents-of-change within the UK. On the analysis of our commentators the ruling class is too entrenched and the centre/left, dominated by labourism[57], is both imaginatively and practically crippled. In considering exogeneous change it should be noted that the events of 1989-91 in Europe have changed the entire post-Second World War political game. In place of cold war stasis governed for the western part of the continent by the US ideology of Atlanticism, we now see a complex dynamic of change: (i) the EC is moving towards a more integrated political-economy (with the notion of federalism variously invoked); (ii) the EFTA periphery of the EC is rapidly moving to establish eventual membership; (iii) eastern Europe, freed by the Gorbachev-inspired revolutions from the decayed Brezhnev command system, is quickly embracing mainstream European ideas (although quite which ideas is open to debate); and (iv) the USSR/CIS is in process of both internal reform and bi-polar withdrawal. In all this the EC is the key. It provides the immediate political-economic structure within which the UK state must operate and, as John Palmer[58] suggests, its future shape is now being debated.

To conclude, it may be argued that the UK system is essentially pre-democratic and serves the interests of a southeastern trade and finance bourgeoisie, with the centre/left relatively powerless to effect change, a condition which has obtained for most of the twentieth century. At the same time it is also clear that change in the UK is needed to arrest long term relative decline, and, as Marquand puts it, a developmental state is needed. However there is no agent in view, except maybe the general programme of European Community unification.

The structure of contemporary UK political discourse

There is a wealth of material dealing with strategies for the analysis of cultural forms within the marxist tradition, and discussions of the relationship of structures, ideas, and actions are similarly extensive[59]. In

---

56 W. Hutton in numerous pieces in *The Guardian*, from mid-1989 onwards

57 See D. Marquand *The Progressive Dilemma*, London, Heineman, 1991

58 J. Palmer *Europe without America*, Oxford, Oxford University Press, 1987

59 See T. Eagleton *Ideology*, London, Verso, 1991 and G. Turner *British Cultural Studies*, London, Allen and Unwin, 1990. In brief three lines: the humanist marxists, the British marxist

this essay I am interested in the ways in which received political-economic structures have been read into the polity of the UK, both at the level of formal political institutions and discourses, and in the arena of ordinary life. This sphere of routine practical activity and interpretation mediates the relationship of structure and agency: it is the realm of Gramsci's hegemony, and a sphere of competition between the promulgators of differing sets of meanings.

Following the material of the opening section of this chapter, what I want to take from the structural analysis of Nairn, and others, is the idea that the overall structure of UK polity was fixed in place in the late nineteenth and early twentieth century. As Marquand would put it, there was a failure to achieve the political breakthrough which would have established a European-style developmental state[60]. Relatedly the late nineteenth and early twentieth century period of UK development experience saw the familiar structures of the polity fixed in place: the broad sets of ideas; the social groupings and their relationships to political life (patterns of social class); the institutional vehicles (formal political parties), and associated institutions (for example, unions). It is this pattern of structures and associated discourses which shapes our political experience of the present. The underlying form of this discourse has never been questioned: it survived the crisis of the First World War; it survived a crisis in the 1930s when it was rescued by Keynes; and it survived the crisis of the Second World War and the extensive social welfare reforms of the post-war period. Following Nairn's general example I will look at the following: (i) the official ideology of the UK and its extension in the common sense of the people; (ii) the strategies used by the state to ensure that the population remains within the cognitive ambit of the official ideology and its informal extension; and (iii) note an alternative set of ideas drawn from various characterizations of 'mainland social-democracy', and finish with a speculative note on some possible sources of change for UK political discourse.

The official ideology of the UK and its informal extension

The official ideology of the UK, the way in which the system presents itself, comprises a set of ideas which detail and celebrate the particularity of Britain. Against the claims of various political projects derived from cultural modernism the official ideology of the UK reads legitimacy out of

---

historians, and the formal strategy of structuralist work. In a cross cutting area it is mainly the first line which I use.

60 Marquand *Unprincipled*. These European 'developmental states' were not in their first expression bourgeois liberal democracies in Nairn's sense as these were not finally established until after the Second World War. Marquand and Nairn are running slightly different arguments: the former on political-economic development and the latter on political-cultural development.

the history of the country, or more specifically its ruling group. It is a non-ideological ideology which celebrates continuity and evolution, duty and obedience, and an accumulative ideal of prosperity. Nairn characterizes it thus: 'This spirit-essence will...be called 'Ukanian' ... the Geist or informing spirit of the UK...A cultivated instinct historically fostered to replace theory and principle, the feeling for Ukania is fed by palpable exemplifications ... uncontestable images of reassurance and guidance'[61]. The core of Ukania is the monarchy linked to an elaborate repertoire of myths exemplifying 'The Country', and it is clear that the elite are in charge for 'management remains in the hands of an essentially hereditary elite whose chief attribute is knowing how to manage: their 'secret' is knowing the secret'[62]. And what they know, the spirit of Ukania, is

> diffused from above downwards in a process of (occasionally antagonistic) familial articulation signposted by notions like 'fairness', 'decency', 'consensus', plural concessionary 'liberties', 'having one's say', 'tradition', and 'community' - rather than the humourless abstractions of 1776, 1789 and after: Popular Sovereignty, democracy, egalite and so on[63].

Nairn notes that this official ideology keeps Britain lodged within early-modern times, and he adds that it is 'a strategy of deep dissimulation'[64].

The official ideology comprises a core set of ideas: parliamentary sovereignty; representative democracy; the rule of law; constitutional monarchy; plus the rhetorical schema of 'liberal individualism', which is discussed later in this text. This set of ideas could also be taken, after Robert Redfield[65] as the UK polity's 'great tradition', that overarching set of ideas, expressed in particular concrete institutional arrangements and carried by the distinctive patterns of life of the elite, which legitimate and order extant social patterns. Against the great tradition a counter-tradition can be identified, a 'little tradition' belonging to the non-elite and expressing their patterns of life[66].

Many commentators have noted the social distance between elite and mass in the UK, and have looked to separate patterns of life amongst the classes. Clearly this was a theme of the early 'cultural studies' work of Richard

---

61 Nairn *Enchanted Glass* pp.93-4. The notion of 'Ukania' comes from Neal Ascherson who recycles an idea from Robert Musil parodying the Habsburg Empire with its diverse national groups and overblown central state. The term is often used by Scottish commentators looking at the contemporary UK.

62 ibid. p.97

63 ibid.

64 ibid. p.98

65 R. Redfield cited in J. Scott 'Protest and Profanation' (Parts 1 and 2) in *Theory and Society* 4.1, 4.2, 1977

66 Scott has pursued these issues in the context of peasant life in Southeast Asia and characterizes the relationship of the groups invoking these traditions as involving on the part of the weaker an always provisional negotiated submission.

Hoggart and Raymond Williams[67], and the continuing gulf in UK society has recently been reviewed by Jeremy Paxman[68] writing on the 'establishment' and making it quite clear that it comprises a network distinct from ordinary patterns of life.

On the matter of the great tradition, the quartet of ideas noted here have been discussed earlier in one way or another so I'll not pursue them at length, merely add a few notes and examples of the official ideology at work. Nairn's discussion of Royal-British nationalism offers many detailed instances of the ways in which people actually use the proffered ideological constructs in their ordinary everyday lives. Nairn's text is concerned with Royalty and he discusses, for example, the following: royal work; language-accent; garden parties; dogs; the Royal Family; and the like. All are ways in which the official ideology of Royal-British nationalism is translated into practice and 'consumed'. This same strategy could be followed for the other key elements of the official ideological package: here I will present notes to such an exercise in myth-dissolving.

Parliamentary sovereignty, representative democracy and the rule of law

In the established view the UK parliament is the seat of political power/authority in the UK. It is not popular sovereignty but is cast in terms of crown-in-parliament, the settlement of the English Revolution. It is an elite system. Not merely the vehicle of the southeastern trade-commerce ruling class but also, inevitably, an elite-ordered system: a 'mandarin' system with political power reserved for those on the inside. In popular parlance the establishment.

In respect of the extension of the official ideology into the sphere of political discourse, Marquand speaks of the 'Westminster model' as conditioning the way in which commentators approach these matters; it is, he adds, a very particular form of institutionalized power and authority. The model is a legacy of the nineteenth century, and is 'heavily influenced by the utilitarian individualism of Jeremy Bentham ...who thought that sovereignty was inherently unlimited ... that the Crown-in-Parliament must be absolutely and inalienably sovereign'[69]. Thus was political power/authority concentrated and protected against rival claims, from local or regional government, from supra-national bodies, or from codified bills of rights. The Westminster model was very flexible. It was sovereign and it could order its own affairs and thus it could absorb dissenting groups within its restrictedly tolerant orbit. Marquand[70] argues that the Westminster model suited the nineteenth century liberal market very well,

---

67 See Turner *Cultural Studies*

68 J. Paxman *Friends in High Places*, Harmondsworth, Penguin, 1990

69 Marquand *Unprincipled Society* p.9

70 ibid. chapter seven

but it is no use for a developmental state which requires, amongst other things, power sharing, and explicit central direction (and thus negotiated consent). Thus Marquand diagnoses the core political-institutional machineries of Ukania as deficient for development.

Marquand discusses a slow collapse in confidence in respect of the Westminster system in the wake of the shift of the state to an interventionist role in the 1960s. Following Keith Middlemas[71] he suggests that a long-established system-preference for political stability, even at the cost of economic growth, was fatally disturbed and that once the mystique of the Westminster model was weakened, as it was by failure to secure such economic growth, it rather tended to dissolve away and we are left with a strong and extensive state-system capped by a 'club government' whose inherited authority is seemingly waning.

Parliamentary sovereignty is acknowledged in ordinary speech as an echo or repeat of the official ideology. Thus parliament is recognised and acknowledged, but in a distinctly pragmatic/cynical sort of way. It is seen as a centre of power but is often simultaneously seen as ridiculous: (i) it is a centre of power but it is treated as theatre, a spectacle, to be viewed from the outside, a place that belongs not to 'us' but definitely to 'them'; (ii) it is often taken as ridiculous, as a bear-garden (and television/radio have made this worse), undisciplined, a source of endless amusement for newspaper commentators operating in facetious, or impudent, or irreverent mode - always a style of the relatively powerless; yet (iii) it is also a source of pride - the UK House of Commons is the 'mother of parliaments' in official ideology. Overall one engages with parliament via petitioning or protesting - both are the activities of subjects not citizens and they are likely to be futile anyway.

Turning to the issue of representative democracy in political theory we find that this is contrasted with varieties of participatory democracy whereby the population of a country is routinely and extensively involved in societal decision making. Representative democracy is the political mechanism of English liberalism. David Held[72] characterizes English liberalism as follows: (i) citizens are seen as in need of protection from governors, and each other, thus the role of the state is to protect individual persons and their property; (ii) regular elections enable the sovereign people to choose from competing groupings their representatives; (iii) the state machine is constructed with separation of powers to block any concentration of power; (iv) the system affirms a notion of the rule of law, formal and public statements of agreed rules/contracts, within which individuals can act; and (v) the sphere of state action is circumscribed, state and civil society are in principle separate. In the UK, we may note, bearing in mind both Held's formal model and Nairn's characterization, that we

---

71 K . Middlemas *The Politics of Industrial Society*, London, Andre Deutsche, 1979
72 D. Held *Models of Democracy*, Cambridge, Polity, 1987

have some way to go before we actually establish a liberal political system. The involvement of the mass of the population is reduced as noted above to petitioning, protesting and participating in what Max Weber called 'plebiscitary democracy' via periodic elections.

On this business of the extension of the official ideology into political discourse, Miliband[73] argues that in the UK system parliament plays a central role in that it enshrines the electoral principle and thereby legitimates government and political system. Miliband argues that the UK system, as it has developed since the Second Reform Act of 1867 is not democratic, rather it is capitalist-democratic and whilst individuals and groups can impact upon the system its primary role is one of demobilization. All official life comes to centre on parliament and all extra-parliamentary activity is de-legitimated.

Miliband notes that a stable polity requires that the under-class acquiesce and points out that the Labour Party and trades unions have lent their support to the UK's system of capitalist-democracy and have thus been effective agents of containment. The political philosophy of the labour movement has rarely advanced beyond a rather feeble fabianism, which like the system generally is disposed to elite ordered reform and top-down planning. More broadly, the spread of opinion-makers, the media and intellectuals, have not shown any great independence and the system, with its extensive machineries of control (civil servants, police, armed forces, judiciary, monarchy), has absorbed critics and smoothed over global-system occasioned disturbances and maintained a significant measure of stability. Indeed Miliband, writing in the early 1980s, finds no very obvious grounds for anticipating change, except maybe a drift towards a more openly expressed authoritiarianism.

Yet, more optimistically, the matter of UK's political institutions and culture has been debated over recent years, and Stuart Wier[74], reviewing the first year of Charter 88's activities, notes how the issue of constitutional reform has moved up the political agenda. On the same matter and indicating both how there is a cultural and institutional aspect to all this, Hirst[75] looks to institutional lines of reform of representative democracy, a position of both dissent and agreement with centre/left critics. Corporatist, pluralist, and 'associational socialist' reform strategies are considered, and all three, with latter pair stressed, are commended. Hirst's dissent centres so far as I can see, on his view of 'representative democracy': he sees a genuinely legitimating system/mechanism whilst others see a strategy of demobilization.

Finally, looking to the matter of the rule of law, we have a part of the liberal-democratic package where in theory the judiciary is independent of

[73] Miliband *Capitalist Democracy*
[74] S. Wier in *New Statesman and Society* 1 December 1989
[75] P. Hirst in *New Statesman and Society* 19 October 1990

particular groupings or individuals and its decisions are binding on all. In the political philosophical tradition of liberalism, recalling Held's analysis, the rule of law serves the crucial function of establishing an agreed and legitimate framework of rules whereby sovereign individuals can contractually order their affairs[76]. The body of agreed rules must be independent of the interests of both particular groups and the state. In the official discourse of the UK polity the body of agree laws, and the institutions which are the vehicle of that law, are read in these liberal terms. However, K.D. Ewing and C.A. Gearty[77] in a recent critical discussion suggest that the official reading of these matters is seriously awry, and whilst noting that up until as recently as the 1960s there was confidence in the system they identify a subsequent rapid and severe collapse. Reviewing in brief fashion the judicial system of the UK they point to a slow decline in the judicial independence established in the late seventeenth century as the crown and parliament lost power to the executive and note that the 'lack of any real constraints on the executive branch has led to a crisis of overgovernability'[78]: governments can make law with little effective check (unlike either the USA or mainland Europe). Further the power to make key judicial appointments lies with the executive. In regard to civil rights Ewing and Gearty identify a particular failing on the part of the UK system as civil rights are nowhere positively defined, instead they are merely a residue: 'Freedom is not something that can be asserted in opposition to law; it is the residue of conduct permitted in the sense that no statute or common-law rule prohibits it'[79].

Ewing and Gearty then go on to review a series of issues related to civil rights and in doing so illuminate not only the weak status of such 'rights' but also the growing power of the state-machine. In turn they consider: (i) the extension of police powers, where they find that these extensions have gone along with increasing public unease and half-hearted and incoherent attempts at regulation via self-regulation; (ii) the interception of communications, where they look at telephone taps, and identify a state-practice recently forced into the open but not yet subject to any real accountability; (iii) the matter of public order, where they note that the authorities have wide powers and discretions and that police and courts have been quite ready to extend the reach of the law against minority groups, and where in respect of Northern Ireland they note the dissemulating use of the judicial machine as a cover for the state's counter-insurgency activities; and (iv) the extent of the national security state, where they note only a slow shift from executive discretion towards regulated activity. Ewing and Gearty conclude that it should 'be clear that civil liberties in Britain are in a

---

[76] See Plant *Modern Political Thought* for an exhaustive review of the liberal search for such a body of formal rules - Plant concludes that the search is hopeless.

[77] K. D. Ewing and C. A. Gearty *Freedom under Thatcher*, Oxford, Oxford University Press, 1990

[78] ibid. p.6

[79] ibid.p.9

state of crisis'[80]. They go on to add that the 'major source of the problem ... is a political system which has allowed the concentration of power in the hands of the executive'[81], and rejecting as palliatives those solutions which call for more parliamentary scrutiny, or a human rights commission, or a bill of rights, they insist that the 'need is for major surgery to the body politic'[82] in order in effect to democratize the system, yet the authors are pessimistic and end by remarking that 'there never has been a democratic culture in England'[83].

In the UK common discourse the idea of the rule of law is accepted, however, as noted, lately there has been some scepticism about the extent to which extant institutions and post-holders do manage to secure the rule of law in practice: the police are now seen as occasionally or routinely dishonest and incompetent; the judiciary are now seen as occasionally or routinely 'out of touch'; and the law itself is doubted, thus, 'one law for the rich and one for the poor'. But all this scepticism seems to be inchoate.

Constitutional monarchy and the notions of civility and individualism

In conventional terms the sovereign authority in the UK is that of 'crown in parliament', so the crown is crucial for the UK system. It is called a constitutional monarchy as the crown takes a somewhat indirect practical role, and a colossal ideological role that is all too direct. Given the extensive role of the monarchy the 'constitutional' label is rather misleading as it makes it sound benign. All this has been addressed by Nairn who offers, in the opening section of his *The Enchanted Glass,* an ethnography of contemporary UK polity. The start of the analysis is the matter of the great popularity of the monarchy, which is both continuing and deep. Nairn notes that 'Britain's Windsors are like an interface between two worlds, the mundane one and some vaster national-spiritual sphere associated with mass adulation, the past, the State, and familial morality'[84].

Unpacking this mystery requires looking behind the surface to discover just what roles, and how, the monarch plays in the lives of contemporary Britons, and Nairn takes note of the vast industry of publishing that feeds off the Royals, and details its character: the stress is on the personalities of the Royals and the directness of the revelations made, and thus the intimacy with the readers achieved. The persons of the Royals and the institution which they exemplify fuse in a popular fashion that offers the intimately-known Royals as a model for the UK: the ideology offers, or constitutes an aspect of, an identity.

---

[80] ibid. p.225
[81] ibid.
[82] ibid. p.275
[83] ibid.
[84] Nairn *Enchanted Glass* p.27

The identity offered by the Royals links directly to those more familiar identities of class. Nairn notes that whilst the 'Monarchy may be relayed to a British mass audience through an endless strip-cartoon of jokes, scandals, smut and Schmalz, from which the 'idea of Britain' seems remote ...[it provides] ... the structure of authority which defines other speech, conduct and people as ...merely those of a class or region'[85]. He continues against those who would dismiss any concern for culture understood in this way, that in fact social manners express 'the deeper structures of society and state. All societies and States rely on such social customs and concrete verbal and body languages in reproducing themselves'[86]. In the case of the UK a peculiarly archaic pattern of manners, which celebrates the division of society into elite and mass, also serves to provide an overarching mechanism of unity: 'The glamour of Royalty and the neurosis of 'class' are two sides of the single coin of British backwardness'[87].

In Nairn's view the monarchy, the institutional character of the state, and the present popular understanding of these matters come together to form a cultural construct which he dubs the 'spirit kingdom of Ukania'; the ethnographic object of his subsequent enquiry, and the cultural formation which must be transcended if the UK is to shift to the modern world. Popular monarchy is thus the ideological cap-stone of the present pre-modern UK polity[88].

Following Nairn the key notions of the official ideology of the UK polity in their informal extension, could be taken to come together in the notion of civility. In its UK form this would embrace: reasonableness, the preference for understated political and social life; decency, the preference for acquiescence in received common opinion and action; and moderation, the preference for limited appetites, demands, and consumption. It is important to be clear that this familiar pattern of ideas cannot be equated with the mainland notion of the public sphere, that area of routine citizen political engagement, and nor can it be equated with the notion of civil society, the sphere of private economic activity. In the UK the habits of civility are expressed in a restrictedly democratic political environment: the population is demobilized and all that's left is useless deference or equally useless protest[89].

The curious status of the complex of social manners which I have summed as 'civility' can be underscored, and their limitations made clear, by turning to another key notion in the routine life of the UK population, that of individualism. The idea of individualism, following the informal expression of the political philosophical theory of liberalism, affirms the ontological

---

[85] ibid. p.61

[86] ibid. p.62

[87] ibid.

[88] See C. Hitchens *The Monarchy: a critique of Britain's favourite fetish*, London, Chatto, 1990

[89] A. MacIntyre *After Virtue*, London, Duckworth, 1981

priority of the person. Informally, there are only individuals, and thereafter there are those institutions which individuals freely contract, and finally there is the generality of individuals, the mass. Each individual confronts the social world thus understood as a realm of potential gain and loss, with other individuals as potential allies or opponents.

It is clear that the notion of individualism is deeply lodged within UK common culture, nonetheless there is a tension in this pairing of individualism and civility and the relationship of individual to collectivity within the sphere of UK political culture has been discussed on many occasions: it was a significant element of that late nineteenth and early twentieth century set of debates which issued in the outline of the received structures which we inhabit[90]. The political-cultural tension is resolved in the UK public sphere with the social styles of reasonableness, decency and moderation. In the UK individuals are free to defer, to acquiesce, to conform; and the notion of community, the sphere of collectivity, appears only as an approved realm of self-help and ritual display (community centres, local sports teams, village fetes, and so on).

Machineries of universe maintenance

The focus of our attention now moves to the strategies used by the state and political class to ensure that the population remains within the cognitive ambit of the official ideology. Recalling Alasdair MacIntyre[91] on Stalinism, the ideology promulgated by a ruling group can be open to inspection or protected. MacIntyre analyses Stalinism as an ideology of industrialization-presented-as-democratization, which used show trials as a means to keep the ideological circle closed. Once on the inside it all did make sense. In regard to polities the open-ness or closed-ness of their public discourse is thus a key question.

The core of the Habermasian project of political reform is the democratization of societal decision making. The rejection of the strategy used by government, parastatal and private market organisations whereby decision making is defined as technical and thus necessarily out of the proper sphere of democratic discourse and accountability. The Habermasian political project entails the broad affirmation of democratization: citizenship requires participation, and this requires rejection of spurious claims in regard to the technical quality of certain discourses. The

---

[90] See for example: S. Collini *Liberalism and Sociology: L T Hobhouse and Political Argument in England 1880-1914*, Cambridge, Cambridge University Press, 1979; A.K. Dasgupta *Epochs in Economic Theory*, Oxford, Blackwell, 1985; P. Abrams *The Origins of British Sociology*, Chicago, Chicago University Press, 1986; and P. Scott *Knowledge and Nation*, Edinburgh, Edinburgh University Press, 1990 chapter two.

[91] The expression 'universe maintenance' I take from P. Berger and T. Luckman *The Social Construction of Reality*, Harmondsworth, Penguin, 1976. The example is from A. MacIntyre 'A mistake about causality in social science' in P. Laslett and W.G. Runciman eds. *Politics, Philosophy and Society Series 2*, Oxford, Blackwell, 1962

language-carried minimum democratic ethic of discourse (with equality of contribution and neutral argument-quality resolution) provides the evaluative criteria against which present social arrangements can be characterized. The ethical-political project looks to open dialogue, and any practical-political programme will have to judge given circumstances.

Set against the model of open discourse presented by Habermas it is easy to see the routine of secrecy practiced by the UK state/government. Generally political and administrative decisions are made within the state apparatus, perhaps after 'appropriate consultation', and thereafter announced. Thus, in the 1980s: the decision to run down the steel industry; the decision to run down the coal industry; the decision to embark on privatization; and the decision to split up the NHS into levels of service. Such examples could of course be multiplied. More formally, on government secrecy Clive Ponting has written that the 'extent and nature of official secrecy is the missing ingredient from most historical discussions of modern Britain ... Britain has one of the most extensive systems to control the flow of official information of any Western democracy'[92].

On the question of the repression/absorption of dissent in the UK we can note that there are a spread of familiar strategies: the institutional bases of possible dissent can be repressed (for example, the abolition of GLC, or attacks on Trades Unions); the institutional bases of possible dissent can be undermined (for example, routine attacks on local government); and institutionally based semi-independent groups can be pressured (for example, the legal, medical, and academic professions). In a similar way we could note that dissenting groups can be coopted/absorbed (for example, the race relations industry, or the pressure for equal opportunities for women); that dissenting groups can be demonized/marginalized (for example left groups such as Militant, or CND, or environmental pressure groups, or in the1989 Euro-election the Green Party with its 18% support and no seats); and that deprived groups can be stygmatized/disregarded (thus the poor and welfare users).

If we take note of the actual discourse of public political life in the UK, what those in authority say, then here we find routine evasion. It is evident in the manipulation of statistics (which is arguably superficial if damaging); in the manipulation of argument (which is the familiar 'slippery talk' of politicians), again damaging on any discourse-model of democracy; and increasingly evident it seems the strategy of making blunt denials of reality in favour of convenient untruths. In this last case, arguably the fullest expression of what J.K. Galbraith[93] calls the 'institutional truth', the sets of ideas to which an organisation is committed, we discover straightforward misrepresentation. Routine use of 'institutional truths' and 'convenient lies' destroys the very language of political discourse. Overall, we can

---

92 C. Ponting *Secrecy in Britain*, Oxford, Blackwell, 1990 p.1

93 J. K . Galbraith in *The Guardian* 28 July 1989

summarize by saying that the UK state-regime makes routine use of a battery of techniques of demobilization which are designed to keep the population safely within approved cognitive boundaries.

European social democracy

Marquand[94] argues that there is a particular intellectual-political legacy to the English Revolution. The UK political class, which apparently responded successfully to the industrial revolution, has proved unable to deal with the subsequent changes in their global-system circumstances. In the late nineteenth century, argues Marquand, the UK political class effectively locked itself into an intellectual-political-institutional posture that ensured relative economic decline. In sharp contrast the Germans, Americans, Japanese, and northwestern Europeans variously managed to secure extensive development. In place of the UK political class' celebration of the market they established the political, institutional and cultural bases of developmental states. What Marquand seems to have in mind when he speaks of developmental states is European social-democracy, understood as a political project informed by the modernist project. In the late nineteenth century the UK political class choked-off such a political project.

Anderson pursues these matters, noting first that 'The single market of 1992, and the impetus towards federal institutions beyond it, will constitute the critical new dimension of British politics'[95]. From this context Anderson picks out the idea of social-democracy which he characterizes as a union-based working class movement within northwestern Europe which emerged in the late nineteenth century in those countries which had industrialized early: England, Germany, Belgium, plus Austria, Scandinavia and The Netherlands as a privileged periphery. Anderson notes that only in the UK in the pre-First World War period was there no formal social-democratic party. After the First World War he sees these parties as having their first chance in government yet being overtaken by the depression period of the 1930s. It was not until the aftermath of the Second World War that northwest European social-democracy, with its technical apparatus of Keynesianism, gained its real political chance, and whilst the tide ebbed somewhat in the 1950s the programme's apogee came in the mid-1970s. Overall, these parties were the beneficiaries of the post-war 'long boom' and in Sweden and Austria the linkage of trade-union based party and economic success was fixed in place. This was not the case elsewhere and when the 'long boom' came to an end in oil crises and inflation the inability of Keynesian theorized social-democracy to make effective reply opened the way to the largely Anglo-American New Right.

---

94 Marquand *Unprincipled Society*
95 Anderson *English Questions* p.307

Anderson goes on to take note of the experience of southern Europe, and traces the route out of autocracy via ideologies of eurocommunism to the 1980s spread of social-democratic regimes in Spain, Portugal and Greece. The story here is different and the success of these governments, which looked to the model of the northwest European social-democratic countries, is best read as the establishment of liberal-democratic parliamentarism rather than classical social-democratic social and economic success. In the period of the 1980s, that is after the 'long boom', the global system did not offer such a favourable economic environment[96].

Anderson thus sees a distinctive political-cultural tradition, and associated politics, which can claim some significant success in shaping contemporary European polities. Aspects of social-democracy might be these: citizenship, there is routine and acknowledged membership of society in contrast to the UK situation of elite/mass; the public sphere, there is a realm of citizen participation in political decision making in contrast to the UK where the elite rule and the mass are passive/demobilized; and civil society, there is a realm of private and family activity-in-community in contrast to UK tendency to privatized consumption[97].

In this context Kenneth Morgan[98] looks at the post-Second World War experience of the UK and diagnoses a fourfold missed opportunity: the economy is not ordered; the state has lost much of its legitimacy via neglect of reform plus inefficiency; class division in society remains; and no clear view of the UK's position in the world has been generated. Comparing the UK with the mainland, Morgan comments that whereas they have learned the lessons of the Second World War the British have preferred a nostalgic complacency, and the possibility presented by wartime dislocation of reaffirming the modernist project in the UK was missed. If we speculate on likely sources of change then a rational judgement entails pessimism. Yet this holds only for endogeneous change. As there is now a broader global system change in process which must impact on the UK, complex change in Europe might be expected to lead to internal democratization. As Benton puts it, looking at the possibilities for systemic change in the UK: 'The mould is more likely to crack from without, than to be broken from within'[99].

---

[96] ibid. pp.314-325

[97] On this idea see J .Keane *Democracy and Civil Society*, London, Verso, 1988

[98] K . Morgan in *Times Higher Education Supplement* 19 October 1990

[99] S. Benton in *New Statesman and Society* 1 November 1991

Conclusion

In summary, at this point we can now see both how the phases of the development of UK capitalism have sedimented particular political-cultural patterns in the polity, and how these established institutional, ideational, and cultural patterns serve to inhibit endogeneous change. Nonetheless the global structures which enfold the UK economic, political and cultural space are in process of change. It is my speculation that these patterns of change within the global and European systems are likely to require quite extensive reforms within the UK.

3 The ideology of liberal-individualism

Introduction

In the preceding chapter I discussed the political-economic and political-discourse structures of the UK. One element of the discourse of politics was noted but not pursued, namely the omni-present ideology of liberal-individualism[1]. The relationship of this package of ideas to the UK official ideology sketched in chapter two is difficult to specify directly. It draws upon the four elements of parliamentary sovereignty, representative democracy, constitutional monarchy and the rule of law insofar as these are all shaped to some extent or other by the same seventeenth century English Revolution and its ideology of liberalism; however in the contemporary UK liberal-individualism is at once less stressed, and much more influential. One might say that it is here that we find the day-to-day working area of the official ideology: the sphere between the public voices of authority and the private voices of the ordinary inhabitants of the UK, where received political discourse merely 'runs-through-our-heads', and is manifest in the ordinary small change of conversation[2].

The idea-set of liberal-individualism has received much attention amongst critics of extant states-of-affairs, and all seem to have it in common that they identify particular social, economic and political incapacities as

---

[1] In this chapter I pick-up an idea mentioned in chapter two and treat it in detail as an element of the UK political culture.

[2] On ideology see T. Eagleton *Ideology*, London, Verso, 1991

flowing from its cultural prevalence and extension. Various criticisms are made and remedies advanced for example in the matters of political-economic policy making and political-cultural self-understandings. David Marquand[3], whom I will come to later, remarks that the core of the 'British disease' is the ideological/philosophical commitment to the ethic of liberal-individualism. It is this vision of the nature of humankind, individual and collective, which fatally undermines all attempts at effective collective action, and is the root cause of the inability of the UK polity to construct and put in place a developmental state of the sort mainland Europeans established. And in a similar vein Alasdair MacIntyre[4], whom I will also consider later, analyses the rise of the modern world from the perspective of moral philosophy and details the replacement of Aristotelian and religious ethics with the psuedo-morality of liberal-individualism. A fragmented ethical experience is the lot of today's population of the West which is effectively bereft of any ethic of community. MacIntyre looks to the reconstitution of democracy.

In the light of such strategies of critique and commentary I will consider the ideology of liberal-individualism in this chapter in a series of ways: firstly, with reference to the work of political philosophers I will tackle it as a delimited-formal ideology; then secondly, relying on a spread of commentators I will look at the pervasive-informal extension of the idea-set, that is how it shapes the thinking of persons and groups within UK society; and finally, I will add a comparative perspective by noting the outline of the counterposition of formal and substantive democracy.

The delimited-formal ideology of liberal-individualism

The tradition we understand as liberalism, which can be taken to comprise a sequence of specific statements where each is a context-appropriate elaboration of preceding material, finds recent expression in the 1980s work of the New Right. The sets of ideas were first presented in the seventeenth century by Hobbes and Locke, and as C.B. Macpherson[5] points out can be taken to have been both novel and progressive. They were novel in that they advanced the idea of possessive individualism, where individuals were sovereign over their own persons and could enter into a variety of contractual social exchanges to secure autonomously arising needs and wants. All this, Macpherson makes clear, should be seen in contrast to contemporary religious and feudal-system related ideas which firmly lodged persons within a social hierarchy of duty, obedience, and deference.

---

3 D. Marquand *The Unprincipled Society*, London, Fontana 1988

4 A. MacIntyre *After Virtue*, London, Duckworth, 1981

5 C. B. Macpherson *The Political Theory of Possesive Individualism*, Oxford, Oxford University Press, 1962; and C. B. Macpherson *Democratic Theory*, Oxford, Oxford University Press, 1973

The delimited-formal ideology was progressive in that it offered a legitimating interpretation for the political project of the rising mercantile bourgeoisie in their struggle against feudal absolutism, both state and church[6]. In brief, it was the theory of the nascent English bourgeois revolution[7]. The work of the theorists of market liberalism, Bentham and James Mill, is added later and we have utilitarian ethics and theories of government action[8].

The mid-nineteenth century saw the influential presentation of liberal-democracy in the work of J.S. Mill, and Macpherson[9] argues that this was the one major attempt to reply to the democratic critique of liberalism. However, Macpherson takes the view that the democratic elements included are extra-liberal and represent an attempt to co-opt pre-seventeenth century notions of democracy where the notions of humankind affirmed made human actions intrinsically valuable; in brief the Aristotelian-derived scheme of civic virtue and the flowering of natural capacities. In contrast the liberal model of human beings affirms that man is a bundle of appetites in search of satisfaction. In these two theories there are different ideas of power, which Macpherson, echoing Isaiah Berlin's[10] famous distinction between positive and negative liberty, characterizes as an ethical-developmental notion (power-to-do), and a neutral-descriptive idea (power-over). J. S. Mill runs these two ideas together and uses the descriptive concept in analysing social arrangements but turns to the ethical concept when offering justifications of extant states of affairs. In Macpherson's view Mill's work represents an heroic attempt to repair liberalism by attaching elements of democracy, but the result is a logically incoherent failure[11].

For the present day Macpherson takes liberalism to be outmoded. The core of liberalism is the model of man as an autonomous bundle of appetites in search of satisfaction, and whilst this may have been progressive when deployed to usher in the world of mercantile capitalism, it seems irrelevant and harmful to the political circumstances of the present. Like J.K. Galbraith[12], Macpherson takes the bourgeoisie's 'battle against material scarcity' to have been won long ago. It is now time to humanize the productive system of the modern world by reaffirming the ethical concept of powers, the core of the political philosophical tradition of democracy[13].

---

[6] Barrington Moore Jr. *The Social Origins of Dictatorship and Democracy*, Boston, Beacon Press, 1967

[7] For a broader treatment see S. Pollard *The Idea of Progress*, Harmondsworth, Penguin, 1971

[8] D. Held *Models of Democracy*, Cambridge, Polity, 1987

[9] Macpherson *Democratic Theory*

[10] I. Berlin *Four Essays on Liberty*, Oxford, Oxford University Press, 1969

[11] Macpherson *Democratic Theory*

[12] J .K. Galbraith *The Affluent Society*, London, Hamish Hamilton, 1958

[13] See P. W. Preston *New Trends in Development Theory*, London, Routledge, 1985, in particular the essay entitled 'The ethico-political notion of development' which expands on the argument noted here.

In sum, liberalism can be taken to comprise a coherent delimited-formal ideological package which involves a set of core elements: the ideas of possessive individualism, the notion of contractual social relations, the affirmation of the centrality of the market, and the theory of the minimum state (all of which are contested by critics). In regard to this set we can note, firstly, that the affirmation of possessive individualism represents the central claim of the liberal philosophical tradition: in brief, that persons are autonomous agents who both know their own minds and are themselves the seat of unlimited consumption desires. This ontological claim has been criticised by many who argue that persons are essentially social and that the model of possesive individualism is pernicious.Then secondly, the characterization of social life as essentially contractual flows from the affirmation of the centrality of the autonomous individual. The trans-individual or social sphere is taken to be constituted by the myriad contracts individuals enter into either directly or indirectly via involvement in established social institutions. Again, this is criticised by many as this view effectively eliminates the idea of the social, and with it notions of community, tradition, interdependence and so on. Thirdly it is clear that the affirmation of the centrality of the market is a key element of the Locke, Smith, Bentham line. Broadly it is claimed that autonomous action in the open market place will maximize human welfare. A progressive position when turned against proponents of restriction (from feudal and church absolutism down to mercantilism) but regressive when recast in the late nineteenth century as neo-classicism and deployed against ideas of democracy. This line has recently been invoked by the Anglo-Saxon New Right to buttress the reactionary programme which they have presented in the wake of the collapse of the post-Second World War social-democratic compromise (and against Habermasian schemes of democracy). And finally the theory of the minimum state follows on from all this, and on the liberal view the role of the state is merely rule-keeper. In New Right formulations democracy is merely a technique for recruiting office holders and is not a substantive ethic. Yet against this it is clear that the role of the state is much more extensive and that it can be an agent of formal and substantive democracy[14].

Overall, when the notions of liberalism are invoked in ordinary discourse we are dealing with political-cultural resources which have a great depth of tradition. We can thus detail the historical occasion of sets of ideas that come down to us as 'received ideas', and we can see how they represented group-specific responses to given sets of circumstances: the outcome of historically located dynamics of structure and agency.

---

[14] An issue much debated amongst development theorists, see J. Toye *Dilemmas of Development*, Oxford, Blackwell,1987

The pervasive-informal extension of liberal-individualism

Over the post-Second World War period the UK's political-economy has had a quite specific embedding within the global system and a political discourse to go along with it. The immediate context of contemporary received ideas lies in the period of post-Second World War US hegemony. This has generated a particular variant of the ideology of liberal-democracy. If the official ideology of the UK with its four great tradition concepts offers an idea of historical continuity, of a depth of tradition, no matter how the historical truth gets handled or mishandled, then the public sphere of the present, the way in which contemporary political life is viewed, has been dominated over the post-Second World War period by the idea of the 'free west'. This of course is an ideological package which transcends the cultural bounds of the UK. An American hegemonic idea, it expresses the subordinate position of the UK within the USA's post-Second World War economic and political sphere. The political-ideological package of the free west runs together ideas of free speech, free trade, free markets, and freedom-in-general in an all embracing celebratory liberalism which was recently represented as the 'end of history' by Francis Fukuyama[15]. The dominance of the UK public sphere by ideas of liberal-individualism thus represents the day-to-day sphere of working of the UK official ideology as it is modified by US hegemonic culture. And together the great tradition and the content of the public sphere generate a flow of ideas that suffuse in a myriad ways the common sense of the population creating an 'acquiescent little tradition'.

The idea of the free west was constructed and deployed in the immediate post-Second World War period. On the exposition of Gabriel Kolko[16] it was produced by the USA in order to assert and legitimate its post-war political and economic hegemony in the West. In the war years on this account, the USA quickly established 'war aims' and these centred on the establishment of a global open market economy which inevitably would have the US as its metropolitan centre. This goal entailed establishing institutional vehicles, such as the UN, IMF, World Bank, and GATT, and the removal of obstacles, chiefly the European colonial empires[17]. It also required resistance to possible counter-visions of post-war arrangements, thus the active assertion of US interests via institutional mechanisms (plus, of course, the overwhelming economic/military power of the US) was coupled to an alternative-blocking strategy aimed at the European and American left: hence the whole cold war machine of thought-control[18]. The

---

15 F. Fukuyama *The End of History and the Last Man*, London, Hamish Hamilton, 1992

16 G. Kolko *The Politics of War*, New York, Vintage, 1968

17 On the business of the displacement of the UK by the USA see Kees van der Pijl *The Making of an Atlantic Ruling Class*, London, Verso, 1984, and for the UK reading of the episode see C. Hitchens *Blood, Class and Nostalgia*, London, Vintage, 1990

18 R. Aron *The Imperial Republic*, London, Weidenfeld, 1973

USA presented an ideology of the free world to block the European/American left in particular, and the USSR more broadly. Both targets were subsumed within a claimed project of rolling back 'International Communism'. D.F. Flemming[19] discusses the diplomacy of the cold war and argues convincingly that the whole business was made in the USA and that the USSR made repeated, and futile, attempts to negotiate a resolution. Later the USA invented modernization theory as the newly decolonized territories became a zone of conflict between the great powers[20].

It is the case that the ideology of the free world, having been made in the USA, was then exported to the UK and Europe more generally, and this hegemonic idea-set has governed thinking about US/UK relationships ever since. But at this point we could note the many ambiguities of this UK/US relationship. At the level of informal political theory we find that there is in the UK a desperate repetition of claims that there is a 'special relationship' between USA/UK (expressed by Harold Macmillan as the UK's Greece to the Rome of the USA), and this despite massive and widely accepted evidence to the contrary. The general issue here, as indicated by Christopher Hitchens in *Blood, Class and Nostalgia*[21], is the reaction of the UK ruling class to its displacement by the USA as the key metropolitan power in the global capitalist economy, and the way it read this displacement into public discourse. Noting all the ambiguous elements we could say that in the UK the ideology of the free world has been presented as a further extension or variant of the UK great tradition. Thus the UK, in affirming the ideology of the free world with its US hegemony, is merely re-affirming its own traditions of liberty. The present-day natures of the US and the UK states, and their relationship, are all assimilated to an historical unity-in-development-of-liberty which is wholly spurious. In the UK the ideology of the free world celebrates the notions of free markets, free societies, free speech and freedom-in-general, and goes on to contrast all this with the unfreedom of socialist totalitarianism in the old eastern European block. The contrast between free west and totalitarianism runs deep: Thatcher's Brugges speech where the idea of a united European system was attacked as 'socialistic'; or Thatcher's Church of Scotland speech where Christianity is annexed to the project of Thatcherism[22]. However all this is familiar material so I will not pursue it further, instead I will turn to the way in which the great tradition, and the contents of the post-Second World War public sphere with its focus on liberal-individualism, run through commonsense thinking.

---

[19] D. F. Flemming *The Cold War and Its Origins*, New York, Doubleday, 1961

[20] F. Halliday *Cold War, Third World*, London, Radius, 1989

[21] Hitchens *Blood, Class, Nostalgia*

[22] J. Raban *God and Mrs Thatcher*, London, Chatto, 1990

Acquiescent private voices, a UK little tradition?

In the work of James Scott[23] the idea of a 'little tradition' is pointed to in contrast to the great traditions of high culture, the sphere of the elite, and is characterized as the autonomous moral community of localized peasant life. This local form-of-life is maintained in an essentially conflictual relationship with the overarching culture and it affirms distinctive ethics of action based on local cultural resources. The little tradition also offers the moral resources for dissent, both articulated and informal.

The extent to which it might now be possible to speak of UK little traditions, in the rather different sense of non-metropolitan integrated groupings, is an issue that remains both open and unclear. Tom Nairn[24] argues that the nineteenth century saw the development of industry-based regional particularisms in the UK. Victorian cities were built, and they had strong local governments. These centres of economic, political, and cultural power were separated from the metropolitan centre and from core groups of UK ruling class; that is, they were industrial capitalists not commercial, landed, or mercantile traders. Through the twentieth century these groupings have been in slow decline and over the decade of the 1980s under Thatcher's centralizing drive regional power has been further weakened. Relatedly other theorists have looked to characterize the responses of non-core groups: Richard Hoggart and Raymond Williams[25] established what is now labelled 'cultural studies' with their celebrations of the coherence and value of industrial working class culture in the inter-war, and early post-war, periods. Frank Parkin[26] has identified a series of cognitive-ideological responses on part of 'working class' ranging from deference, acquiescent turning away into local community, through to opposition. Williams[27] has considered the exhaustion of the political power of the mainstream non-elite, and has looked to marginal groups offering critical opposition over brief periods. Over the 1980s the UK saw a series of 'local rebellions', from an upsurge in peripheral 'Celtic nationalisms', through to inner-city riots, the miners strike and poll-tax protests. However, such expressions of resistance seem to have been merely transient disturbances in the process of the smooth articulation of metropolitan political, economic and cultural power.

The line of thinking which I am following picks up from Nairn and Ralph Miliband and looks to the idea of demobilization. If there ever were little traditions it is difficult to see them now. One might say that if the UK does have little traditions, sets of ideas and actions distinct from those of the elite

[23] J. C. Scott 'Protest and Profanation: Revolt and the Little Tradition' in *Theory and Society 4* 1971

[24] T. Nairn *The Enchanted Glass*, London, Radius 1988

[25] Discussed in G Turner *British Cultural Studies*, London, Allen and Unwin, 1990

[26] F. Parkin *Class Inequality and Political Order*, London, Palladin, 1972

[27] R. Williams 'Base and superstructure in marxist cultural theory' in *New Left Review 82*, 1972

groups, then they surely are not autonomous and local as the world of regional or clearly marked class identities must have begun to move to its close in the early post-war years[28], rather they would represent sedimentations of broader sets of ideas, the way in which non-elite have read and taken up elite sponsored ideas: one might say that the UK has an acquiescent little tradition, and its substance is 'individualism' together with 'civility'. What we can see is an extensive set of ideas surrounding liberal-democracy which block the presentation of a richer set of ideas, broadly individualism bereft of any very obvious notions of citizenship or community.

In sum one could say that the great tradition offers four broad ideas of representative democracy, parliamentary sovereignty, constitutional monarchy, and the rule of law, all of which have informal extension, and which have a further expression in the guise of the ideology of liberal-individualism, as modified by the post-Second World War hegemony of the USA into an element of the broader package of the free west, and that together these override any local and autonomous cultural schemes and act therefore to construct an acquiescent little tradition. The official ideology in its informal extension combines both 'civility' (reasonableness, decency, and moderation) and 'individualism' (with its scheme of autonomously arising wants secured contractually in the marketplace), and although these exist in some considerable tension it seems to me that the set centres on liberal-individualism. This cultural sphere is thus the realm of an elite-disseminated pervasive-informal ideology which forms the vehicle of obedience to the status quo and the block to the emergence of alternative little traditions. I will pursue the thought via the accumulation of a set of examples: they illustrate the acquiescent little tradition and its internal tensions, where collectivity connotes constraint and individualism connotes freedom.

Freedom affirmed: the informal and the eccentric in English-British thought

The informal connotes the not-restricted. The ideal of negative liberty as freedom from restraint is here affirmed. Formality is constraint and informality is the absence-of-restraint, or freedom. The acknowledged social is dangerous, it is either the sphere of the state, seen as necessarily restrictive, or the realm of individuals aggregated, the mass. Both spheres imply unfreedom, de jure or de facto.

Within the broad spread of English culture the informal is widely stressed in celebrations of the un-structured, the un-ordered, the spontaneous. The following are examples: UK ideals of countryside which celebrate the rural scene as one of small-scale intimate reassurance, familiar and dignified by

---

[28] See R. Kee *1939 The World We Left Behind*, London, Weidenfeld,1984; or R Williams *The Long Revolution*, London, Chatto, 1961

long historical existence, and celebrated in the visual arts, thus Constable or the many portrait painters of the UK rural squirearchy[29]; UK art-form of garden-making with its careful recreations of what is seen as unstructured countryside, and the related celebration of Garden Cities[30]; UK celebrations of village life and architecture (and cottage gardens) as somehow representing the essence of England, again with the stress on the organic growth and pre-modernity of these forms, the 'village' of common understanding is almost a refuge from the contemporary world[31]; UK anti-modernism in architecture and the preference for the styles of earlier years generally, from medieval through to nineteenth century Victorian houses, forms of urban living which accumulated over time and which were not rationally designed or laid-out[32]; and relatedly in pubs, a quintessentially English institution, the old, the scruffy, the bric-a-brac stuffed[33].

Such affirmations of the unstructured, the unconstrained, extend to replies offered in regard to patterns of behaviour prescribed by the state. Thus people object to seat-belt laws in terms of it 'infringing upon personal liberty' notwithstanding its demonstrated benefit in terms of safety. Restrictions on smoking cigarettes in public places are similarly resented (by smokers). Again, people object to proposals for a formal ID card system on the grounds that it infringes personal liberty notwithstanding the fact that a formal system of necessity would be a codified system and hence a signal advance upon present state habits of security record keeping (that is, an uncodified equivalent of an ID card system) and notwithstanding the fact that all sorts of other identification means must be used in ordinary life (for example, to support a cheque).

The ethos of informality can be given specific vehicles in the persons of eccentrics. Thus within English-British received political culture we have: Francis Drake, a war hero who took time off to finish a game of bowls before sailing into battle; Robin Hood, a man who lived in a forest and stole from the rich to give to the poor; Nelson, characterized by Linda Colley as a 'hero in his own epic'[34], another war hero, who refused an order to retreat by putting his telescope to his blind eye so that he could not see the signal, and then ordering the attack; Sherlock Holmes who is a late Victorian hero who lives alone, plays the violin, takes opium in a ten per cent solution and invents the science of detection; various criminals, Kray

---

[29] J. Wolf *The Social Production of Art*, London, Macmillan, 1981

[30] J. Ryder and H Silver *Modern English Society*, London, Methuen, 1985

[31] P. Jennings *The Living Village*, London, Hodder, 1986

[32] P. Wright *On Living in an Old Country*, London, Verso, 1985

[33] And we might note that one of the most succesful popular groups in recent years has been CAMRA - dedicated precisely to preserving 'the traditional British pint of beer'.

[34] L. Colley *Britons Forging the Nation 1707-1837*, London, Yale, 1992. See chapter four which deals with how the UK ruling class reacted to defeat in America by selfconsciously reconstituting itself as a 'service elite' and many British males took themselves to be 'heroes in their own epics' (pp.177-93).

twins, Great Train Robbers; and relatedly most politicians when they appear in their biographies (no matter how dull they may have been in reality). And this celebration of the eccentric can extend to whole episodes which are remembered in a glow of informality: thus the Second World War was won by brave individuals (the few); eccentric rag-a-muffins (Dad's army); the scruffy (airforce personnel); with the whole enterprise exemplified by the make-it-up-as-we-go-along informality of the little-boats at Dunkirk (itself an informal episode). And there was a black market, with spivs, and scrounging. And for humour, ITMA, and later the Goons. Against this we can note that as the myth of informality was created the reality, now hardly detectable in UK common political discourse, was of a command-economy in the UK, with the USA and USSR providing money, munitions and armies.

Umberto Eco, in *Travels in Hyperreality*[35], discussing the use made of historical reproduction museums in the USA, speaks of hyper-reality, which designates the particular cultural resource obtained by this process of the very careful reconstruction of elements of reality. Such reconstructions are taken by Eco to be vehicles of identity-affirmation: it is through such hyper-real exemplifications that we tell ourselves what sort of people we are. With the UK celebrations of the 'informal' what we are seeing is an affirmation of an identify of withdrawal from the explicitly social and public sphere which is taken as threatening. The sovereign autonomous individual is threatened by rational social order, and informality becomes a reassurance.

Freedom assailed: the mass, law-and-order, and the bureaucrats

Breakdowns in law-and-order can lead to mob violence and the rule of the mass. In eighteenth and nineteenth century political commentary fear of the mob figured quite strongly[36] and in the UK over the post-Second World War period there have been a series of 'moral panics', mostly focusing on the young, which recorded various 'threats to the fabric of society'[37]. If we tease out the logic[38] of liberal-individualism in this informal, or folk-form, as it is routinely evidenced in the day to day discourse of 'ordinary people' in the UK[39] (reasonable, decent, moderate), it is clear that adherents of liberal-individualism take the view when confronting the realm of what is ordinarily taken as the social that there are only individual persons. The

---

[35] U. Eco *Travels in Hyperreality*, London, Picador, 1987

[36] G. Rude *The Crowd in History*, London, Wiley, 1981

[37] The classic sociological text being S. Cohen *Folk Devils and Moral Panics*, Oxford, Martin Robertson, 1972

[38] My formal intellectual sources here are Held *Models of Democracy*, Macpherson *Democratic Theory*, and MacIntyre *After Virtue*

[39] See S. Lukes *Individualism*, New York, Harper and Row, 1973, who shows how the notion works differently in different western countries - I am looking at the Anglo-Saxon variant.

social and the public sphere consequently is a realm of aggregated individuals, the mass, which is taken as inherently unstable and disorganised. So it is governed by imposed rules. Rules for the convenience of individuals. The social and public sphere is not taken to be routinely and extensively structured. Law and order are imposed. However, within the essentially unstructured sphere of the mass there are islands of naturally given security/surety, most importantly the family (and beyond that the larger family of Nation).

A related sphere of potential restriction is found in the state and its agencies, 'the bureaucrats'. Notwithstanding the general 'civility' of UK life the sphere of the state is perceived as latently restrictive. In the tradition of liberalism freedom is understood as freedom-from-constraint, Berlin's negative liberty, and the sphere of the state thus necessarily appears as restriction. A minimum spread of measures may be required to secure 'order', the prior condition of the pursuit of private satisfactions, but these restrictions are both diminutions of pre-given negative liberties and likely to expand. It is the idea that the state's grasp is likely to expand that is picked-up in common discourse, in sum, 'bureaucracy'[40].

Bureaucracy becomes the realm of state-occasioned unfreedom. The bureaucrats are taken to deploy (or stand as the cultural paradigms of these activities) rules, which are fussy, not common-sensical, obscure, foolish, in sum, bureaucratic[41]. On the basis of these rules bureaucrats then interfere in people's lives and business. Such interference impinges upon privacy. It is intrusive, and meddlesome. The bureaucrats are taken as invariably inefficient. They deploy red-tape to enforce their meddlesome rules. They have their own internal agendas[42]. They are often remote, uncaring, unresponsive and rude. Overall what they typically do not provide is 'good service'. They are not deferential. They do not 'know their places' as servants of the public. Revealingly, the business of 'service' became one of John Major's early themes as Prime Minister, and formed the core of his Citizens Charter.

The liberal-individualists take the realm of politics and public to be in essence contractual. A delicate tracery of individual contracts sustains the political sphere which centres on the state, the rule-giver, the guarantor of order. There is no idea in liberal-individualism of collective political life, or action outside the specified institutional arenas. In the UK this becomes what Miliband calls parliamentarism[43]. All political action revolves around/within parliament. There is no other sort of political action: thus riots say, are wholly negative events and the liberal-individualist can only read them as breakdowns, lapses into primal chaos. The idea of a

---

[40] See M. Albrow *Bureaucracy*, London, Macmillan, 1970 especially chapter seven

[41] D. Warwick *Bureaucracy*, London, Longman, 1974 especially chapter six

[42] A recent theme of the New Right, see Marquand *Unprincipled Society*

[43] R. Miliband *Capitalist Democracy in Britain*, Oxford, Oxford University Press, 1982

spontaneous, coherent and retrospectively rationally defensible riot is for the liberal-individualist simply incoherent. In the UK the relationship of individual and collectivity is handled via the notion of the autonomy of persons, the non-existence of society, and the requirement of agreed contracted rules. The idea of citizenship, with its legitimate and encompassing public sphere centered on the republican democratic state, is not available in UK culture.

The free-self: consumer, thinker and actor

Liberal-individualist theory takes unlimited consumption desires arising within the self of the person to be rational and given. Several general comments can be made. Zygmunt Bauman[44], whom I will consider more fully in the following chapter, points out that for those in work consumption has now become lifestyle; the freedom to construct a pattern of life out of proferred consumption goods. This new form of life has been theorized with the ideas of post-industrialism and the related culture of postmodernism. Unfortunately those without the means to consume are taken as failures (not fellow citizens society is duty bound to assist) and are welfare-processed (thus minimum needs are met at the cost of denial of status, personal and social). Galbraith[45] long ago tagged the political-economic consequence of the stress on private consumption as entailing the production of 'private affluence and public squalor': a lesson apparently re-learned by the Anglo-Saxon economies over the period of the 1980s.

All these traits are present in the contemporary UK. The decade of the 1980s has seen a flurry of shopping-centre building as consumer-consumption becomes ever more central in people's patterns of life, and these shopping-centres become ever more cathedral-like in scale and ornament[46]. The worlds of high street consumer choices, the mass media, popular music, sport and advertising have come together in an extraordinary culture-of-display and at the same time the decade of the 1980s has seen public services run-down, a widening of income-differentials, and a sharp redistribution of wealth upwards in line with neo-classical notions of 'trickle-down'. And of course a central folk-figure over the decade has been the yuppie with conspicuous consumption as the core of a life style.

Against this we might note in passing that for the UK, USA and Australia, the bastions of 1980s New Rightism, the upshot is that all now have debt mountains and trade deficits on the backs of shrinking productive

---

[44] Z. Bauman *Freedom*, Milton Keynes, Open University Press, 1988

[45] Galbraith *Afluent Society*

[46] For example in Glasgow there is a marvellous example called the St Enoch's Centre which is contrived as an all glass architectural pastiche of a baroque church.

economies. Susan Strange[47] has coined the term 'casino capitalism' and a recent text edited by Jonathan Michie[48] identified a decade of failure.

As individuals are the reality, so they are the basis of knowledge-claims. In the British empiricist tradition the ground of all substantive knowledge claims is sense-experience, the necessarily individual sensory exchange with the given material realm. The approach is discredited in epistemology but an echo persists in the sphere of social/political claims. In the social/political sphere matters are either quantifiable (and thus taken as objective and, like rules, commanding of obedience) or they are subjective, and command no obedience. In the subjective sphere one is entitled to one's opinion. The absence of a genuinely social sphere means that opinions are valid-as-asserted. That I assert my opinion is enough to validate the claims I make. Claims to fact are judged against reality, naturalism. The sphere of the objective is the quantifiable, but most social, political, aesthetic and moral judgements admit only of opinions, mine, yours, the guy next door's, and in claiming this entitlement to opinion the self which utters the opinion is the ground of its validation. MacIntyre[49] calls the broad moral climate of the West emotivist where this term points to the same view of moral-judgement which I have indicated and is also a pejorative term in the lexicon of moral philosophy[50]. The social/political sphere becomes reduced to a haze of personal, and personally validated, opinions. It is thus rendered inoperative of course. Without the mechanisms of public dialogue the population is in practice demobilized.

For the liberal-individualist action is essentially private. It originates within the sovereign person. Action that is outward oriented must conform to the body of   contracted rules. However this requirement is external/pragmatic, rather than internal/moral: obedience is a pragmatic requirement occasioned by machineries of rule-enforcement. Social rules in this narrow view are restricted to the agreed social sphere, they are not understood, as an anthropologist or sociologist would say, to run-through-peoples-heads. This liberal-individualist position has direct implications for political life and notions of ethics more generally. In establishment politics this view produces the ethic that action is private, but in public rules must be conformed with, so do as you wish but do not get caught!

In regard to ethics generally MacIntyre[51] has argued that liberalism has no ethics, and that with its celebration of individual sensibilities, and disregard for expectations of action carried in tradition, the statements in regard to ethics which it does offer are little more than a mish-mash of bits-and-bobs which together can be characterized as the manipulative ethics of

[47] S. Strange *Casino Capitalism*, Oxford, Blackwell, 1989

[48] J. Mitchie ed. *The Economic Legacy 1979-1992*, London, Academic, 1992

[49] MacIntyre *After Virtue*

[50] B. Willliams *Morality*, Harmondsworth, Penguin, 1972

[51] MacIntyre *After Virtue*

emotivism. Again, in the period of the high-tide of logical positivism ethical injunctions were regarded as meaningless noise, the boo/hurrah theory of ethics. Ethical statements merely deployed an 'emotional charge' and hopefully shifted the person you addressed in the desired direction. Emotivist ethics are thus instrumental. In contemporary UK society ethics find institutional expression as more or less openly scorned ritual; for example the church, or the realm of politics, or figures of authority such as headmasters, or magistrates. The delimited-formal ideology of liberal-individualism blocks the expression or emergence of any ethics-embedded-in-social-practice.

Freedom as tradition, recalled in nostalgia

Patrick Wright in his *On Living in an Old Country*[52] analyses the way in which a sense of history permeates the routine of everyday life. Drawing on the work of Agnes Heller he argues that we can speak of a 'national past' which comprises the stories we routinely assume about ourselves, rather than explicitly tell. Stories about a national past are the means whereby the routine of everyday life, with its usually unreflective particularism, is linked with the particularism affirmed by the wider group with whom we identify, the nation.

Everyday life is the realm of routine and it includes an element of historicity, of the appreciation of being lodged in developing time:

> Everyday life is the historically conditioned framework in which the imperatives of natural sustenance (eating, sleeping ...) come to be socially determined: it is in the intersubjectivity of everyday life that human self-reproduction is wedded to the wider processes of social reproduction. Thus while everday life may well be naturalized and taken for granted ... it is in reality socially formed and complex. At the heart of everday life, therefore, is the interdependency of person and society[53].

Everyday life links structure and agency, it is the immediate local network that we must inhabit.

This local aspect of living is grasped in Heller's notion of particularity, the unreflective self-understanding of those who accept and affirm the norms of the wider group to which they belong. Contrariwise, individuality is a distanced appreciation of the cultural norms binding us. Particularity was made into the core ethic of bourgeois society, the egocentric doctrine of individualism plus the mystificatory notion of the private pursuit of greed occasioning maximum social wellbeing. However, the rise of modernity not only ushered in bourgeois particularity but also a new realm of freedom, of individuality and hence also, insecurity.

---

[52] Wright *Old Country*
[53] ibid. pp.6-7

In everday historical consciousness agents explain their world/selves via plausible tales, stories, narratives, or histories. It is a part of the business of making sense. It is embedded in routine, the sphere of the taken-for-granted. It is also strongly implicated in the response of groups and individuals to change, and here especially the rise of science can be noted with its disenchantment of the world. Wright argues that the national past is thus a story told to inhabitants to render things meaningful and clear in the context of the flux and disenchantment of the modern world. Nostalgia in the UK plays an important role. Wright offers the examples of the model of the old established family, with its below-stairs retainers, the use of craft models of manufacture, the invocation of old character types. All of these act to structure the present, as the inheritor and present expression of the national past. Wright mentions two particular styles the national past adopts: the use of auratic sites where history is taken as most particularly present; and remembered war which is taken as a sphere of non-routine when actions made a difference.

Wright points out that there is a clear political aspect to all this as the group to whom we are routinely enjoined to belong/submit is the nation. We are offered a national past, an official history. The nation replaces other more local communities and it re-enchants the world. A story is woven which tells us who we are, where we came from and where we are going. Wright calls attention to royalty, we have a royal family which exemplifies familyhood and the collective national family. The other matter of particular relevance is 'heritage', the authorized auratic residue of the past, and Wright notes that it has expanded in recent years and 'now includes the local scene alongside the capital city, the old factory alongside the municiple art gallery, the urban tenement or terrace alongside the country house, the vernacular alongside the stately and academically sanctioned'[54]. Wright continues:

> In the end, however, we come back to history in a more familiar sense, for the national past is formed within the historical experience of its particular nationstate. Among the factors which have influenced the definition of Britain's national past, therefore, are the recent experience of economic and imperial decline, the persistence of imperialist forms of self-understanding, early depopulation of the countryside, the continuing tension between the 'nations' of Britain (Wales, Scotland and, most obviously, Ireland), the continued existence of the Crown and so much related residual ceremony, the extensive and 'planned' demolition and redevelopment of settled communities which has occured since the Second World War, and the still living memory of a righteous war that 'we' won[55].

The political issue for Wright lies in the question of whether or not 'everyday historical consciousness might be detached from its present

---

[54] ibid. p.25
[55] ibid.

articulation in the dominant symbolism of nation and drawn into different expressions of cultural and historical identity'[56].

Degraded polity, ineffectual policy

With these examples, and in the context of the wider discussions of liberal-individualism above, it seems to me that we get some idea of how the UK's acquiescent little tradition works. Any appeal to the potentially critical resources of either local non-metropolitan little traditions or available rational modernist democratic ideologies is blocked. It is clear that the repeated invocation of the notion of the individual must act to inhibit any move to invoke a notion of citizenship on the part of UK inhabitants. Individuals inhabit private spheres and the public sphere is the realm of aggregate individuals, the mass, and is conceived as essentially unstructured (except in its market-related, or quasi-market contractual way), and in need of control (so as to secure minimum conditions for private pursuits). There is no rational social and public sphere. There is no citizenship. There are no citizens, and the state bureaucracy represents control. The general denial of citizenship, the reduction of inhabitants to mass-in-need-of-control, typical of liberalism, was exemplified by Thatcher and commenting on the relationship between Thatcherite style and the substance of UK politics, Germaine Greer[57] dubbed her 'the nanny of the nation ... the only adult in the nursery', and she went on to argue that the Prime Minister presided over a degraded and infantilized polity .

Moving on, I turn now to consider more specific critical pieces, that is, the work on political culture and political-economy offered by MacIntyre[58], who diagnoses an emotivist culture in thrall to the related myths of market choice and bureaucratic rationality, and Marquand[59] who identifies liberal-individualism as a crucial factor in the slow and continuing relative decline of the UK.

MacIntyre's critique of the political-cultural implications of individualism

In his text *After Virtue* MacIntyre is concerned to review the contemporary circumstances of moral discourse in modern liberal capitalist society. The conclusions he reaches are highly critical and deeply pessimistic. MacIntyre talks of the market establishing non-citizenship such that the population of the UK is merely an agglomeration of private individuals. A moral subjectivism characterizes the polity. Public discourse now comprises the futile dialectic of moral subjectivist protest confronting the psuedo-

---

[56] ibid. p.26
[57] G. Greer in *The New Statesman* 16 August 1985
[58] MacIntyre *After Virtue*
[59] Marquand *Unprincipled Society*

rationality of instrumental bureaucracy. Present moral-political stasis can be addressed only in the reaffirmation amongst groups understanding themselves as communities of the Aristotelian classical notion of 'virtue', where this designates the community and tradition carried practical ethic of the achievement of decent self-hood. All of which was anticipated, but not it seems pursued, in the ideals of republican democracy current in the eighteenth century at the start-point of the modern world.

The work of MacIntyre recalls that of Macpherson, Arendt, and Jurgen Habermas[60], in that he too argues that it is necessary to distinguish between democracy and liberal-democracy in order to reassert the claims of the former. MacIntyre's contribution is to present this argument in the language of ethics (and to take to task the role of the moral philosophers in the debacle he identified). MacIntyre makes three broad claims: about liberal-democracy; about individualism; and about contemporary moral discourse.

The rise of the modern world has bequeathed to us the pseudo-morality of liberal-individualism. In the period of the rise of the modern world the established power of the church was broken. Aristotelian notions of science gave way to mechanistic theories, and in ethics the Aristotelian/theistic schemes of practical obedience within received traditions, to oversimplify, gave way to schemes which identified one way or the other personal responsibility. These schemes represented the attempts of the theorists of the Enlightenment to reground morality in notions of human nature. MacIntyre thinks that they failed because the project is misconceived. The Aristotelian scheme comprised the three elements of untutored nature, man-having-realized-true-nature, and the precepts needed to guide the transition. The rules of ethics are thus practical. However, the shift to the modern world involved rejecting the Aristotelian notion of man as having an essence. Humankind was taken as material, thus Hobbes. So all that was left to ethical discourse was a notion of untutored nature and sets of rules. It did not make a coherent package any more. When the theorists of the Enlightenment attempted a rational ethics, that is, deriving ethical rules from claims about natural man, all they created were 'individuals', bundles of appetites bound by restrictions, and moral philosophy became an academic backwater.

The consequences of this invention of the 'individual' are manifold. First, the key moral experience of the present is to see ourselves as morally autonomous agents (Kant, or Kierkegaard) confronting others: self-responsibility and manipulative competition are conjoined in a social realm now lacking any notion of shared community. Second, the social world of individuals, with 'rights', has come to have to face the role of bureaucratic managerialism, concerned for 'utility', and disputes over decisions affecting the community collapse into the sterile assertion of rights against utilities - an emotivist moral culture. Third, the claims of bureaucratic managers to technical expertise requires both a realm of morally neutral facts and law-like generalizations about this realm. It turns out that autonomous facts, the disjunction of facts/values, and notions of social laws are all products of the rise of the modern world and none are as self-evidently plausible as our common culture supposes, and the contemporary claims to relevant expertise of the bureaucrat-managers are false[61].

MacIntyre takes the rise of the state in the modern period to be coterminous with the rise of the bureaucrat-manager. In the modern period the state comes to offer legitimations of its actions in terms of knowledge of how to manage social change. MacIntyre is quite content that such knowledge is unavailable, and that the routine invocation of this knowledge serves to obscure the deployment of arbitrary will. The role of the bureaucrat-manager, with the routine claims to expertise, is that of a discrete veil pulled over the pursuit of the interests of governments and corporations.

It is also the case that the sources to which the bureaucrat-manager looks are the realm of the social sciences as they are familiarly understood. The particular intellectual aspiration to which MacIntyre is drawing attention is the routine pursuit of statements of 'law like generalization of strong predictive power'. MacIntyre is content to offer a mild rebuttal, noting first that over the last couple of hundred years social science has not produced any such material, and then pointing out that the social world is suffused with systematic unpredictability.

Contemporary moral discourse is thus a hotch-potch of fragments of the pre-liberal-individualist era plus various modern bits of nonsense. The former would include: the memory of the pursuit of the grounded-ness of ethical discourse which is now no longer expressed in the acknowledgement of the ends to which humankind tends but in claims about simple material human nature; the memory of the affirmation of the practicality of ethical discourse, which is no longer cast in terms of the achievement of community-bound tasks, securing the grounded ends of humankind, but rather in the recognition of sets of rules of behaviour; and the memory of the affirmation of ends, which is no longer cast in terms of the realization of genuine self-hood but becomes rather a matter of control and obedience to rules curbing human nature. The later, modern material, would include rights, utility, protest, bureaucratic expertise, aesthetic consumerism etcetera.

MacIntyre argues that to reconstitute moral discourse it is necessary to reach back to the pre-liberal period where notions of community, tradition, the practicality of moral discourse, and the project of self/community

---

61 MacIntyre *After Virtue*, chapters six through nine

development were available. A sketch of this Aristotelian ethic is available in eighteenth century republicanism. In regard to this project MacIntyre is pessimistic. It is a task for small groups. The broad marxian project was too optimistic. Small groups must begin now, for 'the barbarians are not waiting beyond the frontiers; they have already been governing us for quite some time'[62].

All in all this is a quite remarkable critique: the notion of an essentially degraded polity which presently substitutes a mish-mash of nonsense for ordered discourse picks up critical themes within European social theorizing which are usually left to the submerged counter-tradition and presents them in moral discourse. Of particular interest are three points: (i) the characterization of familiar understanding of moral responsibility, as somehow residing inside the person of the individual, as emotivist nonsense; and (ii) the typification of claims to rights/protest and so on, the familiar language of contemporary public politics, as essentially futile; and (iii) the way in which orthodox social science is so deeply compromised as mere intellectual servants of the social control mechanisms of the bureaucrat-managers, who in turn are the shamans of the real power holders of modern society.

Marquand's critique of the political-economic consequences of individualism

Marquand begins by noting that UK economic agents have 'repeatedly failed to adapt to the waves of technological and institutional innovation sweeping through the world economy'[63] and, relatedly, that 'Britain's political authorities have repeatedly failed to promote more adaptive economic behaviour'[64]. The root of this failure to direct adaptation to changes in the global economy is traced by Marquand to the 'ethos of market liberalism'[65]. The attitude that saw the market-led adjustment of the late eighteenth and early nineteenth century declines in importance as competitors wedded to state-led (Japan) or corporatist-consensual (France, Germany) strategies arrived on the scene. The UK political class did not act: 'At the heart of that ethos lies a set of attitudes to the role of public power, and to the relationship between public power and private freedom, which is unique in Europe'[66]. Where the mainland Europeans, and Japanese, repudiated laissez-faire economics and deployed, variously, Listian style national developmental economics, the UK ruling class did nothing: 'The notion of a developmental state ... met dogged and

---

62 ibid. p.263
63 Marquand *Unprincipled Society* p.144
64 ibid.
65 ibid. p.146
66 ibid.

uncomprehending resistance'[67]. And this reaction was not technical incapacity, so to say, as the command-economy of the Second World War showed, it was rather a product of ideas so deep seated in UK culture as to be invisible-by-virtue-of-familiarity. Sounding very much like Nairn, Marquand remarks that following the seventeenth century English Revolution the UK did not establish a mainland-type state and that 'Its inhabitants are not citizens of a state, with defined rights of citizenship. They are subjects of a monarch, enjoying 'liberties' which their ancestors won from previous monarchs'[68]. As regards the government, Marquand notes that 'Executive power is still, in an odd way, private rather than public. It lies with named individuals - ministers of the Crown, legally responsible for the activites of their departments - not with the state'[69]. Overall, the 'political culture which all this reflects and sustains can tolerate reactive intervention, designed to respond to pressures which have already made themselves felt or to buy off trouble .. It cannot provide a moral basis for discretionary intervention '[70].

The historical occasion of this fundamental political-cultural posture is the settlement of the English Revolution. Like Nairn, Marquand sees a partial, incomplete, and presently disasterously ineffectual, revolution against feudalism - much of the old was brought along to deform the new: 'The end product was a political culture suffused with the values and assumptions of whiggery, above all with the central Lockean assumption that individual property rights are antecedent to society'[71]. It is this cultural-political posture which blocks any attempt in the UK to articulate a notion of the public-social and to identify a developmental role for the state.

It is a public-social sphere ordered by a developmental state that is in evidence in the succesful polities of Germany, Austria and Sweden[72] - sometimes called 'neo-corporatism' after Philippe Schmitter[73]. In the UK all that ever happened was Keith Middlemas's 'corporate bias'[74], which in the 1960s acted to destroy a political compromise between UK capital and labour without effectively establishing an industrial-developmental strategy. Indeed on Marquand's analysis the episode of nineteenth century industrialization looks in retrospect to have been, for the ruling class,

---

[67] ibid. p.147

[68] ibid. p.152

[69] ibid.

[70] ibid. pp.153

[71] ibid. p.154

[72] See P. Katzenstein *Small States in World Markets*, London, Cornell University Press, 1985

[73] P. Schmitter 'Interest Intermediation' in S Berger ed. *Organizing Interests in Western Europe*, Cambridge, Cambridge University Press, 1981

[74] Cited here in Marquand *Unprincipled Society* p.161

something of a side-show[75] with the early nineteenth century interest in active capital replaced by the late nineteenth century with passive rentier capital. Again one is reminded of Nairn, the crucial UK centre is the outward oriented southeastern bourgeoisie.

In sum, Marquand argues that the particular intellectual-political legacy of the English Revolution left the political class unable to respond effectively to subsequent changes in world economic system circumstances. Having apparently coped succesfully with the industrial revolution, in the late nineteenth century the UK political class effectively locked itself into an intellectual, political, and institutional posture that ensured relative economic decline. In contrast, the Germans, Americans, Japanese, French, and northwestern Europeans contrived variously to secure economic and social progress: in place of the celebration of the market, made by the UK political class, they put in place the political, institutional and cultural bases of developmental states. For the UK Marquand is pessimistic: the cultural-political mode of possesive individualism, plus the cultural-institutional vehicle of the Westminister model, combine to block change.

Marquand advocates a general programme of decentralization and democratization in pursuit of a dialogue-educative political culture, but whilst the material is certainly marvellous, the author never directly addresses the question of whether or not the UK ruling class are commited to the goal of the pursuit of effective nationstatehood. Marquand apparently takes this for granted but, as Nairn points out, ruling class success is perfectly compatible with national decline. Relatedly, Marquand offers nothing by way of clues as to the likely impetus for the changes (entirely sensible and laudable) which he proposes, and again, this can be compared with Nairn who is consistent and actually writes-off the chance of establishing republican democracy (his focus is more political) until the present British state breaks up.

The model of formal and substantive democracy

Following Macpherson I would assert that the traditions of liberalism and democracy can be distinguished and that the latter represents a submerged counter-tradition to the familiar schemes of liberalism, presented as liberal-democracy. I will add a note on these matters, looking at the central claims of the idea-set and then at the situation of the UK.

In respect of the model of formal and substantive democracy, we can begin by noting that the European cultural project of modernism centres upon the deployment of human reason to natural scientific and social

---

[75] An idea echoed by Hutton in *The Guardian* 7 June 1993 in the course of a review of P. J. Cain and A. G. Hopkins *British Imperialism*, London, Longman 1993. Hutton goes on to argue that the UK will have to 'reinvent itself'.

scientific problems and issues. The cultural project of modernism in respect of social science centres on the commitment to the rational apprehension of the dynamics of complex change. Lodged within this cultural social scientific project, and acting both as criterion of ethical evaluation and analytic orientation/focus, is a commitment to the maximization of democracy. I take the position that the late nineteenth century saw the marginalization of the democratic project of the Enlightenment in favour of the affirmation of the restricted model of liberal-democracy. Such a marginalization would have been accomplished differently in the various European states. After Barrington Moore we could speak of routes to the modern world in Europe, where the complex interchanges of classes in the process of the construction of nascent modern polities would issue in definite patterns of institutions, parties and traditions of political discourse. All matters which exercised nineteenth century theorists of social science. Nairn remarks that the process of the establishment of liberal-democracy in mainland Europe was in fact long drawn out and rather late, indeed post-Second World War. It was this delayed development, in terms of realizing the models proposed by the nineteenth century theorists, which permitted the UK ruling groups to deny so successfully and for so long the archaic character of the UK polity.

Like liberalism, the idea of democracy has its history. The late eighteenth century put the notion of democracy firmly on the political agenda of the modern period, and ideas from the classical democratic theory of Greece, via the Renaissance humanists, are represented: listed by David Held[76] we have liberty, equality, citizenship and law. The French Revolution is anticipated by the American War of Independence, and Anderson[77] takes the USA as the first model of a modern republican democratic nationstate. Its celebrated theorist is Tom Paine.

In the nineteenth century there were, argues Arthur Rosenberg[78], a series of failed democratic revolutions throughout Europe. It is here that we can locate the work of Marx. In the *Paris Manuscripts*[79] we find the ethic that drove Marx's work and it is a philosophical anthropology of humankind centred on creative human social labour, all approached via the notion of alienation, the present condition of complex self-loss in capitalist society. The demand for free expressive labour was latent in alienated labour, so it is all an emergent or tendential ethic of radical democracy. Thereafter his project of the critique of political-economy aimed to produce a systematic analysis of the dynamic of society such that key group could act to overcome condition of alienated labour: the critique was from German philosophy of especially Hegel, and the systematic analysis was the language

---

[76] Held *Democracy*

[77] B. Anderson *Imagined Communities*, London, Verso, 1983

[78] A. Rosenberg *Democracy and Socialism*, London 1938

[79] K. Marx *The Economic and Philosophical Manuscripts*, London, Lawrence and Wishart, 1957

of UK political-economy. Marx's work has come to be influential within political discourse, ambiguously given its varied 'careers', and the line of work which I affirm is the humanist-marxian.

The notion of democracy is now widely used: a useful survey of received First World Anglo-American academic discourse is made by Held[80]. The democratic line Held approaches by speaking initially of developmental democracy, and offers the usual list: the Levellers, Paine, Rousseau, and Marx. In regard to the familiar 1950s US-inspired pluralists, who noted an absence of conflict and spoke of consensus and the end of ideology, democratic critics including Miliband, Nicos Poulantzes and Claus Offe, pointed out that the modern polity was class divided and the state acted for the ruling class.

The economic and political crises of the 1960s and 1970s provoked two analyses: liberals spoke of the overload of the state, where failure flowed from the overly optimistic and extensive demands placed on state; and democrats spoke of legitimation crises as an economy with heavy state intervention to secure economic growth failed to generate the revenues necessary to secure growth or sustain the compromise of the welfare state with resultant loss of legitimacy. In the 1980s, the New Right citing Friedrich Hayek called for 'rolling back the state' to let the market recover its potency, and the New Left argued for decentralized democracy in place of the over-centralized system of the era of the post-war compromise. All of which can serve to remind us that democracy is a political project pursued in the 'real world' and that it is a project still in process.

The cultural-political project of formal and substantive democracy is complex and can be summarized as comprising a set of claims in respect of ontology, ethics, knowledge and politics. An ontology of the social world is affirmed. Society transcends and enfolds individuals. It runs through them: individuals are complex crossing points of social networks. Relatedly the ontology of persons insists that persons are social animals. They exist in society and society exists in them. Persons are creative agents. An ethic in regard to persons acting in the world flows from this ontology. Human beings make themselves in routine social practice: a double exchange, with others and with nature. Human beings are shaped in society. There is no pre-given model: human essence is tendential, creative and cooperative in essence but the actual expression is context bound (dynamics of structure and agency condition behaviour). The democratic project notes this in the slogan: 'the free development of the individual logically demands the free development of all', and the practical ethic of democracy celebrates individuality and looks to a social world which will serve this end (developmental power is emphasized). An epistemology forms a core element of the democratic position. Classic formal and substantive democracy is rationalist: we can interpretively grasp the cultural dynamics

---

[80] Held *Democracy*

that enfold us (and thus better order our activity via social-political action). These cultural dynamics may be interpretively grasped via the social scientific techniques of political-economic analysis and culture-critical analysis, these are the key procedural strategies of the core of the European received tradition. Finally a politics is implied, emancipatory action in service of progress: details of party programmes can only be sketched in with reference to immediate local circumstances (that is, local determination of political-social projects).

Democracy in the UK

Focusing on the UK experience we find that the late nineteenth century saw the expansion of Empire and with it empire loyalism/jingoism; and the ideological reinvention of monarchy as head of national family; and a measure of social-political reform under the liberals (a theme Marquand stresses)[81]. The institutional sphere sees the extension of the franchise, the rise of unions, the rise of social reform legislation: the basic vehicles of class-conflict expression were set in place and we inherit them. In all, class conflict was contained and with a measure of reform established the familiar balance of class power was established at this time. A reform-minded Liberal Party faces a revived Conservative Party. Later the Labour Party develops with the assistance of the Liberals.The period sees familiar party structures, linkages to wider groups in the community, and ideological-practical stances established. The basic axis of conflict between reform and reform-containment develops. A contested compromise is established. The resultant configuration varies of course depending on the economic and political strengths of the contenders and system opportunities, constraints, and changes.

In the realm of ideas the compromise effected in the late nineteenth century finds theoretical expression in the eclipse of the project of democracy by reforming and ameliorative liberal-democracy. In social theory this is bound up with the schism argument[82] which suggests that the holistic and critical discipline of political-economy fragmented into a series of circumscribed social scientific specialist areas (economics, sociology, philosophy, political science). The key discipline became neo-classical economics constructed around the notion of the market such that issues of production and distribution were ruled out a priori. An element of this schism-process was the loss of the project of democracy. It becomes a marginalized idea bereft of institutional vehicle, or political voice, in a period of class contested-compromise. Nairn/Saville[83] speak of the substitution by the Labour Party of pursuit of welfare reform for socialism,

[81] Nairn *Enchanted Glass*

[82] See A. Giddens *Profiles and Critiques in Social Theory*, London, Macmillan, 1982

[83] Nairn *Enchanted Glass*; J. Saville *The Labour Movement in Britain*, London, Faber, 1988

the late nineteenth century cashing of the modernist project of democracy. The outcome is that socialism becomes equated with the provision of welfare in the West, and as Bauman[84] points out the eastern block came to be regarded as one entire arena of welfare. The project of democracy has been revived in post-Second World War Europe, and to some extent in post-1960s UK where it was bound up with political conflicts and the rediscovery of the style of political dissent, plus the marxian legacy.

The character of UK political institutions and received cultural ideas are such as to block the emergence of a politics of discourse. Extant institutional structures and discourse-forms act to demobilize the mass of the population and 'politics' is reserved unto the elite.

The Westminster model effectively makes parliament a law-unto-itself. In the absence of a republican democratic-structure, with its complex specification of the rights and duties of citizens, and of political representatives and public servants within the formal political institutional system, the resultant political structure is merely an aggregration of piecemeal powers - the present residue of earlier political-economic struggles, and class contested compromises. In Europe the breakthrough to developmental states was made, even if, as Nairn argues, European reaction proved so ferocious that it was not until after World War Two that 'bourgeois democracy' was finally established.

In the UK the ill-defined, and un-defined, powers of the state are available to any party winning a simple majority in a plebiscitary election, and with an electoral system which in Europe is uniquely unsuited to producing a representative parliament, to use in a fashion unconstrained by formal constitutional mechanisms or formally established goals. Constraint and goals are customary only. Recently it was remarked that Mrs Thatcher had much more power in her hands than any eastern European 'totalitarian ruler' ever had. In the UK governments routinely disemulate. Increasingly the media-advertising world is used: photo-opportunities, sound bites, spin-doctors, election campaign advisers using marketing, with all the research repertoire of surveys and focus-groups in order to make the package offered to the voters acceptable.

Against this a model of a discourse-politics is affirmed by Habermas[85]: decentralized political institutional structures; extensive and routine citizen participation; and denial of capitalist defensive-excluding definitions of spheres of commercial-private interest, because industry too is a sphere of legitimate social-public interest. My own view of the UK is that this democratization will have to be imposed, and here present patterns of complex change in Europe might just provide the agent.

---

[84] Bauman *Freedom*

[85] Habermas *Structural Transformation*. For an overview see R. C. Holub *Jurgen Habermas Critic in the Public Sphere*, London, Routledge, 1991

Conclusion

Picking up from Nairn's work on the political-economy of the UK and its official Royal-British nationalist ideology, I have gone on to look at a core element of the UK received political culture: the ethic of liberal-individualism. It is this ideology which pervades the 'public sphere' of UK political discourse: sets of ideas drawn from this characterization of the social-political world run deep within the ordinary conversational discourse of inhabitants of the UK. The upshot of these reflections is that a new notion of citizenship defined with reference to ideas of formal and substantive democracy together with a polity ordered around a developmental state are necessary conditions of progress in the UK.

4 Postmodernism, consumption and common sense

Introduction

In the preceding chapter it was suggested that the UK was in some sense a degraded polity. Characterizations of this sort have typically called attention to certain perceived features of the contemporary UK polity: thus the decline of ideologically-explicit political conflict; an apparent disposition on the part of the majority to withdraw from extensive involvement in the life of the community; the rise of forms of life which seemed to centre on consumption; and most broadly a pervasive sense of the de-politicisation of public life. All of this would be viewed negatively of course, as evidence of some sort of extensive cultural failure. However, a counter-reading has been advanced in the 1980s in the guise of the theory of postmodernism. The core position advanced is that the industrial capitalist system has made an epochal movement to a global knowledge-based post-industrial world. Postmodernists have argued that as the system remade itself, with its new dynamic centring on the globe-spanning knowledge-networks of media, money, and ideas, the relationship of individual to system altered. Most evidently in the new possibilities of consumer life-style construction, but thereafter looking at the matter structurally, in terms of the relationship of individual to political-economic system: where the nexus of individual and system had been the workplace with repression as the technique of control, the key linkage is now to be found in consumption in the marketplace, and seduction replaces repression as the crucial axis of control[1]. Overall, patterns of life grounded in the demands of the economic system and shaped by the tradition-carried resources of culture, have given way to individual life-styles constructed from the proffered array of goods in the marketplace.

In this chapter I want to consider the commonsense level of UK political culture in the light of these sorts of claims. I will proceed by looking at the notion of postmodernism itself and consider in particular the place of the idea of the market within postmodernist thinking. I will look then at the commonsense of UK political discourses, and finally I will introduce an idea of demobilization. In anticipation, I would say that in regard to the character and dynamics of UK polity it seems to me that the work of the postmodernists is not helpful, and in place of their notion of seduction I would rather speak of systematic demobilization.

Ideas of postmodernism

The decade of the 1980s has seen the extensive presentation of a fashionable theory to the effect that we now live in a knowledge-based post-industrial world and that this new political-economic base has definite implications for the sphere of culture and for the individual inhabitant of the new situation, in brief, a post-industrial society underpins a postmodern culture. Much postmodernist material is both intriguing and opaque, and coming at matters from a broadly hermeneutic-critical direction the task of reading their output presents itself as one of separating sense from nonsense. A useful overview is offered by Alex Callinicos who suggests that three cultural trends came together to fashion the final 'global postmodernist' package. The first involved changes in the arts, in particular a 'reaction against the International Style in architecture ... This rejection of the functionalism and austerity prized by the Bauhaus ... in favour of a heterogeneity of styles drawing especially on the past and on mass culture found its apparent counterparts elsewhere in the arts'[2]. In this instance we have the posited shift from the aesthetics of modernism to those of postmodernism. And then, second, 'a certain current in philosophy was thought to be giving conceptual expression to the themes explored by contemporary artists ...[which] stressed the fragmentary, heterogeneous and plural character of reality'[3], and this is the epistemological shift from structuralism to post-structuralism. Then, thirdly, 'art and philosophy seemed to reflect ... changes in the social world. A version of the transformations supposedly undergone by Western societies in the past

---

[1] Z. Bauman *Freedom*, Milton Keynes, Open University Press, 1989

[2] A. Callinicos *Against Postmodernism*, Cambridge, Polity, 1989, p.2

[3] ibid.

quarter of a century was provided by the theory of post-industrial society'[4]. Finally, these three themes in regard to art, philosophy, and political-economic life were run together by J.F. Lyotard[5], in a strategy of extensive cultural criticism, who argued that the contemporary world was best seen as a field of language-games through which individuals moved: a relativistic, provisional, and fragmented social world where received meta-discourses of progress are abandoned as patterns-of-life structured by the practices and cultures of capitalist-industrialism give way to life-style creation within the knowlege-based global system of post-industrial society.

In regard to the aesthetics of postmodernism Frederick Jameson[6], in an influential essay, has argued that postmodernist culture has to be taken seriously as it could plausibly be taken to represent the cultural form of a new stage in the development of the world capitalist system. Drawing on the political-economic work of Ernest Mandel, Jameson proposed that postmodernism be analysed in the context of the notion of late capitalism; a form of political-economy characterized by the power of global multi-national capital. The culture of postmodernism flows from the pre-eminent position in contemporary life of the commercial marketplace. The ideas of progress which we take from the nineteenth century are eschewed. The consumption opportunities offered by global capitalism are all that is on offer. Life-styles can be constructed from these elements. In this vein earlier cultural schedules which distinguished high-culture from low-culture are dismissed. Any product offered on the cultural marketplace is as good as any other. By extension earlier schedules of the socially acceptable and the unacceptable are dismissed: any product may be taken up into a life-style package. Indeed in the marketplace-centred non-aesthetic/non-ethic the production and consumption of novelties because they are novelties becomes prized. The pursuit of what J.K. Galbraith once called private consumption expands to become in effect the sole logic of the common culture of late capitalism. Overall Jameson identifies certain key characteristic of postmodern culture: depthlessness, in place of structural analyses/understandings the surface image is stressed; ahistoricism, in place of analyses/understandings that place events/processes in history, the present is stressed; intensities, in place of considered ethics/aesthetics, subjectivist emotionality is stressed; technologies, in place of a view of technology-as-servant the power of technology is stressed; pastiche, in place of realism the play of invention is stressed; and episodicity, in place of the coherence of sequential discourses, the broken nature of discourse fragments is stressed. Against those who would dismiss postmodern culture as some sort of fashionable nonsense, Jameson urges that over recent years it has become

---

[4] ibid. pp.2-3

[5] F. Lyotard *The Postmodern Condition*, Manchester, Manchester University Press, 1979

[6] F. Jameson *Postmodernism: Or the Cultural Logic of Late Capitalism*, London, Verso, 1991

clear that this cultural logic has come to enfold us and we needs must attempt to grasp it.

One important aspect of the postmodernist material is its insistence that received patterns of social theoretical argument are now in need of radical renewal. Above I noted, referring to Lyotard, the claim that the familiar confidence of our culture in respect of historical dynamics of progress could no longer be sustained. In place of the experience of continuous intelligible progress, the experienced world of postmodernity has become one of partial truths and relativistic subjective perspectives. In our ordinary lives we are invited to select from proffered consumer alternatives in order to construct a life-style, and in the realm of social theorizing we are similarly enjoined to reject received traditions aspiring to universal knowledge in favour of the local, the partial, the contingent, the gestural. Whilst I would reject global postmodernism it remains true that there is some considerable force to many of the epistemic claims made in the name of postmodernism. In this area an influential idea has been 'discourse', which is perhaps most readily associated with the work of Michel Foucault whose method is a mixture of philosophy and history invoked to make a history of the present. In respect of the work of Foucault we can identify discourse: reality is constituted in the commitments we make, mostly unconscious or routine, in ordinary social action; we are, fairly directly, making up the world as we go along. Relatedly we can speak of epistemes: the sets of assumptions invoked or drawn upon in discourse. Discourses/epistemes constitute historical blocks of meaning, discontinuous and incommensurable, like paradigms. Then we have genealogy: the records of successive transformations between discourses and epistemes. It is all the quasi-structuralist presentation of the sets of conditions underlying patterns of more or less self-conscious thinking/acting. However, it is clear that this idea of the 'meaning-drenchedness' of taken-for-granted social practices has been a feature of much of the social philosophical work of the twentieth century, and one strong theme of this work has been with the critique of patterns of received thinking, that is with the elucidation of patterns of meaning, and expectations of the outcome of such exercises in critical elucidation have been informed by the classical modernist project, the thought that clarity was an aid to the further deployment of reason, itself a condition of social progress. It seems to me that the epistemic contributions of postmodernist work to the ongoing traditions of European social theory will have to be slowly uncovered, and the problem of disentangling sense from nonsense is complicated by the tendency of epistemic reflection to overlap with the global postmodernist packages.

There is a wealth of available material in regard to the political-economic system changes which are taken to underpin this shift to a postmodernist culture, and these are detailed and ordered by David Harvey[7], who eschews talk of post-industrialism and elucidates matters around the Gramscian-regulationist school distinction between fordist and post-fordist modes of production: the former characterized in terms of mass production, extensive state regulation, corporatist industrial relations, and mass consumption of essentially common products; whilst the latter is characterized in terms of flexible production, restricted state-regulation, market-based industrial relations, and 'personalized' consumption from a varied menu of consumer goods.

This broad characterization is unpacked by reference to the detail of the political-economy of both Western and non-Western countries over the period since the First World War. The 1930s are read as the confused episode of the construction of the fordist system; from New Deal politics in the USA and Keynesianism in the UK, through to National Socialism in Germany. The essence of the productive system was the mass production of standardized products for a mass consumer market and the technologies, patterns of industrial organisation, patterns of political ordering, and expectations in regard to consumption of the output, all took time to fix in place. Indeed, the shift to a widespread use of fordist modes of accumulation and regulation is taken to be post-Second World War, the period of Keynesian demand management and the post-war 'long boom'.

The shift to post-fordist accumulation and regulation strategies is dated with reference to familiar political-economic and political events; once again the episode of inflationary pressures compounded by the oil-price hike of the early 1970s is cited, and these are taken to have tipped the fordist system into crisis. The post-fordist mode of production is thereafter taken to be in process of construction and theorists point to a new rapidity in technological innovation, and to patterns of production which are decentralized, probably multi-plant and multi-national, and which adopt the strategy of flexible specialization such that a wide range of products can be made with designs and specifications quickly changed. This new pattern of production requires an educated, adaptable, and complaisant workforce, and government de-regulation of the market.

Harvey relates this broad scale political-economic theorizing, for at base what we have here is an old-style marxian analysis of changes in the economic base occasioning consequent adjustment in the superstructure, to the problem of inevitable capitalist overaccumulation crises evidenced by idle plant and men, and stocks of unwanted materials and capital. Fordist mass production resolved just such a crisis of accumulation in the early years of the century, and the shift to post-fordist flexible accumulation looks like a further strategy for resolving the crisis of overaccumulation which came to a head in the 1970s. However, Harvey suggests that it is all

---

[7] D. Harvey *The Condition of Postmodernity*, Oxford, Blackwell, 1989, see chapters seven through eleven

speculative and it is by no means clear whether the system has changed fundamentally or the 1980s have just seen somewhat unusually reactionary political regimes in power.

The influential text of Lyotard *The Postmodern Condition*, offers an early and sophisticated specimen of the construction of culture-critique around the idea of postmodernity, what I dub the 'global' strand encompassing the more circumscribed exercises. Lyotard draws upon Wittgensteinian notions of discrete language-games underpinning forms-of-life, in order to argue that the two great nineteenth century metanarratives of progress which were constructed alongside the rise of science-based modernity, the French-inspired ideas of the Enlightenment and the German-inspired systems of speculative idealism have undergone a dual process of decline: intellectually they have undermined themselves in shifts towards either state-linked bureaucratic control, or abstract, formalized, and finally empty disciplines of learning (especially philosophy); and in practical terms the political-economic systems in which they operate have become dominated by the pragmatics of the power of technical means, and the ends of action, the points of orientation of the metanarratives, are no longer of any great concern. This dual process of decline has allowed, so to say, the expression of a new political-economy and culture. The global political-economy of the present is dominated by flows of knowledge (or information), produced via a natural science oriented to discontinuities and novelties (rather than the task of uncovering a single coherent Truth), and within these flows groups and individuals compete for the means to fashion discrete life-styles. It may all be viewed in an optimistic libertarian fashion, a system offering freedom to choose and construct life-styles from open flows of knowledge (or information), but the pessimistic reading sees a renewed centrality for capitalist market relations (and these are ever unequal)[8].

The eschewal of metanarratives of progress coupled to the market dominated diversity of the present, all buttressed in Lyotardian reflection by Wittgensteinian notions of discrete language games, seems to issue in a new style of social theorizing, a gestural non-discourse of non-progress which is addressed to no one. It is difficult to know how one is to move forward. However, these broad themes of structural and cognitive change (and maybe decay) are pursued by Zygmunt Bauman, to whom we might usefully turn.

---

[8] See Lyotard *Postmodern Condition*, and G. Bennington *Lyotard Writing the Event*, Manchester, Manchester University Press, 1989

Bauman on postmodernity

In *Towards a Critical Sociology*[9] Bauman distinguishes between 'positive-constructive' and 'negative-critical' strategies, and notes that the former approach is exemplified in the work of Emile Durkheim, and then Talcott Parsons. The social world is constituted a reality in itself, and thereafter approached after the style of the natural sciences, as they are ordinarily understood. The practitioners equate explanation with prediction and concern themselves with causal predictive modelling. It is clearly argument-on-behalf-of-the-planners. Bauman urges that a critical sociology of emancipation is needed. These remarks signal a central concern of Bauman's oeuvre, which has been with the changing self-understandings of social theorists and in particular with the subtle exchanges between such self-understandings and the broader dynamics of change within the encompassing political-economic systems.

In his text *Legislators and Interpreters*[10] Bauman returns to these themes in a wide ranging fashion. In this text he argues that the circumstances of the shift to the modern world in the sixteenth and seventeenth centuries called forth the social scientific conception-intent of authoritative control. The role of the legislator informing the political-cultural project of the expert-directed building of a rational society. This project is as yet uncompleted. Recently the project has received criticism from the vantage point of those who affirm a notion of postmodernity. Bauman diagnoses an ambiguous situation. The new situation seems to involve the systemic changes attendant upon the rise of consumer market capitalism, with its substitution of seduction for control, with the consequent loss of the legislators role (the new system needs only technicians). An occasion for intellectuals to feel rather down at the mouth. We also seem to have a recognition of diversity of patterns of life within an increasingly interdependent world which opens the possibility of the role of interpreter. But in Bauman's scheme the old expectations of there being an historical agent, a vehicle for change, an audience for whom theorists could argue, has also gone. The role of the intellectuals is of interpretation for, it seems, no one in particular.

Bauman begins with a series of remarks on the role of the intellectuals in the period of the shift to the modern world. Moving from an analogy drawn from anthropological studies of religion, which permits the characterization of 'intellectual' as both a social role and a political project, Bauman goes on to note the circumstances and activities of the Philosophes as being the exemplars of the role and project of the intellectual. In the confusions and dislocations of the shift to the modern world it is the

---

[9] Z. Bauman *Towards a Critical Sociology*, London, Routledge, 1976
[10] Z. Bauman *Legislators and Interpreters*, Cambridge, Polity, 1987

intellectuals who come to offer to the newly constituted state the strategies and legitimations necessary to underpin its actions.

Unpacking the nature of the project Bauman, citing Foucault, speaks of the concern of the powerful in the newly emergent modern world to exert their control, to bring the confusion to an end, and to establish a regular order. In this task the role of the intellectuals is that of assistant and legitimator. It is on the basis of claims to knowledge of how the social system works that the legitimacy of the rulers comes to rest, and it is the intellectuals who provide this knowledge. Thus we have the role of the 'legislator'. Thereafter, the state and its intellectuals embark on the business of educating the people, of bringing order. Again, this is a political project. The enlightenment project was of establishing a rational state. However after the French Revolution a subtle shift begins to take place, and the intellectuals come to the view that their knowledge is not merely the guide to the state but the key to change. At this point a new political project is forming, and it is that which celebrates the role of the expert. A little later on August Compte says it loud and clear. It is this celebration of the experts that Marx attacks, they have forgotten the real world in favour of ideological recipe-mongering.

Bauman takes this broad modernist project, this celebration of the role of the intellectuals in pursuit of a rational society, with all its conflicts and disputes, to have until recently exhausted all available intellectual space. To engage in argument, even if to disagree, was to affirm the power of reason, and thus to grant the crucial point of the project's advocates. However, in recent years a new position has been advanced, that of postmodernism. From an initially aesthetic discourse on art a broad critique of the present has been made. At this point the ambiguity in Bauman's text sets in. If the postmodernists offer arguments then they will be absorbed into that broad modernist culture they apparently object to. If on the other hand they offer no arguments, then they do not become participants in dialogue, and remain merely the presenters of gestures. Bauman now shifts his line of discussion: where he has operated sociology of knowledge fashion, relating intellectual positions to structural changes, he now turns to focus on what the intellectuals feel has happened. Bauman reports that it seems to postmodernist intellectuals that the role of legislator is no longer available. The system now runs on market-seduction, and it needs only technicians, not intellectuals. In this argument he attempts to read back to structure from a feeling of disappointment on the part of (some) intellectuals. He grants that as yet it is not possible to disentangle genuine system change/cultural change from fashion, but thinks that maybe an interpreter's role is a possibility. But it is also the case that Bauman no longer feels convinced by the notion of agents-of-history, so there is no particular agent to interpret for. At this point Bauman starts to sound like a genuine postmodernist, that is, offering gestures within the non-discourse of non-progress.

The ambiguity of Bauman's work in this matter is further underscored in his text *Freedom*[11] which looks to analyse the contemporary scene. The critique of manipulative reason and political practice is one aspect of his work, and yet there is no clear response in terms of a new political-intellectual project, rather what we find is that some of the arguments of the postmodernists are granted. The shift to the postmodern world is characterized in terms of a reworking of the relationship of system and population. The key exchange is via consumption, and the ordering strategy is via seduction, the offering of consumption goods in the market place. Bauman is unclear as to the progressive reply to this new ordering strategy: optimistically, the critical role of the intellectuals; pessimistically, all that is available is the business of interpreting between divergent groupings within the consumption dominated system.

The ambiguity is not resolved in *Legislators and Interpreters*, and indeed Bauman offers two conclusions to this essay, one for the modernists and one for the postmodernists. The latter looks to the possibility of the role of interpreter within the swirl of a cultural and moral pluralism. But it is not clear that Bauman is convinced, and the first conclusion is more interesting in that it entails a rejection of the childish submission to the seductions of the consumer market place (which, as Bauman points out, simultaneously requires the bureaucratic welfare policing of the lives of the 'failed consumers') and insists on the continuing validity and relevance of the modernist project. It is possible to discern a hint of a resolution of the dilemma. It involves a reaffirmation of the ethic of the modernist project (the emancipatory celebration of reason) together with an acknowledgment of the cultural context-dependency of the epistemology of the modernist project. The celebration of reason is particular to our received culture and may be taken to constitute its core. In the social sciences the central task of scholarship is emancipatory critique and around this other modes of engagement can be ranged. In other words our received cultural traditions are particular and diverse, thus legislation must give way to interpretation, critique, and dialogue if we are to advance the original modernist project. In brief, for our culture the self-images and expectations of the theorist are revised, whilst in regard to cultures other than our own they are changed. The universalist impulse of modernity has to be curbed and here modesty (that is, revision) is not enough and a further step back is needed, acknowledgment of the other. The key epistemic idea becomes dialogue (coupled to interpretation and maybe thereafter involving critique).

The extent to which the judgement in favour of modernity entails affirming a pattern of life that can be taken to be intrinsically ambiguous is made clear in Bauman's *Modernity and the Holocaust*[12]. In this text Bauman argues that sociology should pay attention to the holocaust as an episode that

---

[11] Bauman *Freedom*

[12] Z. Bauman *Modernity and the Holocaust*, Cambridge, Polity, 1989

reveals much about our contemporary modern world: in particular, the extensive ambiguities of the rational modernist project.

The modernist project is seen to be able to create the successes of natural science, and at the same time the technologies of war and control. Relatedly, the modernist project is seen to be able to rationally order society, to enhance civilization, and at the same time to create rational bureaucracies amenable to direction by the state (and thus suffused with violence). And further, the project routinely deploys an epistemic/methodological means-ends rationality, and thus escapes from religion and magic to fashion the secular world that we know, but at the same time renders technical-rationality a 'morality sui generis' and out of reach of familiar social ethics of community, democracy, and so on.

On the holocaust specifically, the bureaucratic-rational state production of death was an expression of modernity rather than an aberration. The possibility for more 'holocausts' is lodged in the form of life that we inhabit. The implications for defensive reform, so to say, would seem to be the democratization of the state (pluralist systems of authority/power), the re-moralizing social science (overcoming the technical-rational model), and the abandonment of grand scale social engineering (in favour of piecemeal).

In regard to Bauman's judgements of postmodernity/modernity, the ambiguity is cleared-up (albeit ambiguously) in the texts *Modernity and Ambivalence*[13] and *Intimations of Modernity*[14] where Bauman apparently comes down in favour of a sociology of postmodernity rather than a postmodern sociology: the crucial difference being that all the phenomena to which the discourse of postmodernism has gestured are taken to reflect underlying changes in the capitalist system, changes which can be specified and elucidated, in other words sociology faces a new object of enquiry rather than intellectual dissolution. Bauman looks to the interpretive analysis of the logic of consumer capitalism and as noted earlier[15] the substantive analysis proposed centres on the notion of market mediated seduction via consumer constructions of life-style. However, in an afterword to *Intimations of Modernity* a more familiar affirmation of the notion of emancipatory critique is made; thus he notes that the seductions of consumerism are duplicitous and affirms that the Enlightenment notions of justice and self-assertion (rational autonomy) cannot be dis-invented.

Overall, Bauman picks up from the postmodernist package two elements: (i) the concern to rework conceptions of social theoretic engagement, which he expresses via the metaphor of the switch from legislators to interpreters; and (ii) the concern for the sphere of consumption/mass culture, which he proposes should form the centre-piece of a new object of enquiry, consumer capitalism. Of this much of the material on conceptions of

---

[13] Z. Bauman *Modernity and Ambivalence*, Cambridge, Polity, 1991

[14] Z. Bauman *Intimations of Modernity*, London, Routledge, 1992

[15] Bauman *Freedom*

engagement is acceptable, being drawn roughly from the post-structuralist line of the general postmodernist package; and, again, much of the material on consumption is interesting and arresting.

Against postmodernism

If there is an overall problem with Bauman's presentation it is, perhaps, that he grants too much to the global theory of postmodernism, the gestural non-discourse of non-progress. It seems to me that he could run his own arguments without reference to the postmodernist's global theory. Callinicos, as we have seen, thinks that the package was made up of elements from the aesthetics of art, notions of post-industrialism, and aspects of post-structuralist social theory. I think Callinicos is right to say that much of the post-structuralist material remains interesting after the general postmodernist package has been discarded. Again, Callinicos goes on to say that much of the general package of postmodernism seems to have been the unhappy consciousness of the radical intelligentsia in a decade determined to ignore them, and this is a point hinted at by Bauman, when he notes that postmodernist discourse has reflected the situation of the intellectuals. Callinicos argues that the 'running has been made ... primarily by North American philosophers, critics, and social theorists'[16], and reports that his view is that their diagnoses are specific to the peculiar economic episode of the 1980s. In the view of Callinicos the roots of postmodernism 'are to be found in the combination of the disillusioned aftermath of 1968 throughout the Western world and the opportunities for an 'overconsumptionist' lifestyle offered upper white-collar strata by capitalism in the Reagan-Thatcher era'[17]. It would not be too difficult to suggest that the global theory of postmodernism was a product specifically of the 1980s and is not likely to outlast its context of production. In a similar fashion Harvey summarizes his position by saying that whilst there has been a change in political-economic structures and cultural practices, and that whilst

> strong apriori grounds can be adduced for the proposition that there is some kind of necessary relation between the rise of postmodernist cultural forms, [and] the emergence of more flexible modes of capital accumulation ... [it remains true that] these changes, when set against the basic rules of capitalistic accumulation, appear more as shifts in surface appearance rather that as signs of the emergence of some entirely new postcapitalist or even postindustrialist society[18].

In political-economic terms then, it could be argued that little has happened to the basic system-logic or its system-extension. And in terms of the discourse of society and polity carried by the system what has happened

---

16 Callinicos *Postmodernism* p.5

17 ibid. p.7

18 Harvey *Postmodern Condition* p.vii

is mostly superficial: the global postmodernist package can be rejected. Moving on, and noting that Bauman's work is focused on the Anglo-Saxon world, and narrowing the sphere further to take in the UK only, one could rhetorically ask the author why if seduction is so effective has the New Right state-regime deployed such an extensive repertoire of repression? Better, it seems to me, in place of theories of postmodernity, to ask how the population is intellectually demobilized.

Postmodernism and the idea of the market

It would seem to be the case that the global postmodernist package has been driven largely by US theorists and echoed by other members of the English-speaking world, and it seems to me that postmodernism is certainly an expression of the system-logic of contemporary capitalism rather than evidence of a new political-economic form. At this point however we can note that a clutch of ideas are coming together: liberal-individualism; postmodernist consumerism; the Reagan-Thatcher doctrines of the New Right; and in the background the formal economic theories of neo-classicism.

That there is a link between liberal-individualism and postmodernist consumerism is made clear by Bauman.[19] The idea of positive liberty, what Isaiah Berlin[20] characterized as the freedom of an agent in charge of his own life, is rejected in favour of the idea of negative liberty, the freedom from imposed restriction, the notion of liberty that lies at the core of the liberal-individualist political philosophy. It is argued that the modernist project of democracy, the pursuit of positive liberty[21], was forgotten long ago. Hannah Arendt is cited by Bauman as arguing that the rise of the 'social question' of poverty in the late nineteenth century turned attention away from fully realising the public sphere of positive liberty and the pursuit of democracy declined into poverty amelioration and, at higher material levels, consumption. Bauman argues that the consumption sphere became self-perpetuating[22]. In this way it is argued that consumer-capitalism has both (i) offered freedom-as-consumption (the negative liberty of freedom from the constraint of want and uncertainty) to all, or most; and (ii) effectively blocked the modernist project. Bauman takes the view that the consumer-capitalist system is now stable and successful. The individual and the system are linked via consumption of goods. The failed-consumers are left with bureaucratic welfare regulation.

---

19 Bauman *Freedom*
20 I. Berlin *Four Essays on Liberty*, Oxford, Oxford University Press, 1989
21 C. B. Macpherson *Democratic Theory*, Oxford, Oxford University Press, 1973
22 Arendt is cited by Bauman in *Freedom* pp.96-8

The linkage of postmodernism and liberal-individualism on Bauman's exposition seems to be this: (i) liberty is freedom from constraint; (ii) liberty is freedom of choice; (iii) liberty is freedom to consume; and (iv) liberty is finally understood as chosen consumer life-style. The shift, one through four, is from liberalism to postmodernism. Whether this linkage is logically necessary, or whether it is really an historically contingent set of 'logical slides', the present reality is, following Bauman (and earlier Alasdair MacIntyre[23]), that once inside the circle it all makes perfect sense, and one of the strengths of liberal individualism/postmodernism is that it has been able to keep people inside the circle. As Bauman puts it, the

> strength of the consumer-based social system, its remarkable capacity to command support or at least to incapacitate dissent, is solidly grounded in its success in denigrating, marginalizing or rendering invisible all alternatives to itself except basic bureaucratic domination. It is this success which makes the consumer incarnation of freedom so powerful and effective - and so invulnerable. It is this success which makes all thinking of other forms of freedom look utopian and unrealistic. Indeed, as all the traditional demands for personal autonomy have been absorbed by the consumer market and translated into its own language of commodities, the pressure potential left in such demands tends to become another source of vitality for consumerism and its centrality in individual life[24].

Jameson[25] picks up some of the power of the language of postmodernist politics in a discussion of the notion of the market: here is the locus of the exchange of individual and system, on Bauman's exposition, and here too is the locus of a powerful ideological discourse. Referring to Stuart Hall's discourse analysis, with its concern for the sphere of ideas, Jameson points out that the notion of the market is a political resource which serves the interest of the ruling groups. The pure market never did exist, so debate in respect of it is not debate about real social processes, rather Jameson tags the idea as being a crucial area of 'ideological struggle'. Jameson grants that the language of the market may describe present patterns quite well, after all ideology and reality intermingle, but as a prescriptive programme it is reactionary. Interestingly, Jameson traces the root attractiveness of the idea of the market to the reassurance it offers to conservative anxieties in regard to the complexities of the modern world. As Hobbes provided Leviathan, so Smith provides the Invisible Hand, and in both cases responsibility for action is removed from actors and lodged elsewhere, in sovereign or system.

Jameson regards the recent appeal of the idea of the market as a product of the decline into intellectual sterility of established communism, and its subsequent institutional collapse. As regards the peculiar sexiness of the idea of the market, Jameson traces that to the 1980s linkages of market and

---

[23] A. MacIntyre *After Virtue*, London, Duckworth, 1981

[24] Bauman *Freedom*, pp. 93-4

[25] Jameson *Postmodernism*

media. The realm of media carried consumerism became the illusory exemplar of market freedom. The notion of the market is taken into common thought as both a natural system-given and a realm of freedom. In this realm of market-freedom, so the ideological story goes, the naturally given consumption-desires of humankind finds their expression, and in a fashion where as both neo-classical market economics and Milo Minderbinder[26] put it, 'everybody wins'.

Meanwhile, outside the ideological circle: the poor of the First World consumer capitalism are subject to the control of the bureaucratic-welfare system; similarly, prior to the revolutions of 1989 the citizens of the Second World of eastern European state-socialist systems inhabited a political-economy and culture which, broadly, resembled the bureaucratic-welfare/control system; and finally the poor of the Third World are seen as aspirant consumers but presently they are excluded.

All these groups are controlled and they are not sources of alternative thinking (either actual or potential), they are merely failed or aspirant consumers. Fred Halliday, in a text dealing with the impact of cold war competition on the Third World, notes that the 1980s have seen 'internationalized unemployment in the developed capitalist world and immiseration in the south, as well as, at a more ideological level, of resurrected, designer, Social Darwinism masquerading as enterprise and freedom'[27]. And he continues by suggesting that the 'cultural climate in the developed world has been marked by mass narcissism and historical amnesia ... the belief that we are living in a world of one, ever-freer, 'modern' and universal political culture'[28]. In sum, a cynical, solipsistic celebration of the model of the Free West; disregarding the poor at home and in the Third World, and centrally disregarding the still present task of the pursuit of modernity.

Looking at postmodernism generally it seems that we should distinguish: the revisions made to technical argument machineries (from structuralism to poststructuralism); the work done in opening up the realm of mass culture (from modernism to postmodernism in the sphere of art); the work done in sociology in respect of the nature of the contemporary world (from industrialism/capitalism to post-industrialism); and the ambitious running together of aspects of all three lines to generate global postmodernist theory. In my opinion much of the work on argument-strategies is valuable, as is the work on mass culture. However I am unconvinced by notions of post-industrialism, and I reject the global package postmodernism where it seems to me that the sophisticated work of French theorists has been represented in the hands of Anglo-American ideologues as a full-blown celebration of irrationalist consumerism, an oceanic-individualism. The

---

[26] The eccentric entrepreneur character from the novel by Joseph Heller *Catch 22*

[27] F. Halliday *Cold War, Third World*, London, Radius, 1989, p.1

[28] ibid.

veracity of the theorem in the context of the UK can perhaps be approached by comparing theory-driven claims to consumer-freedom with the mundane detail of the contemporary UK polity. One might say that in the UK of the 1980s we had more repression than seduction, and that the much vaunted culture of postmodernism has amounted to little more than an outbreak of shopping malls, the eccentric architecture of London Docklands, and the televising of David Lynch's *Twin Peaks*. However, these matters I will set aside for the present. I want to move on now to consider the sphere of common sense political discourse in the UK. I will argue that this sphere is not to be seen as the sphere of self-reflection of free individuals contentedly choosing their life-styles, but is rather the impoverished cognitive realm of a systematically demobilized population.

Contemporary political discourse

Contemporary political discourse in the UK has quite definite characteristics, and one can note the style of deference and protest, the orientation to consumption and individualism, and the institutional development and extensive cognitive reach of state-welfarism. Here I want to try to indicate with a few informal examples how received ideology works at the level of commonsense political discourse; and these examples I take to illustrate the situation of an extensively demobilized population.

The style of deference and protest

The demobilized population has no grasp of the levers of power. It has a political role equivalent to that of a spectator: the master style of response is deference. This can be identified in a range of guises. One could speak of the overarching form of deference being oriented to Royal-British nationalism with its official ideology of parliamentary sovereignty and so on, and informal extension in the public sphere as the liberal-individualist celebration of freedom. Such deference being coupled up to scepticism in regard to the actual performance of the relevant institutions and the principles expounded in the received ideology, and cynicism in regard to politicians. But deference plus scepticism entails demobilization, not discourse. Further, deference to the central myth of the monarchy blocks the modernist-democratic critique of parliamentary sovereignty, as Tom Nairn makes clear[29], and acceptance of this myth fuels the UK's extensive class-caste system, a system still securely in place[30]. More broadly, deference to Royal-British nationalism with its vague, incoherent, and often English-nationalist focused myth of the historical evolution of The Nation

---

[29] T. Nairn *The Enchanted Glass*, London, Radius, 1988
[30] J. Paxman *Friends in High Places*, Harmondsworth, Penguin, 1990

engenders a reassured conformity. Acceptance of this nationalism, like any other nationalism, substitutes convenient official truth for messy real truth and in the UK fantasy-history is now a huge growth industry (and in the wake of the 1992 election John Major appointed a government minister for 'Heritage').

The master style of deference acts to disguise the effective situation of personal and institutional demobilization. This is a matter of incapacity being covered-up. However, the master style also justifies effective personal and institutional demobilization: deference here is a tacit acknowledgement of the claimed superiority of the ruling group. They have access to the knowledge and information. They have skills to judiciously govern. They are responsible. They should be trusted, left to get on with the job, not disturbed. Against the global postmodernist view which identifies an open knowledge-market, we can here note the pervasive restrictive interventionism of the UK state-regime: the role of the population is that of deference and obedience to those who know better how things are[31]. The master style of deference both disguises and justifies an essentially oligarchic polity. The situation of the UK is one where neither persons nor institutions are oriented to sustaining discourse-democracy.

In respect of personal demobilization we can say that typical UK informal political discourse might involve rehearsing arguments from media-sources, or appealing to 'common sense', or reporting subjective feelings. The recourse to media sources is in the first instance entirely rational. In a developed democracy one would look to the media as vehicles for the constitution of public discourse. However, in the UK the media typically does not play such a 'facilitating and enabling role', and what typically it does do is offer ready made 'opinions'. Jameson[32] notes that the media are one key area of the expression of the ideology of the free market. The sphere of the media on this analysis is intensively ideological. Social scientific studies of 'the media' have revealed that it is routinely biased towards the status quo[33]. Broadcast media are hamstrung by governmental regulations and the upshot is that television/radio is routinely bland. Relatedly, the print media are both better and worse. Much of the UK tabloid press is little more than 'Tory hate-sheet' or comics, and the quality press is skewed to the political right. The media are increasingly parts of global communications corporations whose commercial interests include publishing, newspapers, entertainments, and specialist information services. It is this concentration of power that postmodernists identified. The sphere of the commercial media has extended enormously, and commercially proffered life-style overwhelms the particularity of the local and

31 For an explicit expression of the technical variant of this see E. Gellner *Thought and Change*, London, Weidenfeld, 1964
32 Jameson *Postmodernism*
33 See for example the work of the Glasgow Media Group

democratic. Herbert Marcuse[34] called this demobilizing strategy repressive tolerance; a general demobilizing which enfolds specifics. The upshot of all this is that the initially rational impulse of the citizen, to consult the media so as to inform himself/herself, is now fraught with difficulties. The major difficulty being that of the receipt of pre-digested opinions. Recalling MacIntyre[35] on the boo/hurrah theory of politics, as I summarized him, the media are now used not to enable and facilitate the creation of a public sphere but to manipulate opinion in the interests of power-holders.

Invoking commonsense has an important role within the informal political sphere, and we could suggest that when commonsense is invoked in ordinary informal political discourse it signals an attempt to run arguments, to invoke little traditions. After Frank Parkin[36] we could speculate that sources of commonsense ideas might be these, moving from local to general: the neighbourhood, with concrete tradition, routine experience, gossip; the locality/region, with folk traditions; the workplace, with the individual/collectivity nexus, critical and realistic thinking; organisations (private, voluntary), with the semi-formal realm, semi-formal opinions, plus perhaps specific knowledge of specific areas; institutions, both state and para-statal, with both presenting official worlds; and the media, offering invented worlds. In this context the state, by denying local power bases and concentrating power in the metropolitan centre, pressures the individual to shift their sources of critical reflection from concrete tradition, which is potentially oppositional, a little tradition[37], to the official realm of Galbraithian 'institutional truths', and thence to the fantasy worlds of the mass media. The mass with their recourse to media, commonsense, or subjective feeling are left with little more than 'arguments from ignorance', and are thus demobilized. Bauman[38] seems to think that all this has been achieved successfully by the system, and that it is more or less permanent. I think this is a false view. The shift has occurred but it is all engineered and needs must be continually re-engineered.

As regards formal institutions and their contribution to discourse in the public sphere we find a similar withdrawal. In the BBC's coverage of politics, for example, they apparently aim at 'balance'. This seems to be the point at which the BBC can maintain some sort of balance-between-contending-pressures. Hence the policy of 'balance' is precisely a political balancing act, that is it has nothing to do with arguments which may be presented in regard to this or that issue. Analysis governed by nothing more than the notion of 'balance' is just a style, formed by deference to extant power-holders. Using the BBC as an 'argument source' for informal

---

[34] H. Marcuse *One Dimensional Man*, Boston, Beacon Press, 1964

[35] MacIntyre *After Virtue*

[36] F. Parkin *Class Inequality and Political Order*, London, Palladin, 1972

[37] On 'little tradition' see J. C. Scott 'Protest and Profanation: Revolt and the Little Tradition' in *Theory and Society* 4 1971

[38] Bauman *Freedom*

political discourse is futile as what they present is pre-digested compromise and no techniques of argument or knowledge. Similarly as regards commercial firms a combination of claims to commercial confidentiality plus PR means that they are broadly invisible in the public sphere such as it is and largely absent from informal conversation. These firms enter public conversation either as villains (when they have been caught out) or hero's, as when they advertise themselves as being for example 'a Great British Company'. One feature of the post-privatisation corporate scene has been the rush to advertise; now the 'viewing public' is reassured that large companies 'care'. Again, relatedly, as regards the state machine the habit of secrecy and absence of rights of access to information mean that most parts of the machine are remote and unapproachable. Yet the reach of the state cannot be underestimated, a point eloquently made by Ralph Miliband[39]; and by Shirley Williams who commented on the results of the 1992 election by noting that the 'power of the executive in the UK, based on the myth of parliamentary sovereignty, extends to a system of patronage that shapes civic society; that web of governing bodies, consultative committees, commissions, and agencies to which the government of the day appoints its loyalists'[40], and went on to lament the drift towards an elective one-party state which ensured that civic society never received inputs other than ruling party thinking. Of course, the ideological role of 'technical matters' has been stressed by Jurgen Habermas: the claim to the status of technical-discourse acts to remove from the public sphere issues which might otherwise be taken to be a matter for societal consideration. In sum, it remains the case that in addition to a monopoly of the means of legitimate violence the ruling class has many techniques of political rhetoric which help secure its position.

Chua Beng Huat[41] has analysed the contemporary political culture of Singapore and from an initial position which rejects ideas of depolitization, advanced by Chan Heng Chee and H.D. Evers[42], argues that politics continues in Singapore outside and away from 'official channels'. In Singapore 'politics' emerges as gossip and rumour, or amongst marginal groups claiming they are doing something else. In my terms Chua rejects depolitization and substitutes demobilization, and in Singapore the pressure of the state to control political life and thought, that is to demobilize, is relentless but not in essentials different from the UK. Given the lack of institutional vehicles for a discourse-democracy in the UK, and given the strategy embodied in the official ideology of misleading (with foolish, or false, material in respect of the UK) and disabling (with the promotion of

---

[39] R. Miliband *Capitalist Democracy in Britain*, Oxford, Oxford University Press, 1982

[40] S. Williams in *The Guardian* 15 April 1992

[41] Chua Beng Huat 'Reopening ideological discussion in Singapore' in *Southeast Asian Journal of Social Science 11.2*, 1983

[42] Chan Heng Chee and H. D. Evers 'National identity and nationbuilding in Singapore' in P. Chen and H. D. Evers eds *Studies in ASEAN Sociology*, Singapore, Chopmen, 1978

an emotivist culture in place of a public sphere), which makes citizenry routinely unable to run arguments appropriate to the public sphere, then we might speculate that political argument emerges elsewhere. In the UK, after MacIntyre[43] and Raymond Williams[44] it emerges in the activities of marginal groups and it also emerges as the cultural habit and political style of protest. Of this we may note that protest is the political life of those outside either the establishment or the parliamentary-political sphere. Finding examples is straightforward, and we might instance the following: (i) the UK Muslim community's protests against Salman Rushdie's book where this group has no links to the establishment, or any effective base in the parliamentary-political sphere, and consequently they have been unable to lodge their objection in any institutional sphere which admitted of possibility of rational discussion, and so they have had recourse to strategy of protest; (ii) and similarly, the long campaigns of opponents of military and civil nuclear power programmes, where the extant institutional locations of political power have simply ignored them, and their only scope for action has thus been protest; (iii) or again, the way in which the lack of formal mechanisms of legal review forced those rightly convinced of the innocence of those convicted in recent UK 'Irish Trials' to wage long publicity campaigns (in this case eventually successful); and finally (iv) we can note that in the UK even established citizen-involvement mechanisms can be disregarded if the citizens get the wrong answer (recall Brecht's joke) as with the issue of the location of London's Third Airport which was twice rejected for the town of Stanstead after formal public enquiries, and has now been built at Stanstead. As cultural style protest is well developed and in the UK we have parades, marches, events and so on. In sum an informal folk-politics, usually futile, but occasionally having an impact. On protest generally, MacIntyre[45] suggests that the modern world has come to neglect democracy in favour of a ridiculous confrontation between essentially subjective protest and bureaucratic pseudo-rationality.

In sum it is not possible to regard the UK as an open society. Power is reserved unto the elites and the population are better seen as a mass rather than a citizenry[46]. This status is both reflected in and in part created by their active demobilization as citizens. For the majority politics reduces to deference and protest.

---

43 MacIntyre *After Virtue*

44 R. Williams 'Base and superstructure in marxist cultural theory' in *New Left Review 82*, 1973

45 MacIntyre *After Virtue*

46 One recalls A. Kornhauser *The Politics of Mass Society*, London, Collier, 1958 from another period of conservatism

Consumption and individualism

If deference and protest represent the sphere of active demobilization then there are also passive demobilization strategies. This is the sphere picked out by Bauman[47] where freedom is understood as consumption or life-style. Analysis of the sphere of consumer culture has been a major concern of the postmodernists. Where other theorists have tended to be dismissive, seeing the realm of consumption as system-derivative and thus suffused with the ideas and practices of the capitalist system as a whole, the postmodernists have insisted that the sphere be considered directly, and read as valid in its own terms. Mike Featherstone[48] reports that it is possible to identify three broad approaches to the analysis of consumer culture: the critical, the elucidatory and the affirmative.

The critical line traces back to the analyses of Georg Luckacs and the Frankfurt School who presented notions of mass culture, the superstructural form of fordist modes of production. In brief the new realms of popular culture and mass consumption were taken to be both degraded cultural forms (low culture) and demobilizing politically (paradigmatically Hollywood, the 'dream machine'). Activities which had been undertaken in private time according to private, or local cultural norms, become part and parcel of the mass cultures of entertainment or leisure. One familiar line of objection to such analyses is noted by Featherstone, the suggestion of elitist disregard for the ways in which consumer cultural forms were read by those participating in this realm.

An approach to such questions can be derived from cultural anthropology and the issue becomes one of the use of commodities as cultural markers, where such markers announce social position, often class. In this analysis the use of commodities within society is accorded a more straightforwardly social scientific analysis: the use made of commodities by people is complex and subtle, and thus presents itself as a realm for investigation. Featherstone cites the work of Pierre Bourdieu[49] and his notion of 'habitus' - the ways in which the class position of an individual is inscribed in patterns of consumption, bearing, taste, speech and so on. In regard to the theorists of postmodernity it is here that they begin their efforts: the contemporary world comprises a profusion of commodities amenable to subtle and routinely reworked significance. Indeed, as Featherstone notes, the contemporary consumer world throws-up its own experts, para-intellectuals, those who teach consumers how and what to consume.

---

[47] Bauman *Freedom*
[48] M. Featherstone *Consumer Capitalism and Postmodernism*, London, Sage, 1991
[49] For a review see D. Robbins *The Work of Pierre Bourdieu*, Milton Keynes, Open University Press, 1991

Finally, there is a line of reflection which traces back to pre-modern notions of excess which might be found in the institution of carnival, or the fair (where rational market exchange and expressive consumption are important). Such forms of activity come down to the present, it is suggested, in the form of departmental store or shopping mall. Again, it is suggested that the critics of the Frankfurt School have missed an important issue, that of popular culture.

All of this 'consumption and individualism' feeds into ordinary discourse of politics. What we find is the routine displacement of the political into the consumptionist as issues are read-out of the political sphere and read-into the market sphere: (i) green politics becomes green consumerism; (ii) freedom of action becomes freedom of consumption; (iii) freedom of thought and association becomes life-style choice; and (iv) scholarship as central to discourse-democracy becomes expert advice in respect of ameliorism (at best).

It seems to me that Featherstone is right to call attention, as do the postmodernists, to the realm of expressive consumption. Clearly it offers scope for fascinating ethnographic study, but the questions posed by the Frankfurt School remain, and much of what the postmodernists say is compatible with the view of consumer culture as system-derivative and suffused with the norms of the capitalist system.

State welfarism

In the post-Second World War period the UK 'welfare state' is usually taken as one of the great success stories. The provision of social welfare has been seen as central to the political-cultural project of the Labour Party. However there are problems: one line of attack comes from the New Right who have spoken of a 'dependency culture'; and another line of sceptical unease, rather than outright criticism, has come from those who doubt the bureaucratic-regulative tendency of labourism.

The former can be dismissed as varieties of apologies for the status quo coupled up to gut-prejudice. However, in regard to the latter the debate gets much more interesting. The Labour Party has affirmed an idea of community. It has pursued social welfare goals on behalf of the community-as-it-conceives-it. But the result is distinctly bureaucratic-welfarist, paternalist, and conservative. Above Bauman cited Hannah Arendt to the effect that socialism long ago mistakenly abandoned the pursuit of citizenship for the pursuit of welfare. In the UK the Labour Party has for long made 'protecting the weak' central to its social welfarism, but now it is challenged by libertarian notions of decentralization and empowerment, and by a resurgence of concern for democracy and citizenship where labourist paternalism and conservatism quickly comes to look authoritarian.

John Saville[50] distinguishes between parties of reform and reformist-socialist parties, and notes that it is clear that the Labour Party has ever been the former type. It has struggled against a reactionary and powerful bourgeoisie and secured some social welfare. The posture adopted is one of 'labourism' and can be traced to the defeat of the democratic movement of Chartism which prompted the construction of a dense network of institutions: corresponding societies, unions, cooperatives, churches and so on, all of which were oriented to ameliorating the situation of the working classes. Eventually the Labour Party is formed and it has pursued similar objectives ever since. As regards the period of 1945-51, the parties 'golden age', Saville notes that it saw the succesful achievement of demobilization consequent upon the ending of hostilities, the basic ideas of welfare state were set in place, and the UK became embroiled in the Cold War (in no small measure thanks to Ernest Bevin). The USA became the new hegemonic power and the government failed to realize this, and failed also to democratize, modernize, reduce defence spending or offload the empire. Saville argues that what 'needs to be emphasized for the years immediately after 1945 is that the welfare policies and highly conservative nationalization measures were slotted into a society that had remained unchanged in its fundamentals during the war'[51], and by 1951 'Labour socialism had arrived at a dead-end'[52].

In the commonsense sphere this bureaucratic-welfarism has produced a distinctive discourse: 'something should be done about it', 'there should be a law against it', 'why has the council or government not done something', and broadly, 'I am entitled to'. In brief, extant UK political discourse at an ordinary level is shot-through with the thought-patterns of state-welfarism, and in the UK it seems to me, given its Fabian and technocratic occasion and style, this does act to demobilize the population, and as has been noted by Paul Hirst, Raymond Plant and David Marquand lines of reform to this stance could usefully embrace notions of community, pluralistic decentralization, and social welfare rights[53].

Conclusion

The formal expositions of postmodern theory celebrate the transient, the decorative, the superficial. Ideas typical of modernity and modernism, progress and clarity of design, are ridiculed as aspects of a meta-discourse which has been overtaken by events. In a political-economy which is now very productive individuals relate to the collectivity via marketplace

---

[50] J. Saville *The Labour Movement in Britain*, London, Faber, 1988

[51] ibid. p.112

[52] ibid. p.121

[53] All in Ben Pimlott ed. *The Alternative: Politics for a Change*, London, W H Allen, 1990

consumption rather than workplace production, and 'seduction' replaces 'control'. In place of overarching schemes of societal development, meta-discourses, postmodernists rest content with the gestural non-discourse of non-progress. Postmodernism urges that consumer-capitalism offers the masses a freedom of life-style that utterly seduces them, and the system is thus stable. However postmodernism looks an implausible doctrine. A mixture of interesting technical social philosophy and cultural criticism has been hi-jacked in the 1980s by disappointed intellectuals, and the core ideas of global postmodernism look like a warmed-over 'end of ideology thesis'. Against postmodernist ideas of seduction I have pointed out that in the UK through the 1980s consent has been engineered. The ruling class puts words into the mouths of the members of the subordinate classes, thus do they acquiesce. Finally, by way of a gesture in the direction of a more optimistic future, all this may be compared with the ideal-typical social-democracy of the mainland: a notion of citizenship is routinely affirmed, and the inhabitants of a country are members of that community/polity; the role of the public sphere is affirmed, and the inhabitants have access to a sphere of citizen participation; an idea of civil society is affirmed, and there is a realm of private and family activity-in-community; and the model of a republican state is affirmed, and citizens inhabit democracies.

5 Old right, new right

Introduction

The material of the foregoing trio of chapters has focused on structural issues: first the political-cultural system of the UK; secondly, the discourse of liberal-individualism; and, finally, the extension of official ideologies into the realm of common sense. Recalling Anthony Giddens[1] on the role of structure as constraint and opportunity, these structures are the givens within which a variety of agents order and pursue their particular projects. As the structures were political-cultural the relevant agents are political agents. Out of the spread of such political agents, which includes individuals, groups, classes and so on, I want to look at the actions of formal political parties in the UK. Much of the substance of politics, that is matters of power, may well be taken to lie elsewhere (thus, those individuals and groups strategically placed in economic, cultural, and political networks at domestic, state-level, and trans-state level), but UK public political discourse takes the formal political parties as significant players. In this chapter I look at the party of the right, the Conservative Party, and in the next chapter I turn to the parties of the centre and left.

I will approach these matters of agency by looking at the structures within which they operate, another variant of the procedures of the foregoing chapters. Tom Nairn and Perry Anderson, in chapter two, dealt with phases in the development experience of global capitalism, within which contexts

---

[1] A. Giddens *Central Problems in Social Theory*, London, Macmillan, 1979

the particular experience of the UK was read. It is this idea of discrete phases within a wider system that I will pursue. The approach differs from familiar discussions which typically focus on the UK scene as if it were a more or less closed system. As will become clear, I take the view that such an analytic strategy is wrong-headed. Matters will be addressed as follows: (i) the problem of analysing system-contexts and state-regime projects; (ii) the particular system-context within which the UK operates; and (iii) the internal characteristics of the UK New Right project.

Analysing system-contexts and state-regime projects

The study of international relations does not usually figure very strongly in the work of the core disciplines of social science. It exists 'off to one side', closely linked to the world of state-state relations, of diplomacy. However elements of this material can serve to buttress the work of the various lines within social science that have stressed the trans-state contexts of the actions of individual states[2]. Andrew Linklater[3] argues that orthodox international relations work has focused on either realist analyses of the power relations of states, or rationalist analyses of the inter-state structures ordering these exchanges. In my terms realist analyses are liberal-individualism writ-large. The inter-state system is anarchic and order is maintained only via balance-of-power mechanisms[4]. Rationalist analyses contradict the realists by pointing to the existing international relations system where there are many mechanisms for constructing and maintaining order.

Linklater discusses both realism and rationalism, and then goes on to look at marxian work: (i) realism is criticised for its arbitrary treatment of state-state exchanges in isolation from other linkages (that is, structure); (ii) realism is criticised for a spurious technical-neutrality in its analyses; (iii) both approach and results (an anarchical system governed by logic of balance of power) are rejected; and (iv) whilst rationalism offers a variant on realism by arguing that state-state systems do have normative underpinnings, and that these are typically implicated in the normative systems within states, and there is thus a sort of international society carrying an ethic in regard to political action, they neglect the material base of the global system[5]. In brief, both lines of the orthodoxy abstract state-state relationships from the encompassing networks of economic, political, and cultural linkages to which political-economy points. However, Linklater

---

[2]Indeed Giddens criticizes sociology for its society-equals-nationstate habit of thought: drawing on marxian work he advocates a world system contextualized modernist project as a more appropriate theoretical object.

[3]A. Linklater *Beyond Realism and Marxism: Critical Theory and International Relations*, London, Macmillan, 1990

[4] ibid. pp.10-14

[5] ibid. pp.15-21

reports that the marxian political-economy of international relations has been rediscovered, and that this approach looks to lodge state-systems within a broader scheme of the development of global capitalist system. A critical reading of the marxian tradition is required to enable debate to move towards the goal of a 'critical theory of international relations'.

As regards the marxian political-economic traditions approach to the analysis of the global system, Linklater identifies a series of problems: (i) in dealing with the causes of change, where the marxian tradition has focused on economically occasioned class-conflict as the motor of change and this essentially economic reductionist approach has blocked attention being paid to other causes, thus for example, state/nation dynamics[6]; (ii) in dealing with the role of the state, where Marx rather tended to look at class-conflict within a state-unit and the business of state-state conflict within a trans-state system was not pursued; (iii) in grasping the role of nations/nationalism, where the marxist focus on class-driven change has left nation/nationalism to one side, often regarded as a distraction; and (iv) in grasping the relations of trans-state and state systems, where the ideas of imperialism (Lenin) and world system (Wallerstein) have been used to address the issue, but, arguably, have never solved it[7]. Linklater, citing Giddens, takes note of the notion of a 'post-marxist approach' and for the future looks for a transcendence/synthesis of international relations work and marxist political-economy in a new approach centring on Habermasian-style schemes of evolution and critique. A critical international relations will be oriented to the expansion of trans-state spheres of community.

The upshot of Linklater's reflections is that any substantive analysis of international relations, which the author would then slot-into an evolutionary and critical emancipatory frame, must look to configurations of the world system, the complex meshing of structures within which agents (that is, a state or regime) necessarily operate, and at how specific agents read such configurations and thus order their actions. The corollary of this, relevant to looking at the UK right, is that the actions of any regime cannot be understood as endogenously occasioned, rather they have to be seen as subject to extensive exogeneous constraint. The agents in question, in this context, will be those able to wield the power of the state, and thus we might speak of 'state-regimes'. In any analysis the actions of the state-regime must be subject to an immediate and extensive contextualization: the situation within global economic system; the situation within global political system; the position in regard to domestic political-economic structures and agents; the scope for possible actions by regime-in-control-of-state; and thereafter the actions of a regime can be taken to embody an ethic or

---

6 On this see T. Nairn *The Enchanted Glass*, London, Radius, 1988

7 On this issue generally see O. Munk *The Difficult Dialogue: Marxism and Nationalism*, London, Zed, 1986

programme (which of course must be acknowledged, characterized and judged).

Analysing system-contexts

The track records of particular state-regimes can be read as exemplifying a series of projects, where such projects represent creative responses to the enfolding dynamics of the global capitalist system. A context-sensitive analytic strategy dissolves the actions of the state-regime into a much more complex trans-state system. Analysing state-regimes as if they were autonomous units is misleading, and the familiar talk about nationstates, taken as somehow essentially self-contained, is an error which reifies a contingent set of relationships thereby obscuring the very processes under consideration.

Over the post-Second World War period, by way of an example, this is precisely how orthodox development theory analysed problems of Third World development. The early expectations of the First World theorists, shaped in a period of optimistic decolonization and bi-polarity, the high-tide of fordism, were that the Third World would recapitulate the historical experience of the West. The discourse of development saw the elaboration of a complex package oriented to the goal of the pursuit of effective nationstatehood which the experts imputed to the replacement elites of the new nationstates of the Third World. This ideal goal can be unpacked to reveal a triple task involving the engendering of political and cultural coherence, the securing of political and social stability, and the achievement of economic growth and welfare. However the assumptions built into this model are extensive, and when examined untenable. There is a triple claim to knowledge (of claimed development sequences), to expertise (in regard to ordering the process), and ethic (in regard to the obligation of First to Third, and the nature of the overall goal of liberal-democracy). The model slowly collapsed because the experts did not have the knowledge or the expertise, and their Western ethic was only dubiously relevant.

As the model collapsed First World development work divided into three broad channels: state aid programmes continued for various reasons (which may or may not have included 'development'); practitioner groups looked to small scale 'empowerment', a much more plausible engagement; and relatedly theorists looked to revise the whole panoply of received expectations. Here we find a shift away from exporting recipes to analysing the detail of actual economic, social, political and cultural processes using the established repertoire of concepts carried in the central tradition of European social science. The upshot has been a return to core concerns with the interpretive and critical analysis of complex change within the context of the on-going development of the global capitalist system.

Once the new nationstates have been put back into their global system contexts, so to say, a plausible way of handling the development experiences of these new nations is generated. In place of evaluations of track records according to the model of the pursuit of effective nationstatehood, which often generates tales of breakdown or falling away from liberal democratic grace[8], we can look at track records as exemplifying the political projects of state-regimes. Such political projects represent the agency of state-regimes within the structural circumstances they inhabit, and in practice, of course, all this is fraught with the usual problems of coalition building and conflict control internally, plus reading global structures and thereafter formulating practical programmes. In the case of Singapore, for example, we find a successful state-regime has pursued a project of upgrading and extending its economic linkages to the global system whilst securing the support/acquiescence of its population with material rewards and basic welfare (schools, health, housing, food). The state-regime project can only be understood in terms of the response of an agent to structural circumstances. In terms of the ideology of the pursuit of effective nationstatehood Singapore has succeeded, and at the same time has submerged itself ever more deeply in trans-nationstate systems. The general point that countries operate within wider systems was very well illustrated by Clive Hamilton[9] on the Four Little Tigers of Asia, where a review of their track records indicates how internal class-groupings came to power and then seized the opportunities provided by expanding global economic system to carve out distinctive economic spaces.

In sum, the material of development theory considered in the light of the remarks on international relations theory reveals that to grasp the nature of a particular state-regime it is necessary to consider the projects these agents pursue within the context of global system structures.

Analysing state-regime projects

There are a variety of approaches to the analysis of the projects of state-regimes, and all revolve around the political-economic and culture-critical analysis of the dynamics of the exchange of internal and external systems, where these structural dynamics constrain the possibilities open to agent-groups. An interesting approach is presented by Susan Strange[10] who looks to construct a political-economy of international relations. Orthodox international relations work is deficient because it focuses exclusively on the relations of governments. Similarly, orthodox economics and political-science are also rejected as both inhabit closed intellectual spaces and take

8 B. N. Pandy *South and Southeast Asia*, London, Macmillan, 1980; see also R. H. Jackson *Quasi-States: Sovereignty, International Relations and the Third World*, Cambridge, Cambridge University Press, 1990

9 C. Hamilton 'Capitalist Industrialization in East Asia's Four Little Tigers' in *Journal of Contemporary Asia* 13, 1983; see also W Bello and S Rosenfeld *Dragons in Distress: Asia's Miracle Economies in Crisis*, San Francisco, IFDP, 1990

10 S. Strange *States and Markets*, London, Pinter, 1988

their spheres of enquiry to be similarly closed: economics is blind to issues of power, and political-science typically ignores economics in its focus on governmental machineries. Work from outside these usual areas is invoked: development economics; historical sociology; and economic history. Yet liberals and marxists are rejected as ideologues. In regard to the familiar social scientific issue of valuation and engagement, Strange notes that 'What I am suggesting here is a way to synthesize politics and economics by means of structural analysis of the effects of states, or more properly of any kind of political authority, on markets and, conversely, of market forces on states'[11]. The key is an idea of the basic needs of any polity in respect of wealth, security, freedom, and justice. Strange takes the view that any polity will evidence some mix of these four. An international political-economy approach can lodge agents (states, or polities) within global structures of power and thus uncover the trans-state mechanisms which underpin given empirical configurations of wealth, security, freedom and justice.

Strange distinguishes structural and relational power where the former sets the broadest of agendas, the frames within which people and groups have to act, and the later focuses on specific episodes of agent exchanges. A final useful notion is that of 'bargains', the compromises struck within a given situation that order subsequent relations. Most broadly, Strange offers the model of a world system comprising a variety of power structures within which agent-groups, primarily states, move, and where the specific exchanges of agent-groups and global structures generate the familiar pattern of extant polities. In all, Strange offers what is in effect a softened-liberalism with the notion of the global system as an overarching frame. That there might be discontinuities in this global system, and in the historical trajectory of capitalism, are not allowed. Nonetheless, this schematic approach does offer a preliminary way of grasping some sort of overview of the wider system within which perforce a state-regime will operate.

On Strange's analysis structural power is found in the four spheres of security, production, financial credit, and knowledge; where the first is the familiar realm of state-state relations, the following pair note the crucial role of economic power, and finally the importance of the subtler sphere of culture is acknowledged. The first noted, the security structure, comprises the networks of relationships between states which revolve around, and order, the use of force. These structures are extensive, and cover diplomatic, military, and security linkages. In regard to the second pair, the production structure, the sphere of the military overlaps in the history of the development of the modern First World dominated global system with the rise of industrial production and global trade. Strange acknowledges recent arguments in regard to the new international division of labour and notes that the production of material goods now takes place in the context of

---

[11] ibid. p.13

a world-wide integrated system. Relatedly, the financial structure comprises an integrated global network, with major centres in Europe, the USA and Japan. This network is the source of credit, and the ability to generate credit confers significant power. Finally the knowledge structure is one of the underpinnings of the entire system, and Strange has in mind the production not merely of scientific and technical knowledge, but also social technologies of management, the business of putting the knowledge to work.

These networks of power constitute the underlying structure of the global system, and whilst resources of power, production, finance and knowledge are unevenly distributed they provide the start-point for the activities of any extant state-regime. Overall, the idea that the author is after seems to be that of a world system comprised of a variety of power structures within which states (and other actors) are agents: lines of power are relatively fixed and the polity itself given shape. The text is naturalistic, takes the world economic system for granted, and looks to a value-neutral analytic machinery, nonetheless what we have is a strategy of analysing the axes of structural power which necessarily constrain/enable the actions of state-regimes (as agents). In place of state-state relations we have a picture of many states-within-the-global-system enmeshed in a network of power relations.

One particular problem with Strange's international political-economy approach is that it rather reduces the business of the internal make-up of any state-regime to a reflection of trans-state flows of power. A corrective to this can be found within that broad marxist tradition which Strange discards, in particular the work of the regulationist school who have offered not dissimilar analyses which do pay attention to the internal dynamics of state-regimes within the shifting patterns of power of the global system. The literature flows from the work of Aglietta[12] and centres on the identification of patterns of accumulation and regulation within state-regimes and across wider sweeps of the global capitalist economy. This school gives us the recently familiar analysis of the post-oil shock shift from fordist to post-fordist political-economic modes of accumulation and regulation[13].

The regulationist school has subsequently become diverse[14], and one line, which stresses the international aspect of class formation, is the Amsterdam regulationist school. Analytically, Henk Overbeek[15] proceeds to look for a series of class-compromises, serving particular class-fractions, and understood via hegemonic ideas, through the stages of the development of the global capitalist system. The interesting notion for present purposes is

---

[12] M. Aglietta *A Theory of Capitalist Regulation*, London, Verso, 1979

[13] See J .Allen and D. Massey eds. *The Economy in Question*, London, Sage, 1989

[14] See B. Jessop *State Theory*, Cambridge, Polity, 1990, chapter eleven

[15] H. Overbeek *Global Capitalism and National Decline*, London, Allen and Unwin, 1990

that of the reading of the world which is promulgated through the polity (thereby achieving hegemony), the comprehensive concept of control. This

> consists in a coherent formulation of the 'general interest' which transcends narrowly defined fractional interests and which combines mutually compatible strategies in the fields of labour relations, socio-economic policy and foreign policy on the basis of a class compromise entailing specific economic and/or ideological rewards for the dominated classes and class fractions involved[16].

Overbeek points out that these concepts of control express the dynamic tensions between competing class-fractions (clustering around circulating and productive capital). These comprehensive concepts of control

> represent the unity of: a more or less coherent set of ideas and programmes; a 'critical mass' of interests forming the socio-political basis for such a programme; and the constellation of (national and international) economic and class forces providing the structural context in which interests are politically articulated[17].

Bob Jessop has offered a similar strategy of analysis which is concerned to 'develop a range of concepts which identify the institutional forms through which civil society, the state and the economy are linked to one another'[18], and he suggests that 'the notions of 'social base', 'accumulation strategy', 'state strategy' and 'hegemonic project' are helpful constructs through which to organise political analysis'[19]. These four elements are unpacked at length and together are taken to display the structural mechanisms underpinning surface phenomena.

The social base of the political order is 'a set of social forces which support - within an accepted institutional framework and policy paradigm - the basic structure, mode of operation and objectives of the state system in its role as the official representative of civil society'[20]. The social base thus points to the wide extension within the population of the extant political order: institutions, ideas, compromises, and collectively affirmed policy orientations.

The idea of accumulation strategies points to a core economic project 'or model, of economic growth together with both its associated social framework of institutions (or 'mode of regulation') and the range of government policies conducive to its stable reproduction'[21]. The accumulation strategy expresses the state strategy and is the ideal model, in

---

[16] ibid. p.26

[17] ibid. pp.26-8 These points were originally listed, I have made the presentational ammendment

[18] B. Jessop et al. *Thatcherism A Tale of Two Nations*, Cambridge, Polity, 1988

[19] ibid. p.156

[20] ibid.

[21] ibid. p.158

all its social and economic complexity, affirmed by the key political agents. The role of the state is central, and the notion of a state strategy is deployed. The state sphere is thus an effective agent, and not, say, determined by the logic of capital. It is also a site of conflict. It is not merely the realm of the ruling class. The state-strategy is 'a pattern of intervention in the economy'[22] which supports a particular accumulation strategy and positions and rewards the key relevant groups. Finally the hegemonic project is 'a national-popular programme of political, intellectual and moral leadership which advances the long-term interests of the leading sectors in the accumulation strategy while granting economic concessions to the masses of the social base'[23].

Overall this is a strategy of making an holistic-interpretive political commentary. Jessop deploys this strategy to read Thatcherism, and as such I will come back to it, however one might note here that Jessop rather neglects the trans-state context. The focus of the analytic machineries is largely on matters internal to the nationstate, presented as responding to outside forces. Following, it must be better to begin with a frame that grants more to the trans-state systems of power within which agent-groups necessarily move.

In this light, and for present purposes, what the work of Overbeek offers is a way of integrating the sorts of structural analyses pointed to by Strange with the detail of the internal dynamics of countries which Jessop treats, where such dynamics will issue in the rise to power of a particular state-regime. Such regimes will confront a fluid and changing set of circumstances, both internal and trans-state, and it is their reading and response which will shape the historical dynamic of the polity in question. Overbeek claims that this approach, unlike Jessop's, can link structure and agency, and notes that

> Every comprehensive concept of control contains at least four central elements ... (1) the relationship with the outside world and the aspired position of the national bourgeoisie in the world class structure; (2) the balance of forces between the social classes within the country; (3) the role of the state in the accumulation process and the overall relations between state and civil society; (4) the relations between the different fractions of the ruling class and the way in which these can be induced to subscribe to the dominant concept of control[24].

Overbeek then adds the substantive point of his text: 'It is my thesis ... that 'Thatcherism' is a reasonably coherent and comprehensive concept of control for the restoration of bourgeois rule and bourgeois hegemony in the new circumstances of the 1980s'[25] and this specific issue I will pursue

---

[22] ibid. p.159

[23] ibid. p.162

[24] Overbeek *Global Capitalism* p.178. These points were originally listed. I have made the presentational ammendment.

[25] ibid.

below. However, what Overbeek accomplishes is to make it completely clear that any discussion of the actions of a state-regime, in this case the UK New Right, must take note of the trans-state structural context. In sum: we can look at the New Right, and Thatcherism, as a political project; we can read the position of the New Right, and Thatcherism, as an agent-response to given structural configurations; we can note that our analyses must be holistic and multidisciplinary (so as to catch the complexity of such a project), and must lodge the projects in question within their true, trans-national (or global) context; and we can note that only thereafter might we focus on the 'internal' aspects of any such project.

Global-system contexts of the UK

As I noted in chapter two, Nairn[26] argues that the UK shifted from feudal absolutism before any other part of Europe and did so in a backward looking and partial fashion (thus with the model of the Renaissance city states in mind the new commercial bourgeoisie did not replace older aristocracy, rather they were displaced from the economic and political centres). The early nineteenth century class struggle against proponents of democracy in the UK, the Chartists, saw victory for the bourgeoisie and a defeat for the 'working classes'. Subsequent late nineteenth and early twentieth century revisions fixed this system in place and gave us the outline of today's polity. In a more general endpiece to his analysis in *The Enchanted Glass*, Nairn compares the UK situation to other parts of the metropolitan capitalist heartland, and comments that the shift from absolutist feudalism to modern bourgeois democracy has only been completed in Europe in the post-Second World War period with final dissolution of empires and the defeat of reaction. For a long period the UK looked relatively advanced but now the truth of backwardness is revealed. Writing before the 1989-91 period, Nairn looks to the future with pessimism: it may be that the relatively successful southeastern commercial bourgeoisie will take the UK into Europe, as a further episode of outward directed development, but this will not help the provinces whose future looks marginal. The various class and regional groupings within the UK now have clearly different interests, and Nairn has spoken of the break-up of Britain.

The current phase of the development of the UK can be further illuminated by sketching in some of the contemporary structural context of the UK situation. To grasp the project of the New Right we must look to structures and agents. After Overbeek's proposal, and in the fashion of Ferdinand Braudel, we can identify a series of relevant time-scales: (i) long term relative decline of the UK (late nineteenth century onwards); (ii) post-

---

26 Nairn *Enchanted Glass*

Second World War absorption within the Atlantic sphere (that is, US hegemony); and (iii) the post-1973 collapse of Keynesianism and the rise of New Right.

Analysing long-term decline[27]

Overbeek[28] follows the broad Nairn/Anderson thesis in regard to the historical occasion of present political-economic and cultural patterns. The hey-day of UK industry is taken to have been the mid-nineteenth century. Thereafter the industrial bourgeoisie were slowly absorbed by the ethos of the aristocracy, and relative decline set in from the mid-nineteenth century as the industrial bourgeoisie both failed to establish themselves as the dominant class-fraction and equally failed to respond effectively to new overseas competition.

Colin Leys[29] sees this as the first period of hegemonic crisis, the dissolution of an historical block, when in response to the arrival of industrial competitors the UK's ruling groups reacted defensively. Overbeek suggests that the polity's response to competition was empire, a sideways expansion, and not reform of the political-economy and culture. In the late nineteenth and early twentieth centuries, reports Overbeek, the UK exported vast amounts of capital, and the power of the class-fraction associated with trade and finance, the City of London, rose steadily. In a similar fashion David Marquand speaks of a shift from active to passive property, as the dynamism of the early phases of the industrial revolution fade away in a defensive alliance of rentier capitalism, both old style aristocratic landed-agricultural and the newer style industrial, against new working class groups. What was important and continues to be important, argues Marquand, was the 'counter-revolution of dividend receivers against owner managers: of consumers of property against users of it'[30].

In regard to the polity the UK class structure was shaped in the eighteenth century, reproduced in the nineteenth century, and congealed around the turn of the century instead of moving on in the face of US and European rivalry. It is at this point that Marquand speaks of the failure of the UK polity to contrive a developmental state. We might note that this covers the period when Nairn takes Royal-British nationalism to have attained its current form and role. The working class were absorbed into the system via empire-patriotism, and when the Labour Party was formed it quickly became an establishment party.

---

[27] There is a large literature on this topic. For a useful survey see chapter one of A. Gamble *Britain in Decline*, London, Macmillan, 1990; a short rather puzzled survey is offerd by A. Sked *Britains Decline: Problems and Perspectives*, Oxford, Blackwell, 1987

[28] Overbeek *Global Capitalism*, chapter 2

[29] C. Leys *Politics in Britain*, London, Verso, 1989

[30] D. Marquand *The Unprincipled Society*, London, Fontana, 1988, p.167

Marquand[31] too looks to this period as having fixed, in essentials, UK political institutions, groupings, and patterns of debate. Marquand notes that many tried to fashion reform from the social imperialism of Joseph Chamberlain, to the proto-Keynesianism of Lloyd George and Oswald Mosley, through to post-war Keynesianism, but none of them succeeded in establishing a developmental state, and nor did the subsequent attempts of Harold Wilson or Edward Heath. The situation was summed up by Keith Middlemas[32] as one of corporate bias, but adds that this did satisfy a desire on the part of contending classes for political stability. The upshot is that the present UK inhabits a pre-modern political structure which lacks the capacity to contrive a developmentalist state.

The inter-war period is analysed by Overbeek in terms of the exchanges of various class fractions against the backdrop of a broad system change to fordist production and control. In straightforwardly economic terms the inter-war period saw crisis in the form of an extensive and deep depression. The responses to these problems were varied. Overbeek reports that in

> Germany extremely protectionist and counter-cyclical economic policies were combined with reactionary political and social practices and nearly full militarization. In the United States and Sweden, on the other hand, political liberalism was combined with the first prototype of the welfare state and with a strong orientation towards international free trade ... In Great Britain, economic policy throughout the depression could be characterized as neo-orthodox: protectionist but pro-cyclical (currency devaluation, tariffs, cartellization)[33].

The response of the UK is characterized in terms of contending capital-fractions, and Overbeek identifies four: the financial and commercial aristocracy linked to City; the liberal bourgeoisie of industry in the nineteenth century; the state monopoly bourgeoisie of heavy industry; and the new corporate liberal bourgeoisie of the new fordist industries. These four manoeuvered for position throughout the inter-war period. Within the context of empire-block protection the new fordist industries of mass production were successful. However, the dominant class-fraction was the state monopoly bourgeoisie and thus fordism never fully captured the polity. Overbeek summarizes the period in these terms:

> The coalition of the first two generations of the bourgeoisie, the financial/commercial aristocracy hegemonic since the beginning of the nineteenth century, and the old liberal bourgeoisie dominating the first wave of industrialization in Britain ... had still prevailed ... The old staple industries, however, were not able to restore their prewar prosperity ... When the crisis hit, these old industries were so severely affected that the old liberal bourgeoisie could not effectively defend its position. Instead, on the wave of protectionism engulfing the globe, a third generation of the British bourgeoisie came to the fore ... the iron and steel capitalists (and other heavy industrialists) ... From 1931 until the advent of the Second World

---

[31] ibid. chapter 5

[32] K .Middlemas *The Politics of Industrial Society*, London, Andre Deutsche, 1979

[33] Overbeek *Global Capitalism*, p.59

War it occupied a relatively strong position vis a vis the City, whose room for manoeuvre and general influence suffered from the conditions pertaining both at home and abroad[34].

It is the complexity of the pattern of changes in the political-economy and culture in this period that is stressed by many commentators. In terms of the regulationist school analysis of the shift of patterns of production and control the inter-war period in the UK sees the very slow and hesitant introduction of fordist patterns of production and control. Overbeek points out that 'the corporate liberal bourgeoisie proved unable to articulate its functional interests into a concept of control that could also express the interests of other fractions of the bourgeoisie or the working classes'[35].

Marquand[36] details the political and policy debates of the period citing four key episodes: the debate around the return to the gold standard in 1925, a ritual reassertion of Britains pre-war role that implied a reaffirmation of a free market system that no politician could in practice pursue; the failed proto-Keynesian modernization projects of Lloyd George and Mosley, blocked by an alliance of Treasury and Labour Government, neither of whom could comprehend the notion of a demand-led recovery; the shift in party political power from Liberal to Labour, which was locked into an ameliorist welfarism and whose core support was the old heavily unionized industries; and the switch to a National Government in 1932 and the strategy of imperial preferences, again, a defensive reaction to the march of events. In all, Marquand identifies a failure to seize the opportunity to construct a developmental state, and overall, Middlemas argues that after the upheavals of the 1920s class-compromise issued in a disposition to favour political stability and not economic growth. The period is important generally as it marks the point at which economic problems ceased to be soluble inside the UK economic space. The stage was set for further relative decline. Henceforth the UK acted within the ambit of the US sphere.

Absorption into the Atlantic sphere

On the matter of the exchanges between USA and Europe, Kees van der Pijl[37] looks at the Atlantic system which embraces the UK, and identifies a series of stages in Atlantic capitalism, reaching back to the nineteenth century US railway boom. The shift in power from the UK to USA begins quite early in this century and by the time of the First World War the global financial centre had become New York. The inter-war period interrupted extant dynamics of change, with trading blocks and

---

[34] ibid. pp. 59-60
[35] ibid.
[36] Marquand *Unprincipled Society* pp.136-43
[37] Kees van der Pijl *The Making of an Atlantic Ruling Class*, London, Verso, 1984

protectionism alongside depression. In the inter-war period in the USA it was the bourgeois corporate-liberal fraction that came to the fore via Roosevelt's New Deal programme. Their comprehensive concept of control drew on fordism, and Wilsonian democratic universalism. In the Second World War this was deployed by Roosevelt as re-oriented New Deal: corporate liberalism. This ideology of corporate liberalism was the basis for an Atlantic cohesion of class relations. Thus for van der Pijl the construction of fordism was a matter of USA/European class formation. In the post-Second World War period the USA was dominant in what was now a changed political-economic and cultural system[38].

On the matter of the UK collapse/absorption Gabriel Kolko[39] has argued that US war aims centred on making the world safe for business, especially US business, and that this necessitated the demolition of the European, and especially British, colonial empires. In the wake of the war's end the moves to assert US objectives against the newly elected Labour government were swift, with for example the ending of lend-lease and the requirement to move to currency convertibility[40]. Kolko also points out more broadly that US war aims also involved shutting-out socialism, both in western Europe, in eastern Europe and in the dissolving colonial territories. Hence the development of the ideological package of the free west, and the institutional vehicles of NATO, the UN, the IMF, the GATT, and the World Bank[41].

The UK situation was that of tension between extensive US links and the geographic reality of proximity to a European mainland in process of political-economic and political-cultural reconstruction. The issue of empire and commonwealth generated further complexities and confusions, as was the case for other European colonial powers. In the UK Overbeek notes that the

> whole period of the late 1940s through to the 1960s is indeed coloured by the tension between the 'special relation', the need for a strong partnership with the United States as the ultimate guarantee for Britain's position as a late imperial power, and the need for closer associations with Western Europe where the fastest growing markets were located for Britain's Fordist industries[42].

It is also clear that the response of the UK over this period was ill-conceived. Ernest Bevin's 'Churchill option' attempted to situate the UK between USA, empire and Europe[43]. As the empire and commonwealth

---

[38] On US/UK relations see C. Hitchens *Blood, Class and Nostalgia*, London, Vintage, 1990

[39] G. Kolko *The Politics of War*, New York, Vintage, 1986

[40] See Gamble *Britain in Decline*, chapter 4 for a general discussion. For a marvellous recollection/reconstruction of the period see P. Hennessy *Never Again*, London, Jonathan Cape, 1992, pp.94-100

[41] See D. F. Flemming *The Origins of the Cold War*, New York, Doubleday, 1961

[42] Overbeek *Global Capitalism* p.88

[43] ibid.pp.93-94

declined into a generalized outward-directedness, and as Atlanticism strongly predominated over Europe, the interests of the City and internationally oriented industry came to the fore, and the UK economic space was internationalized with the City predominant and increasingly detached from UK markets.

Jessop notes that the post-war 'consensus around Keynesianism, international liberalization, and Atlanticism was as significant for what it precluded as for what it included: above all, it ruled out any serious attempt by the state to coordinate a domestically focused strategy of industrial regeneration'[44]. Overbeek too notes that there were post-Second World War 'fordist offensives', that is attempts to modernize, and he cites: Attlee, Macmillan, Wilson, and Heath; but all these failed, and on all this Sidney Pollard[45] speaks of UK industry as doing a good job, but never receiving full backing from state such that every passing crisis in the economy has been met by a city/treasury inspired recession designed to protect the currency and thus the City's outward-directed mercantilism.

Returning to the general level of theory, Overbeek sees the basis of the US mode of production as the mass production industries, what Gramsci dubbed fordism, and notes that the

> stage of the development of capitalism can therefore be characterized as Fordism when considered at the level of the organisation of production, as the era of the Keynesian welfare state when looked at from the level of society and state, and as the Pax Americana when looked at from the perspective of the overall organisation of the capitalist world system[46].

The period is dominated by the USA, and the fordist-Atlantic system lasted until 1971/3 when a combination of President Nixon ending the Bretton Woods system plus the oil shock (with depressed industry and vast credit supplies from recycled petro-dollars) broke the system. The collapse took place on both sides of the Atlantic: Joel Krieger[47] discusses the politics of Reagan/Thatcher as responses to decline. More broadly, van der Pijl sees new patterns of economic power emerging, and at this point theorists look to the notion of post-fordist production and control.

---

[44] Jessop et al. *Thatcherism* p.164

[45] S. Pollard *The Wasting of the British Economy*, London, Croom Helm, 1982

[46] Overbeek *Global Capitalism* p.87

[47] J. Krieger Reagan, *Thatcher and the Politics of Decline*, Cambridge, Polity, 1986

Instability, collapse, and New Rightism/Thatcherism

Overbeek[48] records that after the 1973 oil-shock there was an hegemonic crisis. The post-Second World War period fordist-Keynesian-Atlanticist hegemonic block was disintegrating. The global crisis impacted severely on the only partially fordist UK economy, and the impact was accentuated by the dominance of the City. The crisis presented three alternatives to the UK government: (i) do nothing and hope for rescue by the EC (Heath) or the revival of the world economy (Wilson/Callaghan); or (ii) institute a national-economic-space recovery programme, this was the Alternative Economic Strategy (AES) of the Labour left; or (iii) free-up the economy and open-up the market system, the strategy of the New Right.

From the Heath years on the New Right organised via a network of research groups, friendly journalists, and sympathisers within the Conservative Party. In the broader public sphere the government of James Callaghan accepted proto-monetarism in 1976 with the IMF visit, and the late 1970s saw the intellectual and political collapse of Keynesianism in the face of emergent New Rightism. Overbeek argues that New Rightism/Thatcherism is a coherent project. It is the specific UK variant of neo-liberalism. Its objective, its concept of control, is to advance the interests of circulating and transnational capital fractions whilst buttressing its position via authoritarian-populism. Overbeek argues that Thatcherism in the UK looked to de-construct fordism, with its Keynesian based class compromise, and looked to a post-fordist accumulation regime[49].

The detail of the Thatcher period is familiar, but in regulationist vein Jessop unpacks the state-regime project in terms of its social base, accumulation strategy, state role, and hegemonic project[50].

Jessop reviews support for the New Right, including voting trends, regional patterns of support, class alignments, and rather like Krieger diagnoses a new manipulative political style, and concludes that it does seem to be the case that they have constructed a new coalition, a new social base. A debate that re-surfaced after the unexpected defeat of the Labour Party in the 1992 election, when the Conservative Party retained their share of the vote more or less intact in very unfavourable electoral circumstances, a matter to which I return in the following chapter[51].

The elements of the neo-liberal accumulation strategy are detailed by Jessop in terms of four elements: a commitment to privatisation of state industrial, commercial, and utility assets; the deregulation of the City and the financial system generally; a weakly sponsored drive for market-led

---

48 Overbeek *Global Capitalism* chapter 6
49 ibid. chapter 7
50 Jessop et al. *Thatcherism* chapter 9
51 This was a familiar theme in the post-election press commentary

industrial recovery, the supply side measures; and the hope that the 'synergic effects of tricontinental multinational presence will transform the UK economy into a dynamic multi-national space'[52]. The upshot of all this is an open economy, with large flows of capital moving inwards and outwards. However, unlike other major economies the UK has no core group of industrial concerns (where the Japanese have robotics, electronics, and high-tech consumer goods; the Germans have chemicals, high-tech capital goods, and cars; and the USA military and aerospace). The UK now has an open economy without either core-industries or a government committed to state intervention on behalf of local capital, and

> amongst the major capitalist economies, what distinguishes the recent UK experience is the complete absence of a national strategy for capital restructuring ... This is no mere ideological quirk; rather it reflects the fact that because of the degree of internationalization and multinationalization of the UK economy there is simply no significant block of domestic UK capital that might provide the base for such a strategy[53].

Jessop comments, as do others, that a market-led recovery cannot reverse de-industrialization and that increasingly the UK economy will become subordinate to American, Japanese, and German multi-national companies, and that such activity is likely to be concentrated in the relatively prosperous southeast of the country.

The accumulation strategy has been ordered by a liberal and authoritarian state. Effective power has been concentrated in the state machine. As against the Keynesian legacy 'Thatcherism has proved exceptionally adroit in circumventing, riding out and abolishing the social democratic apparatus of intervention and representation'[54]. The accumulation strategy, and the authoritarianism, have been legitimated amongst the constructed social base via what Jessop refers to as a 'two nations hegemonic project'. Essentially a redistribution of privilege from poorer sections of the community to the better off, and from the public to the private sector, those forming elements of the new social base. In sum, this 'extreme liberal strategy might perhaps be characterized as a comprador strategy. Since 1979 British capital has increasingly been denationalized'[55], and I will return to aspects of this debate in later chapters.

In sum, in this section dealing with the global-system context of the UK I have argued that three time-scale problems have run together in the New Right period: long term relative decline; post-Second World War relative decline; and the recent post-1973 collapse of fordism. These three time-scale problems have structured the response of the New Right agent-group,

---

[52] Jessop et al. *Thatcherism* p.171

[53] ibid. p.173

[54] ibid. p.175

[55] Overbeek *Global Capitalism* p.203

and the response takes the form of a neo-liberal accumulation strategy where the UK becomes a base for finance and international capital.

Internal system character of UK New Right

The present UK state-regime has pursued a coherent political-economic project. In response to a set of structural circumstances that encompassed long term relative decline, comparatively recent absorption into the US sphere, and post-1973 crises, the UK state-regime has pursued a neo-liberal accumulation strategy. This political economic project is the vehicle whereby the interests of the class fractions of finance capital and UK based international manufacturing capital might be realized. The political-economic project, in brief, is the pursuit of an open economy, and was presented through the 1980s in the familiar realms of politics and ideology as Thatcherism. The actions and arguments (ideologies) of the Thatcher governments can be understood within this system-context framework. I will begin with actions, rather than the arguments. In the case of Thatcherism the actions flow from structural context, whereas the arguments are ex post facto, that is designed to explain away, to justify retrospectively, to excuse, to mislead, to demobilize.

Actions and arguments of the 1980s state-regime

Nairn[56] characterizes Thatcherism as representative of a southeastern commercial-international bourgeoisie, the British par excellence, bent upon re-imposing their power/authority upon the rest of the territory of the UK. There are two elements to this project: de-integrative, and re-integrative.

A key de-integrative strategy revolved around policies designed to advance the priority of the market sector within the political-economy by reducing the extent and depth of democratic institutions and mechanisms; it removes control from public sphere and shifts it into the market sector, and it is in line with neo-liberal ideas of democracy-as-technique only. This generated attacks on all centres of institutionally-based potentially independent thinking, where such centres are necessary conditions of formal and substantive democracy. We can note instances in respect of local government, para-statal bodies, professions, media and the law, cumulatively an attack on the UK polity's public sphere/civil society: (i) local government (noted by Nairn as base for nineteenth century industrial bourgeoisies non-metropolitan power base) has been brought under central government control; (ii) London city government was abolished[57]; (iii) para-statal advisory and regulatory bodies have been reformed, or

56 Nairn *Enchanted Glass*
57 K. Livingstone *If Voting Changed Anything They'd Abolish It*, London, Fontana, 1987

abolished, in favour of direct central regulation, or market sector regulation, or no regulation at all; (iv) professional groupings have been attacked, the law, medicine, and the universities, which are traditionally parts of the establishment but seen as threats by New Right; (v) the independent media has been subject to routine attack, for example the revision of the official secrets act (making things worse), or the broadcasting reform (to introduce competitive tendering for franchises and thus drive down standards), or specific attacks have been made (including on the BBC for the *Zircon* programme, on Thames TV for *Death on the Rock*, on Yorkshire TV for programmes on the Birmingham Six); and (vi) established standards of civil liberties have been eroded, and K.D. Ewing and C.A. Gearty[58] detail the mundane way in which liberty has been disregarded and diminished as relatedly the role of the police and security services have been enhanced, and similarly Hugo Young has reviewed the effect of the policies towards Northern Ireland upon civil liberties in the UK and diagnoses a pervasive degradation[59].

A second de-integrative strategy, the corollary of the foregoing, is the centralizing of political power in the UK in the Whitehall-Downing Street machine, a futher narrowing of the public sphere. The UK executive has been powerful and unconstrained in contrast to the other modern states ever since it was constructed in the period of the English Revolution. However, under the UK New Right/Thatcher long established centralizing tendencies have been massively reinforced. Krieger[60] points out that both Reagan and Thatcher insulated themselves inside the state-machine from the usual institutional and political controls: in Thatcher's case summarized in the question attributed to her, 'is he one of us?'. And the new premiership of John Major can be seen as a continuation of the Thatcher regime, and I will pick this up in section five below.

It is clear that there has been a systematic attack upon independent voices within the UK polity and a strong centralizing drive. Jessop[61] speaks of a liberal and authoritarian state and adds that much of this power-concentration has been unpopular but the UK parliamentary-electoral system both allows it and makes reform challenges, for example Charter 88, fairly hopeless. The matter of authoritarianism we pick up later.

A third de-integrative strategy focuses upon the sphere of economic activity. A key area of attack has been upon the assumptions, institutions, and established patterns of activity of the post-Second World War contested compromise of Keynesian growth and welfare. Jessop's summary of the economics of the UK New Right's project specifies four elements: the

---

58 K. D. Ewing and C. A. Gearty *Freedom Under Thatcher*, Oxford, Oxford University Press, 1990

59 Young has written on this in *The Guardian*, see also P. Foot *Ireland: Why Britain Must Get Out*, London, Chatto, 1989

60 Krieger *Politics of Decline*, chapter 1

61 Jessop et al. *Thatcherism* chapter 9

commitment to privatisation; the deregulation of the city; a weakly sponsored drive for market led industrial recovery; and the hope that a 'multinational presence will transform the UK economy into a dynamic multinational space'[62]. Jessop is pessimistic and anticipates this open economy strategy will fail: economic growth will be MNC sponsored and geographically predominantly southeastern, but recall Nairn, class success is perfectly compatible with national decline.

The detail of the Thatcher-regime's economic record has been much discussed. Overbeek looks at industrial policy, liberalizing the city, pushing back the state, business organisations, and concludes that the policy is virtually a comprador strategy with British capital 'denationalized'[63]. He is pessimistic for the future. Relatedly, Pollard[64] diagnoses a 'bias against production' because in the UK economic policy making is dominated by Treasury and neo-classical economics, and the result is almost guaranteed failure. In a similar vein Keith Smith[65] identifies a lack of an industrial policy, and Marquand[66] more broadly speaks of a failure to establish a developmental state. And on the resultant detail of the economic performance William Keegan[67] has spoken of continued failure. Tony Thirlwell[68] has made the charge to the effect that future economic historians would look back on the Thatcher period with amazement, a view broadly shared by the contributors to the collection edited by Jonathan Mitchie, who notes in his introduction that

> The British economy in 1992 is just as peculiar as it was in 1979 in terms of the bloated role played by the City of London, short-termism regarding productive investment, the relatively high burden of military spending, the disproportionate share of research and development which goes on military rather than civil purposes, and the relatively high proportion of investment directed overseas[69].

Over the 1980s, in sum, the UK economy has been opened up and groups linked to City and UK based transnational capitalism have prospered. But there is no sign of a widespread industrial recovery, and nor are service industries looking as if they will replace declining manufactures. Prosperity is geographically concentrated. It is also class concentrated, and on this Krieger[70] speaks of an 'arithmetic politics' and Jessop[71] speaks of a two-

---

[62] ibid. p.171

[63] Overbeek *Global Capitalism* p.203

[64] Pollard *Wasting of British Economy*

[65] K. Smith *The British Economic Crisis*, Harmondsworth, Penguin, 1984

[66] Marquand *Unprincipled Society*

[67] W. Keegan has kept up a continual critical commentary on the conservative goverments economic policies.

[68] T. Thirlwell in *The Guardian* 16 April 1989

[69] J. Mitchie ed. *The Economic Legacy 1979-1992*, London, Academic, 1992

[70] Krieger *Politics of Decline*

[71] Jessop et al. *Thatcherism*

nations hegemonic project, comprising those with jobs in new flexible high skill post-fordist industries, and the disadvantaged unskilled rest, a policy financed by oil money and privatisation revenues.

A fourth de-integrative strategy, hinted at by Jessop's two nations idea, is identified by Krieger in the economics/welfare policy area. In respect of regional disparities, racial divisions, housing provision, and welfare benefits Thatcherism acted to stress division. To break up the Keynesian growth and welfare consensus, which was built in part on ideals of universalistic provision, the New Right stressed particular provision and thus were old solidarities broken down. Krieger thinks this 'dirty politics' and dangerous, old solidarities have been weakened or broken, but nothing has been put in their place. Krieger speaks of Thatcher (and Reagan) as practising an arithmetical politics: 'Thatcherism is based on an arithmetic politics. It relies on the sum of diverse particularistic appeals - on housing, race, anti-labour or anti-union sentiments, entrepreneurial ethos - but does not represent a unified coalition such as that which lay beneath the Butskellite program of the Keynesian Welfare System'[72].

The re-integrative project of the New Right state-regime has focused on the post-Second World War welfare consensus which has been relentlessly attacked as the Right have attempted to build a new conservative grouping around their neo-liberal economics. The re-integrative project has involved this arithmetic politics. Jessop notes that the

> electoral victories of 1983 and 1987 were both premised on an alliance of the privileged nation, which reaped the benefits of the rising real wages of those in employment and the private provision (often tax subsidized) of goods and services, against the subordinate nation, which comprised the long-term unemployed, those employed in the secondary labour market, and those largely dependent on (diminishing) public provision of goods and services[73].

Jessop continues by pointing out that a two nations hegemonic project looks 'first to expand the numbers of those in the privileged nation in the area where its privileges are well entrenched - namely, transport and housing - and second, to widen the scope of their privileges - to pensions, education and health care'[74]. And, finally, this

> project is underwritten, above all, by the uneven impact of economic decline and growth ... and by a major redistribution of income from poor to rich. This entails the widening of differentials within the wage earning classes in line with market forces and arbitrary differentials; a shift of public wealth to individual rich consumers via privatisation; and the political creation of differential access to collectively provided welfare[75].

---

72 Krieger *Politics of Decline* p.86
73 Jessop et al. *Thatcherism* p.179
74 ibid.
75 ibid.

The New Right's re-integrative project has entailed deploying argument. The term 'Thatcherism' has come to be associated with the work of Stuart Hall[76] who characterized the hegemonic project of Thatcherism, in its ideological aspect, as authoritarian populism. Thatcher and the New Right broadly have been assiduous in the promulgation of a set of justificatory theories. We can speak of delimited-formal ideology and, thereafter, the pervasive-informal extension of these ideas.

The delimited-formal ideology comprises a set of core claims: economically, the claim is that free markets are optimally efficient, thus we have claims to maximize material welfare; socially the claim is that as actions and responsibility for action resides with the person of the individual then social or moral worth is maximized in non-state centred, free market, systems, thus we have a claim to maximize human moral values; politically the related claim is that liberalism best expresses and protects the interests of individuals, thus we have a claim to maximize political freedom. A correct policy stance for the minimum state is, therefore, to leave well alone. Free markets will maximize material, social, and political benefits. All of which is buttressed by claims to the scientificity of neo-classical economics, where claims to maximize knowledge are lodged[77].

The pervasive-informal extension of the ideas of the New Right have been successful in that these ideas have linked-up to available prejudices. It is here that Hall[78] can start to speak of authoritarian populism. Thus we may note the following idea-sets, all latent within the UK polity, all of which have been picked-up by the New Right. Firstly, nationalism: Thatcher has played the British nationalist card in the political sphere. This British nationalism generalizes, as Nairn[79] points out a particular English nationalism. In its under-stated form it is a sentimental celebration of a mythic rural past. In its aggressive form it presents itself like all other aggressive nationalisms as exclusive and pre-eminent, it is intolerant, in other words. Then secondly, hierarchy: the New Right insists on hierarchy. Social status is back in vogue. Elitism is back in vogue. Knowledge, expertise and human worth are now taken to be hierarchically ordered. Thirdly deference: habits of social deference are back. The social world comprises superiors and subordinates. Thus managers have the 'right to manage' and unions no rights to consultation. And finally militarism: Thatcher in particular cultivated a reputation as aggressive/resolute; from

---

76 S. Hall and M. Jacques eds. *The Politics of Thatcherism*, London, Lawrence and Wishart, 1983; and S .Hall *The Hard Road to Renewal*, London, Verso, 1988
77 On these themes see R. Dilley ed. *Contesting Markets*, Edinburgh, Edinburgh University Press, 1992
78 Hall *Hard Road*
79 Nairn *Enchanted Glass*

the Falklands War[80] to wars against the 'enemies within'. All these available political-cultural traditions, latent within the UK polity, have been picked up by New Rightism. Neo-liberal economics have been linked to a reactionary social conservatism.

The delimited-formal ideology, and its pervasive-informal extension celebrate neo-liberalism and social conservatism. These two idea clusters shape and inform the New Right politico-cultural project. Additional to this, however, we must note the particular ideological package of the free west. This is in the nature of an officially sponsored area of public political discourse, the way in which the sets of ideas assembled by the New Right are cashed in routine political discourse. This officially sponsored issue or problem complex fills the UK public sphere. Mainstream political discourse revolves around the idea of the free west. It acts to marginalize those who dissent. It acts to demobilize the great majority of the population. It sets an agenda for public politics, and this agenda is that of the post-Second World War political right, organised by the USA, and it is very narrow. Centre/left ideas in the UK have to struggle to be heard, they always appear as marginal, or protests, or utopian, or unrealistic etcetera.

The New Right's project as 'dual parasitism'

The foregoing material on the context-boundedness of state-regime actions prompts a summary view of the efforts of the UK New Right in the 1980s. It has been a project of dual-parasitism. Firstly, political parasitism in the guise of dependency on the USA for status/role. Thus the British Empire is replaced by the special relationship and the post-Second World War continuation of the wartime role as 'premier ally'. This relationship feeds into an enthusiasm for Atlanticism. It is how the UK ruling class have understood themselves vis à vis the world system. Then secondly, economic parasitism upon the European Community which is the UK's major trading partner.

This dual parasitism is the present form of the political-economic posture established in the wake of the Second World War, Churchillism[81]: an open economy linked to Europe ruled by a class grouping in thrall to the USA. Yet, interestingly, it came under severe threat even as, with the Thatcher regime, it achieved apparent dominance within the UK. The threat flows from events in the global system: first, the drive for some sort of unification of the EC (which would undermine the ruling class strategy of economic parasitism by absorbing the UK economy and forcing political and social reform in the UK); and second the dissolution of the power-block system, which removes the American-British political right's enemy, and thus removes the need for the US to have NATO, and a number one ally

---

[80] See A. Barnett 'Iron Britannia' in *New Left Review* 134,1982

[81] Overbeek *Global Capitalism*

(which refocuses on Germany as the key to Europe), and which opens up eastern Europe as the de-regulated low wage economic sphere. The UK New Right thus face the collapse of their strategy of dual-parasitism: politically Atlanticism is dead as the new political centre is mainland Europe, the EC in particular; and economically attention has shifted to Germany, eastern Europe and the EC, and the 1980s UK attempt to make itself Europe's low-wage area is now overtaken by events. Following the changes of 1989 the UK New Right project so forcefully presented by Thatcher looks irrelevant to the new post-block/emergent EC situation.

After Thatcherism 1, the fall

The dramatic fall of Thatcher is evidence first of the ruthlessness with which the UK Conservative Party rids itself of leaders who have come to be seen as electoral liabilities. The removal of Thatcher recalls the demise of Macmillan. But the fall of Thatcher is evidence also of a crisis for the New Right as they confront the dilemmas of the post-1989 world.

That the Thatcher project was inherently unstable was argued for by Krieger[82] who spoke of a project of managing relative national decline where this involved both a dis-integrative strategy of attacking the compromises and consensus views of the post-Second World War Keynesian welfare system and an arithmetical strategy of constructing a new coalition around Keith Joseph's model of a social market[83]. All in all an unstable politics, and one achieved by an activist right which has been quite happy with an aggressive political mode of operation: the upshot has been to create a damaged polity with no very obvious replacement consensus. This broad analysis of the internal instability of the Thatcherite project is echoed in Jessop who analyses the politics of Thatcher as a 'two nations hegemonic project' where the second nation are in effect dropped out of the game and into an underclass[84]. The whole is ordered, and held together, by an increasingly authoritarian state. Robert Chesshyre[85] offers a similar diagnosis: the UK is taken to be a divided society with an incompetent and complacent elite, frustrated business men and yuppies, a bitter working class, and a detached underclass. A recipe for both failure and political-social instability. Chesshyre compares the situation unfavourably with the open-ness of the USA.

By the summer of 1989 commentators were beginning to write about the prospects of Thatcher's removal from the leadership of her party. Andrew

---

82 Krieger *Politics of Decline*

83 On the 'social market' see W. Hutton in *Marxism Today* April 1991. See also R. Mayne *Postwar: The Dawn of Todays Europe*, London, Thames and Hudson, 1983 especially chapter 3 on Ludwigh Erhard who is characterized as a 'planner in disguise' (p.160).

84 Jessop et al. *Thatcherism* p.162

85 R. Chesshyre *The Return of the Native Reporter*, Harmondsworth, Penguin, 1988

Gamble[86] identifies the spring 1989 European elections as a turning point: not only did the Conservative Party lose to the Labour Party for the first time since 1974 but the loss was part of a wider ebbing of Conservative Party relevance. Gamble cites the wider processes of the end of the cold war, the reforms in eastern Europe, and above all the changes in the EC. The Thatcherite programme of authoritarian economic modernization had run out of steam, and new issues had emerged, and Gamble cites both political and cultural modernization as important. Eric Hobsbawm[87] follows up this line, and by the autumn of 1989 is writing that the run-up to 1992 and the next UK election is likely to be dominated by two negatives; that Thatcher is in deep trouble, and that the Labour Party is no longer unelectable. The upshot for all these commentators was the simple question could the Conservative Party dump Thatcher and find a new route to the future?

Marquand wrote in late 1989 that as 'the 1980s stumble to an end, there are growing signs that the 1990s will see a new agenda ... What matters is that the pendulum of mood, aspiration and policy is swinging back from individualism to collectivism'[88]. A litttle later Keegan, at the start of the new year, commented that it 'would be nice to be able to draw a veil across the 1980s and pretend that they didn't exist', and went on to review the consumption boom coupled to manufacturing decline plus deficits that are the record of the 1980s, suggesting that anyone regarding this as success was either deeply stupid, or dupes of the governments propaganda machine[89]. On this last noted, Ian Aitken in the wake of the Trafalgar Square poll-tax riots which the government attempted to blame on the Labour Party, commented that opinion surveys which showed that few people went along with this line 'marked the final collapse of that crucial ingredient in the 11-year success of Thatcherism, the Big Lie'[90]. Aitken added that few governments had 'relied so long or so successfully on the susceptibility of ordinary voters to the constant repetition of untruths'[91].

By late 1990 the valedictory pieces were appearing in the press. Edward Pearce looked at them and at Thatcher's record, and impressed by neither he commented that: 'History will surely assess Mrs Thatcher not on the noise she made or the public and private money she put into a purple-veined advertising chorus; it will look at her aspirations and the extent to which they were reached'[92]. Adding that 'In the matter of macro-economics Mrs

---

[86] A. Gamble in *Marxism Today* August 1989

[87] E. Hobsbawm in *Marxism Today* October 1989

[88] D. Marquand in *New Statesman and Society* 20 October 1989

[89] W. Keegan in *The Guardian* 1 January 1990

[90] I. Aitken in *The Guardian* 9 April 1990

[91] ibid.

[92] E. Pearce in *The Guardian* 28 November 1990

Thatcher ... is hideously vulnerable to historic derision'[93]. Pearce concludes:

> True Thatcherism is monetarism, free markets, plus advertising, ego-tripping and temper tantrums ... Margaret Thatcher was dismissed by her party for a compounded failure, long postponed by oil, opposition division and big loyal headlines, but coming at last as a judgement on a career falling so short of greatness as to miss mediocrity[94].

After Thatcherism 2, Majorism?

The demise of Thatcher may have a considerable impact on Thatcherism. Early analysis on the part of centre/left commentators looked to identify coherent revisions to the political project of the Conservative Party, but there was little agreement. Jessop writing during the election of the new leader spoke, in a piece which did not even mention Major, in terms of Schumpeterian workfare/welfare, where this was exemplified by Michael Heseltine; a version of corporatism, oriented to Europe[95]. Paul Hirst similarly noted that Heseltine was the obvious choice and asks, so why did they come up with Major? The answer offered suggests that Douglas Hurd was too patrician, and Heseltine seen as the man who brought down Maggie with the result that the Conservative Party ethos was now 'set by the lower-middle-class, suburban, and non-university Prime minister'[96]. All of which, given that these self same lower middle class Tories have no idea of the problems facing the UK in the 1990s, opens up a clear chance for the Labour Party, they must become pro-European and radical democratic reformers; in brief Hirst offers Labour the job the Tory's cannot now attempt, that of joining-in and catching-up with Europe. However, the necessary condition of such a project is democratization and here Labour run straight into the impasse of the prior necessity of internal reforms. On both the right and the left then, there was no coherent response to the passing of Thatcher.

Looking to the line of development of the Conservative Party the possibilities seem to be these: (i) Major is Thatcher-with-trousers, or as Ruud Lubbers put it 'Thatcher-minus-handbag'[97], and nothing much is going to change save maybe the over-the-top rhetoric against European unification, with the implication of continuing marginalization for the UK and increasingly rapid relative decline; (ii) Major represents an attempt by Nairn's southeastern commercial bourgeoisie to fashion a new post-

---

[93] ibid.

[94] ibid.

[95] B. Jessop in *New Statesman and Society* 23 November 1990

[96] P. Hirst in *New Statesman and Society* 7 December 1990

[97] R. Lubbers quoted in *The Guardian* 12 December 1991

Thatcher political project which will let it reorientate its outward-directedness towards mainland Europe; (iii) Major is evidence of a loss of nerve, and loss of direction, and there is no clear project in view other than to pragmatically position the party advantageously in regard to elections; (iv) Major represents a reworking of the tradition of one-nation conservatism, a sort of low-level and understated English-British nationalism; or (v) Major is evidence of all four alternatives pursued willy-nilly, where the problem of the Conservative Party is exacerbated by a deep split over Europe[98].

We might thus ask if there is now a clear project being enunciated by the Conservative Party, whether it is a continuation of New Rightism or a new departure, and how does the project of the party fit with the interests of those whom we would take it to represent? However, answering these questions rather involves being clear as to how the UK southeastern commercial bourgeoisie are responding to system changes. The world has changed under their feet, and old alliances with the USA in Atlanticism might be dissolving just as the old political cultural ideological certainties have.

After Thatcherism 3, the 1992 election

The results of the 1992 election established that whatever might be going on within Europe and the global system, and inside the Conservative Party, matters remained constant within the UK polity. The dominance of the conservatives continued as it had throughout the 1980s. In the wake of the results Martin Jacques commented that the most surprising aspect of the election was the stability of the shares of votes accruing to each party, and he pointed out that the figures for 1992 were almost the same as for 1979, 1983, and 1987[99]. Indeed this prompted some to float the notion that the UK now had a Japanese-style elected dominant-party state, and that this would bring problems of corruption, cynical manipulation by effectively unchallenged political and state agents, and overall a possibly sharp decline in the system's democratic characteristics[100].

The post-mortems in the weeks immediately following the surprising election result focused, inevitably, upon both the new Prime Minister and the character of the defeated party, and here a strong secondary element was discussion of the system itself. It was clear that the result was seen as a disaster for the Labour Party, and not too good for the Liberal-Democrats. The election result was taken as a final argument, clearly needed, that the

---

[98] A. Gamble in *Marxism Today* October 1990

[99] M. Jacques in *The Observer* 12 April 1992; W Hutton in *The Guardian* 11 April 1992

[100] H. Young in *The Guardian* 11 April 1992

centre/left had to be re-ordered. In particular this was taken to mean constitutional reform[101].

The broader implications for the Labour Party, in particular, were bound up with what looked like an emergent popular ideological stance on the part of John Major; and the difference revolved around the contrast between a backward-looking labourist welfarism, coupled to public relations gloss, which in the end the electorate simply did not believe, and a forward-looking concern for opportunity and personal advance. Hall summed the ideological contrasts thus:

> Choice, opportunity to rise, mobility within one's lifetime, the power to decide your own fate, where anyone, whatever his or her background, can become anything, provided they work hard enough; this is what Mr Major means by 'classlessness' and a 'society at ease with itself'[102].

As Hall notes, the claim may well be ludicrous, but 'it is exactly the kind of 'accessible classlessness' that millions believe to be desirable and realistic'[103]. An appreciation of the potency of this message requires that commentators acknowledge the new 'sociology of aspirations'. It is against this ideological package that labourism fails. Hall comments that 'in the long years of policy revision and image revitalization, Labour has not found another, effective way of voicing these changed realities'[104]. What is needed, on Hall's analysis, is a new vision of a social-democratic politics adequate to the post-Maastricht Europe, but Hall evidently has no great hopes that the Labour Party has either realized this, or is capable of achieving the broad spread of necessary reforms.

We may conclude by recalling one point made by Marquand, repeatedly over recent years, which is that the Conservative Party is the most successful right-wing party in Europe, and has been in government, either alone or as the dominant partner in coalition, for the greater part of the twentieth century[105]. In the wake of the 1992 election it seems clear that this record is set to continue through the 1990s. It is appropriate therefore to pay some attention to conservatism, where this is taken to be a broader school of thought than the recently influential New Rightism, in order to uncover some secret of their flexibility, appeal, and success. Ted Honderich considers the intellectual resources of the conservative tradition, and having considered familiar claims in respect of ideas of change, human nature,

---

[101] On reforming the system see D. Marquand in *The Guardian* 11 April 1992 and 18 April 1992; M. Kaldor in *The Guardian* 15 April 1992; S. Williams in *The Guardian* 15 April 1992

[102] S. Hall in *New Statesman and Society* 17 April 1992. Also R. Samuel in *The Guardian* 18 April 1992

[103] Hall ibid.

[104] ibid.

[105] This claim runs like a refrain throught the journalism of Marquand - and in the wake of the 1992 election defeat there were some slight signs that maybe the point had been acknowledged if not granted by some sections of the Labour Party

freedom, and so on, argues that in the end it comes down to simple selfishness:

> The conclusion to which we come is not that Conservatives are selfish. It is that they are nothing else. Their selfishness is the rationale of their politics, and they have no other rationale. They stand without the support, the legitimation, of any recognisably moral principle. It is in this that they are distinguished fundamentally from those who are opposed to them[106].

After Thatcherism 4, a dominant-party system

One theme of political commentary in the wake of Major's victory in the Spring 1992 general election was the suggestion that the UK now had a 'dominant-party system', and the model of Japanese politics was often cited[107]. The suggestion was made that all crucial political debate would now take place within the ranks of the dominant party. Such debate would express the concerns of distinct factions within the party. Relatedly, the concerns of the other UK political parties, the Labour Party and the Liberal-Democrats, would gently flow out of the public domain as the ever receding possibility of their actually being elected to government fatally undermined the authority of their views and programmes. It must be said that this thesis was immediately attractive and implausible. Its attaction resided in the brutal data of electoral politics. With the Conservative Party set to rule for an unbroken period of seventeen years by the time of the next election in 1996/7, whilst the technical matter of reordering parliamentary constituency boundaries consequent upon population movements out of the cities into the suburbs promised to rob the Labour Party of up to twenty seats, circumstances seemed to rule-out in advance any electoral victory for Labour. But against this, the ideas implausibility flowed from the implication that a significant UK party could become effectively unelectable and thus irrelevant: surely, the thought came, something will happen to change this pattern.

However, the following months running up to the December 1992 Edinburgh EC Summit did seem to bear-out the apparently rather outlandish thesis of the emergence of a dominant party system. After a long summer recess the UK parliament reconvened in the wake of the total collapse of the government's economic policy following the ejection of the pound sterling from the ERM, and open hostilites within the Conservative Party in regard to the ratification (or not) of the Maastricht Treaty on European union broke out. The autumn months were dominated by a series of political crises, which seemed to leave the government adrift, but safe from both the electorate and the opposition parties. The conflict within the

---

106 T. Honderich *Conservatism*, London, Hamish Hamilton, 1990 pp.238-39
107 An early contributor to debate was M. Jacques writing in *The Observer* 12 April 1992

Conservative Party in the run-up to the Edinburgh Summit was extraordinary and the party displayed an emphatic factionalism in its deliberations, which, of course, became the central political axis of debate as the opposition parties were marginalized. The internecine conflict within the Conservative Party continued, to widespread surprise amongst commentators, throughout the early months of 1993, subsiding somewhat in the summer after the Maastricht bill had finally passed into UK law[108]. At the end of this period the UK government was deeply unpopular amongst the electorate, and speculation began as to the possible replacement of Prime Minister Major[109].

Conclusion

International political-economy offers strategies of analysing the actions of any state-regime in terms of the sets of structures the state-regime confronts. Such an analytical strategy is preferable to more usual strategies which tend to focus exclusively upon the state/society/polity itself. The system context of the UK state-regime can be taken to comprise three spheres, each picking out an historical aspect of the UK context. Thus we can identify the sphere of long term decline (which notes the agedness of UK political-economy), the sphere of the post war subsumption of the UK within the USA hegemonic realm (which notes the Keynesian consensus, plus ambiguous stances vis à vis US/Europe), and the sphere of the post-1973 crisis (which notes the destruction of the Keynesian theorized compromise and replacement by the New Right/Thatcherite policy of neo-liberal accumulation).

The track record to the UK New Right/Thatcher regime can thus be analysed. It is a neo-liberal and social-conservative project to replace the Keynesian compromise. It has successfully de-integrated the political-economy of the Keynesian era, but it has only arithmetically assembled a new grouping. And as Europe unites and blocks dissolve (and intellectual-ideological sureties with them), the UK New Right looks irrelevant, and the fall of Thatcher might well be the first and most dramatic acknowledgement of this, presaging a further episode of UK conservative renewal in the direction of mainland Christian-democracy. One final point in regard to the UK Conservative Party is that it has profited hugely from a divided political opposition, and to this matter I now turn.

---

[108] A final irony to all this being the coincidence of the final passing of the Maastrich bill with the ERM crisis and the shift to wide-bands which many take to have delayed the whole Maastricht programme.

[109] And by the autumn discussion in the press about Major's replacement had become, remarked Hugo Young, 'no longer a bizarre prediction but a banal idea. It has become a given of political conversation' In *The Guardian Weekly* 26 September 1993

6   The UK centre/left

Introduction

Shifting from the party of the right which has dominated UK politics throughout the twentieth century, to the parties of the centre and left reveals at least part of the reason for the success of the Conservative Party. In brief one can point to a mixture of flawed institutions and divided opposition parties. The former include pre-eminently the electoral and the parliamentary systems. Unlike the rest of Europe with its proportional representation systems and written constitutions, specifying the rights and duties of the various elements of the state-machinery, the UK has a 'first past the post' electoral system and no written constitution. The electoral system has the effect of shutting out minority opinion; thus notoriously the UK Liberal Party which for years received popular votes in the three to four million range and only half-a-dozen seats in parliament. This unwritten constitution has the effect of granting great power, free from public or parliamentary inspection, to the executive. Relatedly, in regard to organised party-political opposition to the dominant Conservatives we have to begin with the Labour Party which over the First World War period to the present day has been both the major vehicle of formal political opposition, and committed to an exclusivist vision of its political role and future which has left it disinclined to look for links to other broadly sympathetic groupings. There have been other parties but the electoral and the parliamentary systems have systematically and radically under-represented their popular backing, thus undermining their effectiveness.

Indeed, non-Labour Party centre-left parties have been marginalized since the 1920s.

It seems to me that a significant contributor to the extant UK political discourse, taken overall as impoverished, is the UK Labour Party. Within the literature of political commentary this is an entirely familiar criticism, which broadly I follow[1]. Here I will look at the project of the Labour Party, taken as a particular expression of the modernist project[2], and at the role of the party ideology as a block on centre/left political thinking and action, and finally, I will argue that centre/left critics of labourism will have to acknowledge the routinely achieved conclusion that the Labour Party is not the vehicle of the solution to the problems of UK politics, rather it is itself one of the major problems, and then look to other sources of change.

The modernist project and the Labour Party

The broad intellectual-cultural context of the UK centre-left is the European modernist project of the pursuit of a rational understanding of the natural and social worlds. Political agents draw upon the available ideas of science, progress, reason, materialism, democracy and so on, in order to fashion their broad self-understandings. The Labour Party can be taken as a particular, and context-bound, institutionally-embodied deployment of the broad modernist cultural project. Within the intellectual-cultural context of this broad modernist project the Labour Party understands itself in terms of a political project derived therefrom, 'socialism', the rational and democratic ordering of the polity via collective action, and it is from these intellectual and ethico-political resources that the Labour Party in response to its particular domestic structural contexts and internal party dynamics finally fashions a distinctive party political project, or delimited-formal ideology. In the case of the Labour Party what they came up with was labourism.

---

[1] A lot of ink has been spilled over the Labour Party and I'll not add to it, rather I want to point out that change might be forced upon it along with the UK system generally. I should also make it clear that I am aware that I am making a restricted treatment of centre/left oppositional politics. It is clear that there are a wide spread of regional, issue, and fringe political groups in the UK. There is an extensive spread of centre/left debate (journals, newspapers, campaigns etcetera). After the fashion of J. C. Scott one could say much about this sphere (and much would be positive). But I do not want to become involved for two reasons: (i) the UK post-war period is replete with the efforts of members of the non-institutionalized centre/left to talk-up prospects for change, and all failed, and I do not want to be taken to be offering another, pro-EC, effort at talk-up; and (ii) the real issue is the effective expression of centre/left ideas, and here the lesson is clear for the system in its present configuration blocks any such contribution. The interesting issue in respect of present complex change in Europe is whether or not received structures will alter so as to make political space for such effective contributions in the future.

[2] See Z. Bauman writing on socialism as the critical conscience of capitalism in *Marxism Today* February 1990

The story of the construction and deployment of this idea-set, and the intimately related process of the divergence of rhetoric and reality, is related by John Saville[3]. After the defeat of the radical democratic movement of Chartism in the 1840s the UK working classes settled for a political strategy of social reformism. A network of labour institutions grew up which included unions, coops, churches, corresponding societies and so on. All of these were dominated by the skilled and unionized working classes. This broad movement was essentially defensive, ameliorist and workplace centred (that is, not oriented to the wider public sphere). Through the second half of the nineteenth century the Liberal Party was the major vehicle of social reform. In 1906 the Labour Party was formed when radical intellectuals plus trades unions established it separate from the Liberal Party. At this time the enduring style of the Labour Party was settled; that is, union dominated; committed to ameliorative reform; deferential to extant social system (notwithstanding socialist rhetoric); and committed to parliamentary action. Overall, the political project affirmed: (i) labourism, with its characteristic mix of deference to received authority coupled to a programme of welfare; (ii) the Fabian-inspired affirmation of the role of the expert in ordering social reform; and (iii) parliamentarism, the focus on parliament as the centre of political action and the view of the state machinery as a neutral vehicle of reasonable reform[4]. Recalling David Marquand[5] and Tom Nairn[6] the Labour Party is thus a part of the broad pattern of political life which was put in place in the early years of this century, and which has continued in place ever since. In this way it is all too easy to diagnose the Labour Party, with its dominant position in centre/left politics, as a major part of the problem when it comes to speaking of reform: the democratic tradition in European social theory has no institutional vehicle in the UK, and the core ethic is thus marginalized.

In terms of its self-understanding as a party committed to broad economic and social reform in pursuit of a democratic socialist system, the Labour Party must be seen as an historical failure. Many commentators, looking at its record, would characterize it thus, and indeed this is a familiar judgement[7]. Effective social, economic, and political reform within the UK over the period of the Labour Party's existence has been primarily Liberal Party inspired; first in the pre-First World War period of liberal reformism[8]; and then in the immediate post-Second World War period of welfare reform[9].

---

[3] J. Saville *The Labour Movement in Britain*, London, Faber 1988

[4] R . Miliband *Capitalist Democracy in Britain*, Oxford, Oxford University Press, 1982

[5] D. Marquand *The Unprincipled Society*, London, Fontana, 1988

[6] T. Nairn *The Enchanted Glass*, London, Radius, 1988

[7] See D. Coates *The Labour Party and the Struggle for Socialism*, Cambridge, Cambridge University Press, 1975

[8] S. Collini *Liberalism and Sociology*, Cambridge, Cambridge University Press, 1979

[9] P. Addison *The Road to 1945*, London, Jonathan Cape, 1977

The exchange of labour and liberal traditions, in particular in relation to the contribution this exchange has made, and continues to make, to the dominance of the Conservative Party, has been at the centre of the work of Marquand who has traced out a history of twentieth century conservative dominance precisely in these terms[10]. Over the period of the First World War, and the years immediately following, the Labour Party displaced the old Liberal Party as the main vehicle for the expression of working class political action. The episode is quite distinct, involving splits within the Liberal Party and the rise of the power of organised labour consequent upon war-time mobilization. On Marquand's analysis what the UK polity contrived with this shift of relative power within the centre/left was a means of feeding working class political aspirations into a broad political system which was unique in western Europe. A party dominated by unionized male manual workers coupled to a Fabian-reformist middle class leadership. The typical mainland European solutions to the problem of giving voice to the working classes, broad popular movements ordered around a spread of ideas centring on social-democracy, were not taken up.

This split within the centre/left opened the way to almost permanent Conservative Party rule, either alone, or as the dominant partner in coalition. More broadly, the manner in which the Labour Party understood itself, essentially inward looking, to the unionized working classes that formed its core-group, and the way in which it pursued ameliorative reform, via the Fabian/expert provision of materials for its client groups, effectively shut-out other centre/left groups and blocked the emergence of broad debates in regard to the nature of society which might have been the occasion for the construction of wider political coalitions. Locked into a Fabian reform strategy for its core constituency of the unionized working class, and profoundly disinclined to work for a broader democratic coalition, which essentially would have meant openings to the Liberals, the Labour Party left the way clear for the conservatives.

The Conservative Party is the most successful centre/right party in Europe, and it has survived two world wars, loss of empire, and a strong drive for social reform in the 1940s and although it now confronts the matter of the shift into Europe, which may prove more problematic, it can draw on a legacy of success, a habit of winning. In contrast, even if the Labour Party were to recover quickly from the shock of the result of the 1992 election it is difficult to see them achieving anything, for there are few signs that they have yet grasped the full extent of their problem, that a labourist/Keynesian reform strategy is irrelevant in a post-fordist global situation, much less begun to rethink their role in present patterns of change. The Labour Party continues to represent old themes, to hark back to earlier victories. In this light the period immediately after the Second World War is often taken as a 'golden age', yet Paul Addison reports that

---

[10] D. Marquand *The Progressive Dilemma*, London, Heineman, 1991

this view of the 1945 government and its achievements is a myth[11]. There was a great deal of social reform in this period, it flowed out of wartime upheaval and liberal-establishment reformism, but it effected no decisive break with the pre-war pattern of UK internal politics, indeed Saville argues that what

> needs to be emphasized for the years immediately after 1945 is that the welfare policies and highly conservative nationalization measures were slotted into a society that had remained unchanged in its fundamentals during the war; and which was not to witness any alteration in its basic postulates in the decades which followed[12].

Faced with the depth of the problems confronting them what is remarkable about the period since 1979, when they lost parliamentary power to Mrs Thatcher's Conservative Party, is how little the Labour Party has changed. As Marquand notes, the decade of the 1980s saw a slow falling away of Tory votes, it was by no means a period of enthusiastic cultural change, and he adds that for 'most of the decade, Labour was too weak to provide an alternative to Thatcherism, but it remained strong enough to smother the Alliance alternative'[13]. This ineffective resilience can be traced to the ethos of the party. In its core groups the old labourist view of the world is in place and continues to draw an only slowly subsiding electoral support. The overall pattern of economic and political power within the UK has been little affected by the Labour Party. Reform has been slow and usually Establishment-agreed. Labour's problem remains, argues Marquand, the same as it was in 1920, namely transcending labourism so as to reach new groups in the polity whilst at the same time retaining its commitment to its core constituency[14].

The Labour Party and the political discourse of the UK

Picking-up on the criticisms of the ethos of labourism I want to look at the role of the Labour Party as a block within the political discourse of the UK. The Labour Party presents a distinct style of political argument, and this dominates the centre/left of public political discourse. We can pick out some of the distinctive elements which both help to control the presentation of issues within the party and which have a considerable impact on non-party centre/left discourses.

---

[11] Addison *Road to 1945*

[12] Saville *Labour Movement* p.112. Against this view, arguing for change see P. Hennessy *Never Again*, London, Jonathan Cape, 1992

[13] Marquand *Progressive Dilemma* p.193

[14] ibid. p.207

The style of political discourse of Labour

The labour movement inhabits a relatively closed world of trades unions, party branches, and affiliated organisations (for example, the cooperative movement): what Saville calls the dense network of labour institutions, which grew up in the second half of the nineteenth century and which persist much modified today. It is this network, and the histories and myths associated thereto[15], which is celebrated in the present day as the core of the labour movement.

The Labour Party is dominated by its trades union founders/backers, and in this is unusual, as on the mainland, reports Saville, the parties have dominated the unions, at least insofar as they played political roles[16]. Labour's union base is also quite distinctive. In the twentieth century it has been dominated by the large industrial unions of the skilled/semi-skilled manual working class. In the post-Second World War period large general unions representing public sector workers have also grown up. There have been tensions between the various types of unions, indeed it was conflict between those representing the lowest paid and those representing the more skilled and thus higher paid that brought about the 1979 'winter of discontent' which brought down the last labour government, but this dominance by the general industrial unions has continued. Relatedly the Labour Party is dominated by men, typically drawn from a trades union background, and the ethos of the party in addition to its backward and inward looking defensive celebration of working class community is masculinist; that is competitive/aggressive, paternalist and condescending to the groups it largely excludes (thus, women, minorities, and ethnic groups for example). The ethos of the movement has been quite distinctive, and setting aside the recent impact of the New Right, which has placed intense pressure on this union/labour cultural sphere, one can say that the central posture has been one of acceptance of the status quo. There has been pride in working class life, and reform has tended to look at ameliorative improvements in conditions at work, and in the community. It is anti-intellectual, conservative, gradual, and is of itself a very narrow reading of the broad modernist project[17].

The group for whom the party purports to speak, the working class which is celebrated in the ideology of labourism, is also very particular. It is not a marxist-defined working class. It comprises the skilled, semi-skilled, and un-skilled (male) manual working classes, and labourism imputes to this group sentiments of community, solidarity, warm-heartedness and a

---

[15] ibid.

[16] Saville *Labour Movement*

[17] See P. Hirst *After Thatcher*, London, Collins, 1989, who advocates a 'new ethos' for labour. Again Marquand in *Progressive Dilemma* makes this central - but quite how the new ethos is to be willed into being is not made clear by either author.

progressive social conscience. However, this working class looks more like myth than any structural/cultural social scientific reality[18]. In a similar way Frank Parkin[19], in a well regarded discussion of UK patterns of class consciousness, identified a series of distinctive responses to extant patterns of authority and power. The deferential consciousness was characterized as having two variants: acquiescent ('I know my place'), and aspirational ('I can get on in life'). The defensive response looked to the working class community, and affirmed an us/them model of the social world that insisted that the life-experience of the working class was intrinsically valuable, indeed was a genuine community. Finally Parkin identified an oppositional consciousness, which underlay working class rebellion and bloody mindedness, and which also fed into the political parties of the left. Parkin points out that for the UK it is deference and defence that has predominated.

With the dominance of the Labour Party by the unions and the ethos of labourism there has been no room for intellectuals, indeed the Labour Party has never been a source of new political thinking. This is one of Saville's criticisms, and it is also a point made by Addison who traces the roots of welfarism to the establishment-liberal figure of Beveridge, not to the Labour Party. In regard to the present, new thinking in recent years has happened outside the Labour Party: thus CND, the womens movement, the green movement, Charter 88, peace research and so on. To the extent that the Labour Party has an intellectual basis for its political project then it is Fabianism; a scheme of elite guided social reform. Change is to be ordered from above according to the prescriptions of the experts[20]. Alasdair MacIntyre[21] takes this sort of 'bureaucratic-knowledge' to be a part of the rationalized administered world we now inhabit, and to be more a matter of manipulative histrionics than real expertise[22]. We might note that the familiar style of UK social science, which could be one set of ideas and data which a more energetically minded working class might look to use, has itself been ameliorist and politically gradualist[23]. Geoffrey Hawthorn[24] has argued that this reflects the way in which the intellectual strata have been absorbed into the outer-reaches of government/state.

Marquand stresses that this Fabian-style top-down pattern is one further problem area for Labour and the UK polity broadly. In the absence of a

[18] On this absence, or loss of an 'historical agent' see Z. Bauman *Intimations of Modernity*, London, Routledge, 1992, the appendix which is an interview with Bauman. See also Z. Bauman *Legislators and Interpreters*, Cambridge, Polity, 1987, especially chapter 9

[19] F. Parkin *Class Inequality and Political Order*, London, Palladin, 1972

[20] J. Passmore *The Perfectibility of Man*, London, Duckworth, 1971

[21] A. MacIntyre *After Virtue*, London, Duckworth, 1981 pp.106-7

[22] See also the discussion in chapter three above. Also Γ. Abrams *The Origins of British Sociology*, Chicago, Chicago University Press, 1968

[23] Thus one of the influential traditions within UK social science has been 'poverty studies', a long and distinguished line from Engels through Rowntree to Townsend

[24] G. Hawthorn *Enlightenment and Despair*, Cambridge, Cambridge University Press, 1976

developed political system Fabian-style socialism presents itself not as a socially encompassing and open political project, but rather as welfare intervention authoritatively ordered by elites[25]. A matter for experts and the state to organise and order on behalf of the recipients, the population in general. When the New Right came along, at the end of the post-Second World War economic boom, their otherwise foolishly manichean distinction between state-control and market-freedom did resonate with the ordinary experience of inhabitants of the UK polity. Marquand notes that 'the top-down statism of the left and the neo-liberalism of the right appeared to be the only feasible alternatives. The case for non-statist, decentralist, participatory forms of public intervention was rarely made, and still more rarely heard'[26]. The root of this left intellectual disposition lies, ironically, in the received liberal-individualist culture of the UK. In a realm of sovereign individuals order is a matter of political hierarchy or economic marketplace. There is no genuinely social sphere, or community, the natural arena of a politics of discourse[27]. When the post-war long boom faltered the New Right moved into the resultant intellectual void, and the left had little with which to make effective reply[28]. In sum labourist discourse is quite particular and remote from ideas of formal and substantive democracy, and as Marquand notes labourist discourse blocks the centre/left space of UK politics[29].

Filling the available space

In the UK the parliamentary and the electoral systems have the effect of systematically under-representing minority parties. The effects of the system, together with the ethos of labourism, has the effect of marginalizing non-labour voices, and a broad spectrum of dissenting opinion simply does not get heard. Yet the effective side-lining of nearly all non-labour centre/left opinion leaves the Labour Party in command, and centre/left politics in the UK are thus represented in broad public discourse by labourism, and the tradition of democracy which lies at the core of the European modernist project is marginalized.

On the one hand, then, the Labour Party operates within the confines of a restrictedly democratic system. The internal organisation of the party is similarly non-democratic, revolving around the block votes of unions. The two factors come together, to reinforce the stasis of the party and to block the effective expression of other centre/left voices. As Perry Anderson notes, the

---

[25] See Z. Bauman *Freedom*, Milton Keynes, Open University Press, 1988, where it is noted that many now see socialism as equivalent to bureaucratic-welfare

[26] Marquand *Progressive Dilemma* p.216

[27] ibid. p.218

[28] ibid. pp.219-20

[29] See ibid. chapter seventeen

two voting mechanisms, within the party and outside it, have had symmetrical effects on Labour. Each confers a major advantage secured by procedural artifice rather than political mobilization. The block vote made the recruitment of a genuine mass party, with an active membership capable of sustaining it economically (as well as governing it democratically), of secondary importance. The simple-plurality system avoided the need to win a popular electorate with a free choice of ideological options before it, or to negotiate with competing forces ... The regressive nature of Labourism as a political culture is rooted in the customs and privileges of this legacy[30].

The upshot of this dual-privileging of labourism, this quite particular delimited-formal ideology, seems to me to be a narrowing of the range of public political discourse. In the run-up to the 1992 election Anthony King wryly joked that whilst the result, looking at the opinion-poll data, was too close to call, it was quite certain that a conservative party would win[31].

At the present time in the UK labourism blocks an effective centre/left contribution to public discourse in respect of three crucial contemporary issues: the nature of a post-Tory UK; the matter of European unity; and the nature of a post-block Europe as central and eastern European countries inaugurate reform. The issue here is one of public discourse in respect of these issues, where such discourse is a necessary condition of formal and substantive democracy.

On the matter of a post-Tory UK William Keegan[32] writing in October 1990 argued that the Labour Party needed no new 'big idea' for the good and sufficient reason that Mrs Thatcher was winning the upcoming election for them. Confronted with a spectacularly incompetent government any sensible opposition would sit tight. However, this was, to put it mildly, a minority view. More representative was Marquand[33] who argued consistently through 1990 that the Labour Party had to make some response to the views expressed by the Liberal-Democratic Party, and urged that the aim in the sphere of formal politics should be to construct a coalition of the centre/left so as to ensure electoral success. Outside the formal sphere the objective should be to realize the new ideas, centring on republican democracy, which were being widely discussed.

Similar arguments have been repeated throughout the period of the decline and fall of Thatcher by Stuart Wier[34] and Will Hutton[35], who recently argued that even the IMF had spotted that the era of marketism was over and that this gave the Labour Party a chance to advance its own views,

[30] P. Anderson *English Questions*, London, Verso, 1992 p.350
[31] A. King 'Bring on the Conservatives' in Economist Publications *The World in 1992*, London, Economist Publications, 1991 p.29
[32] W. Keegan in *The Observer* 7 October 1990
[33] D. Marquand in *The Guardian* 2 January 1990, and *New Stateman and Society* 21 December 1990
[34] See S. Wier in *New Statesman and Society* 28 September 1990
[35] See W. Hutton in *The Guardian* 1 October 1990

rather than merely echoing Thatcherist nonsense. On this last element Marquand, in discussing the change in atmosphere that had come over the UK polity in the end-time of Thatcher, centrally a revulsion from individualism and a search for a democratic collectivism, argued that people 'have seen through the full-blooded Thatcherite individualism'[36]. He went on to add that:

> they have been supremely indifferent to the quasi-individualist, sub-Thatcherite concoctions on which parts of the left and centre-left have lavished so much misplaced ingenuity in recent years. They can see that social markets, market socialisms, semi-privatisations and the rest are evasions - clever, but pointless attempts to hunt with the hounds while still running with the hare[37].

In conclusion Marquand asserted that 'they yearn for ... a politics of solidarity, community and mutual obligation, but conducted without patronage and from the bottom up'[38]. In other words, not Thatcherism and not labourism either. Yet, in another piece, Hutton remarked that as regards an idea that shifts beyond being anti-Thatcher the Labour Party have nothing: 'The issue is always dodged, leaving Labour in danger of being cast as the party that will say anything to win votes'[39]. And Ben Pimlott too saw this as a problem, remarking that Labour 'is now at risk of becoming a no-faction, no-philosophy party'[40]. None of these commentators believed that this would be enough to secure an electoral win in 1992. In the event this proved to be the case when against opinion-poll informed expectations the Conservative Party's share of the vote held up, and that of the Labour Party did not significantly advance beyond its 1987 level. The root cause of the debacle was diagnosed by Hall as the profound irrelevance of labourism to the increasingly large tracts of political territory lying outside its labourist heartland[41].

In regard to the complex debates surrounding the dynamic of European integration virtually all that the UK public heard in the run-up to the December 1991 Maastrict Summit on European political union, came from either the Conservative government or from the warring factions within the Tory party. The contributions made by these groupings are wholly opposed to EC integration. And opposition is cast in national and economistic terms. However it is clear that such national/economic objections are absurd for the capitalist system is already trans-national, and recalling Juliet Lodge[42], European integration is already underway and irreversible. Nonetheless, other contributions to public discourse, such as it is, are lost, and the

---

[36] D. Marquand in *The Guardian* 15 October 1990
[37] ibid.
[38] ibid.
[39] W. Hutton in *The Guardian* 5 November 1990
[40] B. Pimlott in *The Guardian* 23 November 1990
[41] S. Hall in *New Statesman and Society* 17 April 1992
[42] J. Lodge ed. *The European Community and the Challenge of the Future*, London, Pinter, 1989

Labour Party does not contribute. Yet Sarah Baxter argues that Labour has performed a silent u-turn and from being an anti-Europe party in 1983 it is now pro-Europe. And the 'breakthrough came at the 1988 TUC conference, where Jacques Delors, the president of the European Commission, unveiled his blue-print for a 'social Europe' and astonished the platform by winning a standing ovation'[43]. However, it has been an understated conversion, and it can be argued that the party has become European by default and has not thoroughly embraced either the goal or the implications[44]. The Labour Party cannot easily embrace mainland social-democratic traditions whilst it remains an oligarchic non-democratic party wedded to a narrowly union based ameliorist politics[45]. Affirming 'Europe' entails affirming 'democracy', and that is something which the Labour Party seems unwilling or unable to do. And in the 1992 election campaign the confusion of the Labour Party was underscored when the issue of Europe hardly figured at all.

Hugo Young took note of this void in the electoral debate, save for ritual posturing in regard to 'Britain's Interests', and traced it to a mix of impotence and dishonesty; with the former noting the extent to which the UK government can actually influence the underlying dynamics of change underway, and the latter its disinclination to let this become known to the UK public. Young comments that the 'silence, therefore, is required as one more subterfuge, now engaging almost the entire political class of consenting adults, in the long dissimulation through which the EC has become the unseen hand behind the politics of Britain'[46]. And for the Labour Party directly there are similar grounds for avoiding debate. As Anderson argues, Labour's future is now bound up with change in Europe yet it remains defensive simply because grasping the opportunities for change in Europe would entail change in the Labour Party, in brief, democratization of both organisation and programme[47].

Finally, in regard to the issues of post-block Europe which have been opened up by the Gorbachev inspired reforms in central and eastern Europe, again we can see that all the running is being made by the political right. The UK and US right has read the reforms in central Europe and the USSR/CIS as evidence of 'the defeat of communism', or of 'victory in the cold war'. Francis Fukuyama has announced that liberal-democracy can now be seen to be the political model to which all polities look[48]. This is of course nonsense, but the debates about the broader patterns in post-block Europe have been the province of the right by and large. Looking at John

---

43 S. Baxter in *New Statesman and Society* 14 December 1990
44 See J. Lloyd in *Marxism Today*, October 1990
45 See S. Wier in *New Statesman and Society* 28 September 1990
46 H. Young in *The Guardian* 1 January 1992
47 Anderson *English Questions* pp.345-49
48 F. Fukuyama *The End of History and the Last Man*, London, Hamish Hamilton, 1992

Palmer's[49] diagnosis of the four possible futures for Europe, the centre right in the UK and USA are pushing strongly for Nato II, a New Atlanticism. These ideas are regressive yet the Labour Party is not articulating a significantly different posture to that of the Conservative Party.

In sum, the UK political system is defective. The Labour Party fills the available centre-left political space. Into this political space it projects the ideology of labourism. Labourism is essentially status quo affirming. The situation is thus that the Labour Party blocks the effective presentation in public discourse of dissenting centre/left ideas (including the formal and substantive democratic).

The need for reform

On this business of the incapacity of labourism and the blocking role they play in political discourse in the UK, the conclusion in principle seems fairly clear, as has been argued repeatedly over the 1980s[50], and both the Labour Party and the UK system stand in need of democratization. However, when one looks for a vehicle to effect such reform it is impossible to find one. The Conservative Party is the beneficiary of the system and is set against reform, and it is no use looking to the Labour Party because they too are part of the problem. On the matter of necessary democratization in the UK the conclusion would seem to be to rule out change arising from within. Yet the condition of advance inside the UK is institutional political reform, and thereafter movement towards a dialogic politics of formal and substantive democracy. At this point one can suggest that if there is no chance of reform-from-within then it is reasonable to consider reform-from-without.

On the analysis of the international political-economists the UK is part and parcel of wider encompassing power-networks. In this context, looking to UK politics two thoughts occur: (i) the present episode of rapid complex change in Europe may place such demands on the UK political-economy and polity that the need for political reform might become overwhelmingly obvious to the public generally (thus, for example, the pressure for some sort of Scottish parliament); (ii) it may be that as European integration proceeds the EC will move to bring UK electoral systems in line with the common practice on the mainland, maybe as a part of an exercise in 'deepening' along with addressing the 'democratic deficit'[51].

In the run-up to the 1992 election it was not possible to be optimistic in regard to the first alternative; however, in the wake of Labour's electoral debacle, in particular with regard to Scotland, one could suggest that at the

---

49 J. Palmer *Europe without America*, Oxford, Oxford University Press, 1988
50 See Charter 88, *Marxism Today*, and *New Left Review*
51 On the democratic deficit see Lodge ed. *The European Community*

very least there will be continuing pressure for internal democratization[52]. However, externally-occasioned change is a stronger possibility, and reform in the UK parliamentary-electoral system might just be occasioned (or imposed) by the logic of the dynamics of change in Europe. Such a change in the technical apparatus of political life in the UK would have profound consequences, and a flow of dissenting ideas would be generated which could rejuvenate UK polity.

My general point here is thus a variant upon the familiar centre/left critique of labourism. In my opinion the UK centre/left must grant the conclusions of its analyses of labourism and write-off the Labour Party together with its long failed political project. In particular, I have argued in this essay that the global system structures within which the territory of the UK is embedded, understanding itself in terms of the political project of 'Britain', are in process of complex change, and that these structural changes (flows of power running through the UK) will occasion the reconfiguration of economic, social, cultural and political patterns within the UK. New patterns of embedding within the wider system will emerge along with new agent-group fostered understandings of those new patterns. After a period of upheaval one might anticipate a new 'contested compromise' and it seems clear that this will centre on some sort of European union. Those who affirm the ethic and political project of formal and substantive democracy, the ethico-political core of the European modernist project, must look to sources of change outside the UK itself, and the evident place to look is the relationship of the UK with the European mainland as the present episode of complex change unfolds[53].

Conclusion

There has been much commentary upon the ideas and track-record of the Labour Party. Commentators are broadly agreed that the ideas deployed in its political project are status quo affirming, and that the party's record is one of failure. This would not matter very much except that the present parliamentary-electoral system ensures minority under-representation. The entire non-labour centre/left is marginalized, and all the centre/left has to offer public discourse is labourism. Reform is urgent, but it will not arise from within the system. It can be argued that centre/left politics will only flourish when change in the system that buttresses labourist dominance is occasioned from the outside. It may be that this is now a real possibility.

---

[52] Commentators in Scotland do think that the drive to a parliament in Edinburgh will continue.
[53] Anderson *English Questions* chapter 6

7 UK public discourse in respect of EC integration

Introduction

In this text I have been concerned to elucidate the structural characteristics of the UK polity, and to note the broad features of public political discourse. I have looked at the exchanges between structures and agents which have shaped the contemporary polity and have followed the arguments of major commentators in regarding the UK as pre-democratic. This polity exhibits a political structure, comprising a configuration of class-groupings and institutional arrangements, which is both extremely resistant to change and highly secretive, political life is largely restricted to the political class. Within the context of this political structure public political discourse is shaped by received cultural traditions of liberalism and a party political debate which is both ritualized (in respect of arguments presented and manner of presentation), uninformative (in respect of information plus argument needed by citizenry in order to participate in a discourse-democracy) and status quo affirming (thus, neither party seeks change, both are content).

Following the lead of the commentators I traced the occasion of this structure-discourse to the early years of this century. As David Marquand[1] pointed out, it is at this time that we find the familiar structures, institutions, and arguments of UK polity fixed in place. This complex pattern of internal structures-discourses has stayed fixed in place more or

---

[1] D. Marquand *The Unprincipled Society*, London, Fontana, 1988

less unchanged ever since, surviving two world wars, the ending of an empire system, and absorption into the US sphere. The extent of changes in patterns of political structure and public political discourse within the UK have been slight. As John Saville comments 'it is one of the remarkable characteristics of Britain during the twentieth century that ... the propertied groups, and their political representatives, have retained their economic and political power unimpaired'[2]. In regulationist terms[3], the UK ruling class (a shifting fractional alliance) has successfully retained control of the internal polity of the UK (and thus economic, social, political, and cultural power) whilst responding (by and large successfully in class terms if unsuccessfully in national terms) to the successive changes of configuration in the international political-economy.

However, at the present time a series of patterns of change within the post-Second World War international political-economy have come to a head. These include the relative decline of the USA's hegemony (economic, political, cultural), the evident relative advance of Japan (economic), the slow relative advance of the EC (economic, political, cultural), the relative advance of Germany (economic, political), and the continuing decline of the UK. To these slowly evolving changes in relative political-economic and cultural power we can add the reforms in the USSR/CIS with Gorbachev, and the reforms in eastern Europe following the 1989 revolutions. At the present time the entire post-Second World War settlement in Europe is undergoing rapid complex change. The shift towards a united EC and the movement towards a post-block Europe are of crucial importance, and the economic, political, social and cultural adjustments implied by such changes for the UK are extensive: in brief, it may be that these pressures as they develop over the next decade or so will be of such a scale as to overwhelm the power of the UK ruling class to protect their internal position. The response of the Conservative Party has been hostile and leading figures have adopted a stance of denial, which has been either subtle-denial (Heseltine, Hurd, Major) or unsubtle-denial (Thatcher, Ridley, Brugges Group). Relatedly the response of the Labour Party has been ambiguous, moving from early denial to a recent affirmation which many see as opportunistic. Overall, the extent to which these matters have been addressed in public political discourse has been slight.

In this chapter I am interested in recording how UK public political discourse has responded to these patterns of political-economic structural change. It is clear that these changes call into radical question the familiar political certainties of the post-Second World War era. There are a series of issues to address: (i) the sequence of blows to the UK political class through 1989-92; (ii) the matter of the dynamic of EC integration; (iii) the matter

---

[2] J. Saville *The Labour Movement in Britain*, London, Faber, 1988. p.112

[3] H. Overbeek *Global Capitalism and National Decline*, London, Allen and Unwin, 1990

of eastern European complex change; (iv) the role of a united Germany in Europe; and (v) the issue of the shape of Europe after the power-blocks[4].

A sequence of blows to the UK political class

The period 1989-92 proved to be devastating to UK received discourse with the old post-Second World War certainties overthrown. At first the UK political establishment resisted but by late 1989 the pace of events had clearly passed them by. Briefly, to recall the scale and shock of the period we can note a sequence of events and occurences:
- the early 1989 debate on short-range Nato nuclear weapons in West Germany, with Thatcher insisting and being rebuffed;
- the July 1989 visit of Gorbachev to the Federal Republic of Germany when he was received as a hero thereby cementing growing links between Germany and USSR;
- the November 1989 decision to open the Berlin Wall thereby putting German reunification on the cards and reopening discussion of the nature of the links between East and West;
- the autumn 1989 revolutions in eastern Europe and the beginnings of USSR's final withdrawal from the old block-system;
- the July 1990 outburst on the part of Nicholas Ridley announces UK ruling class anxieties and Conservative Party splits;
- the October 1990 German reunification which definitively remade contemporary Europe;
- the December 1990 fall of Thatcher, and the end of the phase of optimistic democratic European revolutions;
- thereafter throughout 1991 political and economic reforms continued in eastern Europe and the USSR, culminating in the December 1991 fall of Gorbachev, the dissolution of the USSR, and its replacement by the CIS, which in total announced the end of the block-system;
- then at Maastricht in December 1991 the EC approved the idea of political union to complement the single market;
- subsequently in the autumn of 1992 the UK's pretensions to economic and political power finally dissolved as Major's spring electoral triumph turned into a low comedy of errors which culminated in the ignominious withdrawal from the ERM, and in December 1992 the UK Presidency came to an inglorious end at the Edinburgh Summit;
- then in January 1993 the single market came into effect, and in the summer the UK parliament ratified the Maastricht treaty.

This sequence constitutes a series of blows to the UK political class generally and the New Right's political project in particular. The end of the

---

[4] In this chapter I will make extensive use of the work of a series of commentators writing in the UK press. I want to try to recall and fix in memory the scale and shock of the events of 1989-91 in particular, before the UK political classes assert a new conventional wisdom.

cold war, the reunification of Germany, the revolutions in eastern Europe and the related end of the block-system, plus the drive to further EC integration all point to the collapse of the New Right's strategy of dual-parasitism. The political strategy was weakening as the USA turned to Germany in May 1989, but with Nato increasingly irrelevant the USA no longer needed a number one ally in Europe to confront communism and the particular role which the UK ruling class had fashioned for itself in the wake of the loss of empire became irrelevant. The economic strategy was similarly overthrown by events. When the inner-German border was opened in November 1989, followed by the ripple of revolutions throughout the old eastern block, the UK state-regime's strategy of international finance/trading capital plus home MNC assembly work via deregulation and cheap labour, simply collapsed. On the one hand the opening up of eastern Europe, coupled to the US turn to Germany, gave a wholly unanticipated boost to moves to EC unification, and on the other eastern Europe looked like an even more deregulated area than the UK, and moreover was closer to the emergent German centre of Europe. Notwithstanding the denial of the structural changes in progress made by the ruling UK political class, these changes are of such a scale as to demand response and the construction of a new public politics can be anticipated.

The salient ideas of received political discourse can be taken to express a complex exchange between intellectual tradition, historical-structural conditions, and specific problem complexes. Political discourse in the UK has been premised over the post-Second World War period upon a number of key assumptions which have included: US economic, military, and political leadership in Europe coupled to a particular subordinate role for the UK as principal ally; a continuing adherence to notions of sovereign statehood and national self-determination; and the routine affirmation of an official ideology of liberal-democratic government and free markets. However, the historical circumstances and problem complexes which occasioned extant received political discourse have now unarguably and irrevocably changed: to the gradual changes surrounding movement towards some sort of EC unification were added in the closing months of 1989 the impetus to change of the revolutions of eastern Europe. In Galbraithian terms the UK political 'conventional wisdom' is overthrown by events and we might now expect a replacement to be developed and deployed. A series of centres of debate can be readily identified: government, professions, universities, political parties, issue pressure groups, lobby groups around parliament from business and commerce, the media, and so on. All of these centres will express the views of specifiable groups and will feed ideas, opinions and judgements into an emergent new discourse. There might also be expected to be sources of debate within the sphere of commonsense or lay discourse, that is responses, reactions and contributions to the process of new discourse construction which draw upon informal, traditional, and folk stocks of knowledge.

From these centres of debate and the informal sphere of commonsense a complex set of problems are emerging as disputed issues: nationhood; statehood; sovereignty; relations with the USA; the nature of the emergent European union; and the nature of appropriate policy in regard to particular economic, political and cultural issues flowing from the dynamics of structural change. Over time a new political discourse, with issues, groupings, centres and so on, might be expected to develop. Speculatively, we could look to the dissolution of the ideology of Britishness with all this implies for political institutions and public discourse. The optimistic side of all this we can sum up as the reaffirmation of the modernist project. However, as yet the process of constructing, deploying and sustaining a new political discourse is at a very early stage and its outlines are not at all clear.

European Community integration

UK public political discourse in respect of EC integration has been severely restricted in character. It seems to me that this discourse has been national, economistic, and unreflexive. This narrow and pragmatic focus has blocked discussion of the likely changes which the broader processes of complex change will occasion within the UK.

National-discourse[5]

Discourse has focused on the relationship of 'Britain' with the EC and has been cast in terms of gain/loss and problem/opportunity. This style of discourse is entirely familiar within the UK and it reflects not merely the personalized-nationalism, so to say, of the UK ruling groups whereby 'we' are taken as of one mind, and set of interests, all of which must be necessarily, inevitably and obviously asserted against 'them', in this case the rest of the EC, but also the habit of reading the world through the distorting frame of liberalism, what Alasdair MacIntyre has called emotivism[6]. In this latter case we are dealing with liberalism-writ-large: thus as discrete individuals are taken to interact in pursuit of their autonomously arising needs and wants, so too are nationstates. But liberalism-writ-large is not a plausible characterization of the exchanges between countries. We do not confront the exchange of coherent bounded units, rather it is the case that exchanges across national boundaries are extensive and it is the trans-state system which should be our analytical starting point. It is thus clear that just as any state of affairs within a

5 This heading recalls the earlier discussion of the 'national past', a spuriously unitary construct which frames thinking about past, present, and future. See P. Wright *On Living in an Old Country*, London, Verso 1985

6 A. MacIntyre *After Virtue*, London, Duckworth, 1981

nationstate unit is the out-turn of complex conflicts, so too is any present configuration of the wider system. The trans-national system cannot be usefully analysed in terms of liberalism-writ-large, instead we must look to patterns of structure and agency: what structures are identifiable, and what agents are operating within this environment. In this perspective the nationstate rather drops away, it becomes, as has been pointed out by Tom Nairn and Ernest Gellner, a construct: thus states construct nations, and the notion of nationstatehood is an after the fact rationalization[7]. After this deconstruction we are left with an agent best described as a ruling-group in control of a state machine: in brief a state-regime which is able to act within the ambit of the trans-national structures which comprise the world system.

UK public political discourse has thus far dealt with the dynamics of change in the EC as if it were a matter of the interactions of discrete units. But we have to appreciate the relevant exchange of structures and agents, matters addressed in the work of international political-economy. Recalling the work of Andrew Linklater and Susan Strange[8] international political-economy is constructed against orthodox international relations theory, which is seen to be analytically deficient given its focus on the realm of diplomacy, and against orthodox international economic theory which is similarly analytically deficient given its concern with ahistorical, asocial and apolitical systems of economic exchanges. In place of these resources international political-economy calls on the work of political-economy, sociology, and development theory in order to construct its alternative vision. In this tradition of analysis, on Strange's exposition, attention is paid to the dynamic interaction of structures and agents. Strange identifies a series of structures of power (economic, political, credit, cultural) and within these structures state-regimes appear as agents. In this perspective state-regimes deploy power to control material, financial and cultural flows so as to pursue their own political projects.

In this perspective the lesson for analyses of the activities of the UK state-regime are in broad outline fairly clear: we must avoid analytic strategies which accept the claimed unitary and coherent status of the UK, and which then go on to accept the protestations of the ruling classes to the effect that they are in fact pursuing a project of effective nationstatehood. An analysis which looks to structures and agents reveals the pursuit by the UK state-regime of quite specific political projects in response to structural constraint/opportunity.

The nature of the UK state-regime's exchanges with their partners in the EC has been a matter of concern to commentators over an extended period. There seems to be something of a recurring series of themes in these discussions: the preoccupation of the UK government with the issue of

---

[7] See T. Nairn *The Break-Up of Britain*, London, New Left Books, 1977; E. Gellner *Nations and Nationalism*, Cambridge, Cambridge University Press, 1983

[8] See A. Linklater *Beyond Marxism and Realism: Critical Theory and International Relations*, London, Macmillan, 1990; and S. Strange *States and Markets*, London, Pinter, 1985

sovereignty; the strong UK government preference for intergovernmentalism; and the way in which UK political-agents seem to misjudge routinely their mainland colleagues, thereby generating suspicion.

Bulmer[9] has reviewed the issue, with a concern for the domestic context of the formulation of responses, and identifies a long history of problems with the overall shift in the post-Second World War period being summed as being from isolation to semi-detachment. In terms of the concepts of cooperation and integration the UK has eschewed the latter in favour of the former over the entire period. A central concern has been for sovereignty which not only figures centrally in UK cultural traditions, but also takes a role in public debate where it seems to have become something of a talisman. It has to be affirmed by all participants to public debate in regard to the EC. This peculiar characteristic flows from the way the parties have mishandled the debate, and Ashford[10] speaks of adversarial politics, intra-party unease, and the challenge to the ideological self-images of the parties as guardians of respectively the British national interest and the parliamentary route to socialism. Bulmer[11] argues that whereas the initial group of members, and most of the later joiners, had clear political reasons for setting up or joining the organisation, the UK in contrast was a late, reluctant, and opportunistic member for whom participation was an expression of the failure of their independent line. Overall successive UK governments have found it difficult to engage effectively with the EC as the disposition to semi-detachment is the 'product of a strong institutional logic permeating the political system, economic markets, and public administration'[12]. One way in which this has been routinely expressed is in the systematic preference showed by UK governments over the entire post-Second World War period, for intergovernmental solutions over federal strategies, and George[13] suggests that the most recent restatement of this postition was that of Mrs Thatcher in her notorious Brugges speech of 1989.

The upshot has been a UK pragmatism towards the development of the EC that has jarred with the expectations of the mainland members. On this Edwards[14] notes that whilst integration with the EC at the level of the machinery of government is generally going ahead smoothly, it remains the case that the UK government has been reactive and nationalistic. In particular UK governments 'seem to have a strong tendency to misjudge the policies and objectives of their partners in the Community, epecially their

---

[9] S. Bulmer 'Britain and European Community Integration' in S. George ed. *Britain and the European Community: The Politics of Semi-Detachment*, Oxford, Oxford University Press, 1992

[10] N. Ashford 'The Political Parties' in George *Semi-Detachment*

[11] Bulmer in George *Semi-Detachment*

[12] ibid. p.29

[13] S. George 'The European Community in the New Europe' in C Crouch and D Marquand eds *Towards a Greater Europe*, Oxford, Blackwell, 1992

[14] G. Edwards 'Central Government' in George *Semi-Detachment*

commitment to political integration'[15]. The UK has rather presented itself as the member which drags behind the rest: Taylor[16] notes that notwithstanding the labyrinthine manoeuverings which attend EC politics, as one might expect, the UK is nonetheless slowly going down the integration road. However Bulmer[17] reports that the mainland view of the UK is negative: in matters political it can be taken in Gaullist fashion as merely a conduit for the Americans; and in matters economic as a route into the EC for the Japanese. In my own terms, 'dual parasitism'.

In sum, against the familiar national-discourse we must assert that structural change is already well advanced, and the received intellectual framework of liberalism-writ-large has to be abandoned. The questions which groups within the UK and elsewhere in Europe will now want to ask, whatever their position in relevant political power structures, will be concerned with the analysis of processes of complex change. In respect of the EC the issues centre of the extent of present integration; the depth of its reach within the political-economic structures of extant nationstates; and the pace of integration. Such an approach generates a series of analytical issues, and implies a series of public political discourses, which are far removed from anything presently identifiable within the UK. The present national-discourse in regard to these matters is either an example of the habit of intellectual immobilism in the UK political class, or evidence of routine citizen demobilization so that discourse and decision can be ordered within the closed realm of the political classes.

Economistic-discourse

Public discourse in the UK in respect of European integration has been typically economistic. The original move to associate with the mainland was presented as 'joining the common market', and economic advantages were promised. The recent revival of moves to integration expressed legally as the SEA were presented as establishing or completing the single market, again an essentially economic matter. This was all presented in business-economics terms in the Cecchini Report[18]. Much actual debate in the UK prior to 1989 was cast in technical-economic terms, for example to join or not to join the ERM of the EMS. However, after the annus mirabilis of 1989 there was a change and public discourse recognised that the issue of the EC went wider than the technical-economic, but discussion then became suspicious, attaining its silliest expression in Ridley's suggestion that the whole business was some sort of German scheme to dominate Europe[19].

---

[15] ibid. p.67

[16] P. Taylor 'The new dynamics of EC integration in the 1980s' in J. Lodge ed. *The European Community and the Challenge of the Future*, London, Pinter, 1989

[17] Bulmer in George *Semi-Detachment*

[18] P. Cecchini *The European Challenge*, London, Wildwood, 1988

[19] Cited in R. Fristch-Bournazel *Europe and German Unification*, London, Berg, 1992, p.156

More broadly, it is clear from the commentaries on the relationship of the UK and the EC that the reason for the decision of the Macmillan government to apply for membership was primarily economic: the EEC was seen as a source of trade in a global system that seemed post-Suez to be less hospitable to the UK. This posture was reaffirmed by Wilson, and whilst Edward Heath did see membership of the EEC in terms of a broad reconstruction of the UK, the narrow economic pragmatism was reasserted by the subsequent governments of both Labour and the Conservatives[20].

The early years of UK membership coincided with the end of the post-Second World War 'long boom' and were dominated by issues expressive of the maladaption of the UK to the organisation: the matter of the budget and the CAP[21]. In the case of the former the debate ran on until the Fontainebleau Summit of June 1984 when Mrs Thatcher secured a rebate on the UK's contribution. The issue caused considerable controversy and dissention, and indeed it recently briefly resurfaced at the Edinburgh Summit. The occasion of the problem was the orientation of the trade pattern of the UK, that is outwards with a consequently enhanced financial obligation to Brussels. Relatedly, the difficulties with the CAP flowed from the late accession of the UK and the difference between UK agriculture and state support and the patterns and practices of the mainland. Once again the process of resolution was long and acrimonious. George[22] notes that in complementary fashion the areas where the UK has been most effective have been those which have favoured directly its own interests, in particular the drive to the SEA and the outward directed aspects of EC organisation where the UK has pressed for open trade.

More generally, we might note that what has been assumed in all this debate is that it makes sense to speak of markets or economies in isolation. However, markets and economies are always embedded in societies, and national economies have extensive linkages to trans-national networks. In the case of the UK and Europe these matters have been detailed earlier in this text in the company of Henk Overbeek[23]. The post-Second World War period saw the establishment of American hegemony over an Atlantic economic sphere. It was within this set of structural constraints that the UK, like other European states, had perforce to act. Any realistic discourse (scholarly or group-specific) must address the political-economic analysis of European structural dynamics, and thereafter the culture-critical elucidation of diverse readings of such patterns of structural (and structurally occasioned) change. In other words economistic discourse is wrong because: (i) it extracts economic linkages from broad spread of exchanges (economic, social, political, cultural); and (ii) presents analyses

---

[20] S. George 'The policy of British governments within the EC' in George *Semi-Detachment*
[21] ibid.
[22] ibid.
[23] Overbeek *Global Capitalism*

of matters economic as though these were precisely specifiable matters of the functioning of automatic systems; and (iii) proceeds thereafter to analyse economic exchanges between the UK and the mainland as though these were essentially technically characterizable matters, and moreover, recalling the liberalism noted above, and which is embedded in orthodox economics, as between two more or less sealed, autonomous units. These errors compound the national bias noted above.The reality is of extant trans-Europe political-economic structures, which have to be analysed in appropriate terms.

Unreflexive-discourse

A consequence of the national and economistic approaches has been that discourse in the UK has been unreflexive, which is to say that it has neglected wider issues of complex change and their likely lines of development, and this has hindered discussion of three key concerns: (i) what processes of complex change are underway and in need of theoretical elucidation; (ii) what sorts of process-implied end points can we identify; and (iii) to what extent are these patterns of change accelerating.

Processes to be elucidated

Present patterns of change in Europe have a complex occasion, however it is clear that the drive for reform within the EC system has proved to be of crucial importance. The programme for some sort of EC union, built at present around the SEA, has galvanized thinking and action amongst many groups.

John Pinder[24] argues that the EEC was born of political motives in the wake of the Second World War. It was a movement for federalism with the period of intra-European conflict from 1914 through to 1945 being a sufficient reason to entertain the project. There was also an economic motive in the concern to establish some sort of defence against early post-war US economic and political power. Judged in both terms the EEC was successful. Extensive economic linkages across the territory of the EEC were established and the record of the community countries, measured in orthodox growth terms, was very impressive. Related to these economic linkages the period has also seen the growth of extensive networks of political cooperation. Most obviously in the establishment of the apparatus of the EEC itself.

In the 1980s records Pinder, the dynamic of the EEC faltered as it had before and new economic doubts emerged. The response within Europe was a renewed drive towards realizing the original goals of the organisation, the

---

[24] J. Pinder in Lodge ed.*European Community.* See also J. Pinder *European Community: The Building of a Union*, Oxford, Oxford University Press, 1991

project for the completion of the single European market. The programme envisaged dismantling frontier controls, bringing product specifications into line, establishing rules about government procurement programmes, simplifying and harmonising tax regimes, and freeing capital movements - all of which implied a vast schedule of detailed reforms. The drive to complete the single market also implied a large spread of social, cultural and political change, some sort of commitment to some sort of EC unification, a matter ambiguously acknowledged in December 1991 at the Maastricht Summit.

Given that successive post-Second World War UK state-regimes have, at least in their public utterances and official ideologies, affirmed without reservation a self-understanding as part of what has come to be called the 'Western Alliance', the commitment to a unified EC represents a problem. The self-understandings and policy-orientations of forty years no longer represent the self-evidently correct givens of policy-formulation, but are now themselves called into question. For the UK state-regime the present patterns of complex change in Europe represent a thoroughgoing crisis of identity. Not only is the position of the UK within the wider encompassing capitalist system at issue, but the nature of the internal organisation of the UK is similarly in question: in brief, in terms of the developmental expectations of the major social theorists of the initial nineteenth century formulations of the European modernist project, the mainland is more advanced than the UK.

Building on Pinder's observations we can sketch in some of the wider issues that are opened up by present dynamics of change, and which challenge long established patterns of thinking and acting on the part of the UK state-regime. In the early 1980s A.G. Frank addressed some of these matters, introducing the analysis by noting that his book examined the 'growing disarray and discontent within the Atlantic Alliance'[25] and arguing that these conflicts had to be lodged in economic-structural changes in the world economic system. Frank saw a long-wave crisis coinciding with the relative decline of the two great powers.

In regard to West/West conflicts Frank made a series of points: that there were conflicts over economic policy, a matter of assertion of interests, and those of the USA are not the same as Europe's; that there were similar squabbles over international trade; that there were similar problems over the relation of North to South as the latter is an area of resources vital to both; that there were conflicts over trade with the eastern block where the USA has taken a much harder line than mainland Europeans; and that there had been conflict over the role of Nato, with the Europeans seeing no Soviet threat and the USA keen to keep its very useful and profitable enemy in being. In regard to eastern Europe Frank's view, anticipating much that only became generally clear in UK public discourse after the autumn

---

25 A. G .Frank *The European Challenge*, Nottingham, Spokesman, 1983

revolutions, was that much greater integration with the global system in general and probably Europe in particular, was inevitable[26]. With these problems in mind Frank pointed to a series of political-economic policy strategies that had been tried: beggar thy neighbour competition, the basis of the squabbles noted earlier; monetarism as tried in the USA and UK; supply side stimulus, as tried in particular in the USA with Reaganomics; supply side re-industrialization policies, inspired by Japan, and recommended by US democrats and tried by France in the early 1980s; Keynesian pump-priming as tried by Helmut Schmidt and Francois Mitterand, and as proposed by UK Labour Party AES; and the global Keynesianism of the Brandt Report. In all a confused pattern; however Frank saw one possible optimistic line of development, what he dubbed in the early 1980s when this analysis was presented as a 'Fortress Europe', and this vision was of a post-block Europe freed from the USA.

The theme of the response of Europe to the position of the USA has also been picked up by John Palmer[27]. A series of conflicts were noted within the western block which were expressive of different views and interests: economic, political and diplomatic. Palmer argued that the post-war settlement was collapsing, and a series of patterns of change were canvassed: (i) Atlantic reformism which looks to a continuation of Natoism with a larger European role; (ii) European reformism which looks to a post-Nato system involving European federal integration; (iii) European 'gaullism' involving a post-Nato European nationalism; and (iv) a socialist united states of Europe, both post-Nato and post-free-market. Again, like Frank, the text opens up the lines of possibility now on offer and simultaneously underscores the unease of the existing UK state-regime because the continuation of the post-war certainties of Natoism/free worldism looks decidedly unlikely.

---

26 Expressed in a classic Frankian paragraph: 'In general, the slowdown in growth and productivity in the Soviet Union and Eastern Europe can be traced to the growing maturity of their economies, the increased scarcity and costliness both domestically and internationally of material inputs and the growing scarcity of labour as demographic changes and reduced rural-urban migration militate against supply constrained growth; the difficulties, often bordering on impossibility, of making the transition from mobilising resources for extensive growth to increasing their productivity for intensive growth; the rigidity of economic planning, organisation and incentive motivation that militate against technological change; the simultaneous opening up of their economies to technological imports, exports and world market prices to overcome this limitation externally and the increasingly far-reaching privatisation of economic incentives, rewards and decisions in a more extensive market economy internally' ibid p.71

27 J. Palmer *Europe without America*, Oxford, Oxford University Press, 1988

Grasping these processes, identifying likely end-points

The foregoing section detailed some elements of discussions of processes in Europe which were cast in familiar terms of the economic bases for new patterns of political conflict. But it is possible to come at these matters using a subtler and broader culture-critical approach.

In ironic mode Hans Enzensberger[28] reviews the discomfiture of the established politicians and intellectuals at the autumn 1989 outbreak of commonsensical democratic ordinariness, he has Germany in view but the lessons are offered as general. Enzensberger begins by noting the preference for order manifest amongst what he dubs the political class, all are united in horror that the sentence 'we the people' could ever be taken seriously, however 'it seems very likely that the longed-for stability was always an illusion'[29], and noting that the traditional idea of the state is 'facing a paradigm collapse'[30], he adds that the 'awkward impression which governments are making in the face of the recent changes in Europe is therefore not an accidental embarrassment ... It flows from the impossibility of forecasting the social process and controlling it from above'[31]. Relatedly he notes that the 'spiteful glee of the intellectuals at the humiliation of politics by the tumble of events has stayed within bounds ... No wonder; both imagined they could determine the direction society was to take'[32]. In a preliminary conclusion it is suggested that the states and the intellectuals shared a common error as both 'had fallen for the illusion of the governability of the social sphere'[33].

Enzensberger, having introduced the idea that recent events in Europe challenge not merely the familiar institutional arrangements of the post-war world but that the pattern of changes in train cuts much deeper, now opens up a further layer of possible revision to received ideas: the sets of utopian ideas that have animated the European modernist project. The matter is approached via rationalization, internationalism, and equality. The argument is ironic: these goals of the modernist project have been realized, but in the manner of a fairy-tale where the protagonist's reward of three wishes quickly turns sour.

The optimistic libertarian notion of the withering away of the state now seems to have been perversely realized. The power of the state has become ever more constrained by systems outside its control: economic, political, cultural. Enzensberger comments:

[28] H. M. Enzensberger in *New Statesman and Society* 21 October 1990
[29] ibid.
[30] ibid.
[31] ibid.
[32] ibid.
[33] ibid.

there is no longer any state in Europe which expects of its citizens that they 'believe' in it ... Yet ... the disenchanted state is very far from withering away. It is true that the contention that some individual could 'lay down the guide-lines of politics' has become pure fiction; but at the same time the 'administration of things' expands further and further[34].

Enzensberger goes on to note that the proponents of the European modernist project, in particular in its socialist variants, were not bound by any narrow provincialism or nationalism, internationalism was affirmed. Now it has been realized, however it has been realized by the capitalists: 'what has been established is the anonymous world market, symbolized by a handful of iconic brand names and dominated by the multinational companies, the big banks, and the parastate finance organisations'[35]. Finally,

It is superfluous to provide evidence yet again of increasing social polarisation, even in many rich countries, or describe the desperate situation of many underdeveloped nations. But while real equality cannot be said to exist anywhere, a parodic version of the ideal has been realized in the industrial societies ... Macdonald's has realised the principles of socialism in their purest form[36].

Thus are the three key elements of the modernist utopia realized, however it is at this point that Enzensberger finds a source of optimism in the reaction of ordinary Germans to the events of November 1989. After the celebrations they got on with the task of cleaning-up and rebuilding. The longer term and general lesson is one of modesty on the part of both politician and intellectual: 'They will have to reconcile themselves to the banal fact that democracy is an open, productive, risky process which is self-organising and which evades their control, if not their influence'[37].

In a similar fashion Neal Ascherson[38] looks to read structural changes and political-cultural responses, the ways in which groups read changes and endeavour to act. The future in other words does not have to be determined by high-politics. Noting the broad pattern of present changes Ascherson suggests that there are three possible forecasts in regard to new political lines of action and thinking: the first one is that 'forum politics are going to be the background of all European political behaviour by the year 2000, West as well as East'[39]; the second one is 'that forum politics, with their striking combination of market economics and emphasis of social justice and 'green-ness', are the nascent form of the new European Left for the next century ... [whose] scent seems to resemble that of social democracy in

---

34 ibid.
35 ibid.
36 ibid.
37 ibid.
38 N. Ascherson in *Marxism Today* January 1990
39 ibid.

a new mixture'[40]; and the third possibility is that the forum politics are just a temporary phenomena of rapid change, and that normal political life will shortly be resumed. Of these Ascherson sees the second as the optimistic line for the future. Others too have looked for a 'third way'. Will Hutton[41] has claimed that western European social-democracy and Christian-democracy together do in fact represent such a politics. Evidently the whole matter is still in flux. What Ascherson, following Palmer and Enzensberger, usefully reminds us, is that new patterns in Europe will be the result at least in part of patterns of social life built outside orthodox institutional and ideational frames. The precise patterns are going to be determined by dynamics of structure and agency, not by the deployment of either utopian or bureaucratic-rational recipe knowledge. Nor, against the position of the UK political classes, is it likely to prove possible to abort these dynamics and effect a return to a reworked status quo ante.

Responding to accelerating change

As a result of this unreflexive approach there has been little public political discussion of the long-term relative decline of the UK or of the necessity of fashioning a positive reply, discourse has been narrowly pragmatic. Within the frame of extant political discourse, which remains heavily influenced by the post-war 'growth and welfare' approach, as modified by the New Right's confusions, discussants have not acknowledged that extensive systemic change is underway. However it has become clear that the processes of both EC unification and post-block reconstruction are accelerating.

In terms of an overall sequences of phases in the post-Second World War period, one could probably identify the following: a long period of relative stability for the UK as part and parcel of the US-dominated Atlantic Alliance; the period of UK membership of the EEC when this was conceived merely as a trade block; followed by the present phase of accelerating structural change. The present period of change has its own clear phases: (i) the earliest one being after the signing of the SEA and before any radical changes in the post-Second World War settlement had been made, or if we think of long term structural changes, become clear, but when nonetheless the basis for abrupt and far reaching change for the UK had been laid; (ii) the second phase runs from May 1989 through to November 1989 when the dam of received structures fractured and then burst; (iii) the third phase runs from autumn 1989 through to December 1991, that is the period of interregnum with the old eastern block collapsing, Germany re-uniting, the EC's EMU/PU projects in process but as yet with no new political framework in place; and (iv) and post-December 1991 one

---

[40] ibid.

[41] A familiar theme in commentaries in *The Guardian* published to date since mid-1989

could speak of a new general reconstructive phase, likely to be of long duration, which will see the construction of some new pattern of affairs in Europe. Finally, one might look to the eventual establishment of a new period of stability mirroring the post-war period, but the outline of this is unclear.

The moment when this acceleration in the pace of structural change became evident in UK public discourse was following the November 1989 announcement of the opening of the Berlin Wall. This event obliged UK public political discourse to acknowledge that new patterns within Europe were indeed in process of construction, and the discussions first turned around the December 1989 Strasbourg Summit and the Delors Plan for EMU, with political union added at the Dublin Summit of June 1990. Looking to that first Summit, Palmer commented that

> What gives the Strasbourg European Council historic significance is the interrelated issues of European Community union, the gradual disengagement of the United States as the hegemonic power in western Europe, and the virtual collapse of the Stalinist order in eastern Europe[42].

In the UK media the prospect of the summit and of the EC union which it was suddenly seen to presage was now debated. A key figure, often cited, was Jacques Delors whose speeches as President of the EC had directly presented the notion of EC union. The Delors Plan for economic union, EMU, was bound up with social reforms and institutional reforms which would move towards unification. Palmer[43] reported that after the meeting the view of many EC officials was that 1990 would be crucial for EC unification, and if the process were to be derailed it would take a decade to restart.

Hutton[44] noted the rise of Germany under the energetic leadership of Helmut Kohl, and with eastern Europe and the USSR/CIS undergoing reform, and the USA in economic decline, it was Germany that suddenly emerged from forty years of diplomatic-political tactfulness to take a key and central role in fixing complex change in the EC on the agenda for the 1990s. Palmer reported later that Kohl and Mitterand had decided to ignore any attempted British veto on moves to EC union, and at a meeting in Paris the two leaders set 1 January 1993 as a target date for economic and political union[45]. In July 1990 *The Economist* commented that 'Slowly but surely, the Community is becoming rather less a collection of nation states

---

[42]J. Palmer in *The Guardian* 4 December 1989

[43] J. Palmer in *The Guardian* 11 December 1989

[44] W. Hutton in *New Statesman and Society* 15 December 1989

[45] See J. Palmer in *The Guardian* 20 April 1990, A. Brummer in *The Guardian* 7 February 1990., D. Gow in *The Guardian* 7 February 1990.

and rather more a coherent entity which the rest of the world recognises as a power in itself'[46].

In sum, UK public political discourse with its national, economistic, and unreflexive character has failed to acknowledge the depth of the present changes to European, political-economic and political-cultural structures. Whether this represents a staggering incompetence on the part of the UK political classes or reflects habitual strategies of public demobilization is difficult to judge. It seems clear that neither of the major political parties were operating pro-actively in 1989-91.

Centres of debate in the UK

In the UK these issues of political analysis are variously addressed, and there are a series of centres of debate including professions, universities, political parties, pressure groups, business, finance, the media, and so on, plus the sphere of commonsense conversations. These centres of debate feed into a non-discursive public sphere which is dominated by parliament, with its two major parties. It is here that we find publicly deployed lines of putatively coherent argument in respect of the EC and Europe.

The Labour Party said relatively little in respect of EC integration through 1989-91. Opinion within the party is divided and Ashford has identified five more or less nationalist groupings (with Nairn and Palmer cited as members of a group looking to renew modernist notions in the context of the EC[47]). Traditionally the party has opposed the EC.

In the event, debate has been dominated by the Conservative Party. And it is clear that in regard to the dynamic of EC integration the party is split, and Ashford[48] identifies no less than six groupings, all more or less nationalist. The faction which surrounded Thatcher could be taken to have represented finance capital plus world market focused industrial capital[49]. They have seen the EC as a free trade area, a sphere of opportunity to be exploited by a low wage deregulated UK economy. However, the position taken in public discourse by Thatcher proved to be unsatisfactory, both in the UK where her deep unpopularity came to threaten the continuation in power of the Conservative Party, and overseas as her government was marginalized and indeed ridiculed in Europe.

Palmer[50], in spring 1990, argued that one of the reasons why Kohl became confident in pushing for an acceleration of movement towards European

---

[46] *Economist* 7 July 1990

[47] Ashford in George *Semi-Detachment*. For a general review of the views of European left parties see K. Featherstone *Socialist Parties and European Integration*, Manchester, Manchester University Press, 1988

[48] Ashford in George *Semi-Detachment*

[49] Overbeek *Global Capitalism*, B. Jessop et al. *Thatcherism: A Tale of Two Nations*, Cambridge, Polity, 1988

[50] J.Palmer in *The Guardian* 28 March 1990

unity was recognition of the weakness of Thatcher's position. As the structural conditions of the world system changed, rendering the post-Second World War settlement untenable, the Thatcher government seemed unable to adjust or respond. Discussions amongst EC partners pointed increasingly to a genuine move to some sort of unity and Palmer, noting that other European governments were lining up for 'fast track' unification and that EFTA and eastern block countries were knocking at the door, and that even the Labour Party was modifying its indifference, argued that Thatcher was running out of options and suggested that 'European union ... is likely to prove the issue which seals her political fate'.[51] Over the summer months the crisis of confidence in the Thatcher government deepened. In July one of her closest confidants, Nicholas Ridley, published an interview in which Chancellor Kohl was apparently compared to Hitler. After the Rome European Council of October 1990, when EC leaders reaffirmed their intentions to accelerate movement towards unification, Young commented that matters of UK involvement in Europe were not being adequately addressed within the UK. The relative silence of the Labour Party was one problem, but Hugo Young remarked that the 'main obstacle to such an acting out of democratic consultation is, of course, the Prime Minister ... [who seems to hold a] belief that there was no debate worth having with the British people'[52]. By November in the run up to the Tory Party leadership election Young[53] judged that the Thatcher period in British politics was almost over.

Young argued that Europe 'divides the Conservative Party like no other issue'[54]. Yet on the matter of the splits inside the party it is difficult to be clear how these run. Thus one might want to say that the faction which surrounded Heseltine does seem to be different, it may be that they are rather more Europeanist than Atlanticist. White[55] noted that whilst anti-European sentiment was concentrated and articulated most vividly by the Brugges Group, opposition was not confined to this group. Equally the pro-Europeans, the old Heathites for example, were not by any stretch of the imagination euro-federal enthusiasts. The splits are multiple in regard to Westminster/party debate, and it is only when one pulls back from the detail of day to day politics that a clearer view emerges. An Overbeek/Jessop/Nairn style analysis of the outward-directedness of UK ruling group would not stress these distinctions as the prospect of a unified or more extensively integrated EC represents a threat to the continued dominance of present ruling groups. The conflict inside the Conservative

---

51 ibid.

52 H. Young in *The Guardian* 30 October 1990

53 H. Young in *The Guardian* 15 November 1990

54 ibid.

55 M. White in *The Guardian* 30 October 1990

Party thus seems to be between those who are pragmatists and those like Thatcher/Ridley who seem to be emotional reactionaries.

All these tensions and confusions came to find expression in the debates in the UK surrounding the December 1991 Maastricht Summit on economic and political unity where the UK government of Major deployed its 'dilute and delay' strategy. Marquand comments that the EC was moving towards an informal-federalism with power flowing towards a set of 'interlocking technocracies' in place of real democratic machineries, with the UK taking key responsibility for the fudge[56]. A fudge which William Wallace further argued was irrelevant to the emergent post-block agenda[57]. The Maastricht Summit result was greeted in the UK press as a triumph for John Major. This narrowly national, economistic and unreflexive response was satirized by William Keegan in terms of the ideal-goal of slavery as an off-shore assembly plant for the Japanese, and he went on to note that Britain's 'performance was cheap and tawdry, with the Germans and French looking on in bemused amazement'[58].

The extent of institutional and ideational changes implied by new structural configurations

The extent of changes to UK institutional and ideational structures implied in the dynamics of structural change in Europe is large. They range across a spread of received ideas and for expository purposes can be grouped around the core social science concerns for power, production, and knowledge.

Implied changes in UK structures of power and received understandings

The starting point for considering these matters must be the changing patterns of power within Europe and the UK. It is clear that the remaking of patterns of power will include those elements of the trans-state network which flow through the UK. Following Marquand we might expect a shift away from Westminster towards both Brussels and the UK regions: that is, institutionally embodied power will be relocated both upwards to the new trans-national EC system, and downwards to the newly empowered regions of the UK. Such changes are implied by the federal system which has been latent within the development of the EC over its entire career and which is clearly present in the Maastricht Agreement. Of course for the UK with its strong central state and disregard of regional aspirations to power such implied patterns of change represent a considerable threat, and not merely to present institutional arrangements, but also to received patterns of

56 D. Marquand in *The Guardian* 3 December 1991
57 W. Wallace in *The Guardian* 9 December 1991
58 W. Keegan in *The Observer* 15 December 1991

official self-understanding. As was noted in Scotland over the period of the December 1992 Edinburgh Summit, the idea of subsidiarity, which figured importantly in the talks, implies precisely what succesive UK governments have resisted, a parliament in Edinburgh. In other words, any reconstruction of the present institutional form of the UK state runs the risk of opening up demands for its wholesale democratization, and the London-based UK state-regime has shown no sign of being prepared to entertain such issues. Wallace[59] notes that members of both political parties have expressed fears especially in the particular context of discussions of EMU for 'sovereignty'. Wallace remarks that 'we cannot abandon the myth of parliamentary sovereignty without opening up some fundamental questions about the quality of British democracy and the structure of the British state'[60]. These questions would challenge most sections of mainstream political opinion as

> insistence on Westminster sovereignty became the fundamental principle of ... Unionism, conservatism, and nationhood ... [and] most of Labour's leaders share the same sense of 'English exceptionalism', of unquestioning faith in the democratic character of the British parliament[61].

And if these assumptions are questioned, and their cultural-extension was detailed for us by Nairn in the opening chapter of this text, then the whole construct unravels and we would 'find ourselves not only with a constitutional crisis, but also with a crisis of national identity'[62].

Picking up Wallace's point, Hutton[63] offers an example in the lessons which could be drawn from the proposed structure of the euro-fed for the system of UK democracy: 'the European idea is democratically to incorporate an institution to which is delegated the competence to run monetary policy'. Hutton then asks us to imagine the UK system being ordered as in Germany, with a separation of central bank functions from the private bank sphere (which is not the case in the UK), with representatives of Scottish, Welsh and regional development banks joining in decision making (which is not the case in the UK). And we are invited to imagine how such a system would impact on the highly politicised actions of the UK finance minister. Hutton then speculates about the wide extension within the UK of the principle of independent institutional spheres of responsibility:

> Nor need the principle of independence stop at central banks. The same formula could be use for independent regulation of the financial markets, for independent investment credit banks - and what about a properly independent BBC, an

---

59 W .Wallace in the *New Statesman and Society* 9 November 1990

60 ibid.

61 ibid.

62 ibid.

63 W. Hutton in *The Guardian* 17 December 1990

independent health and safety executive and an independent public sector pay review board while we are at it?[64].

The rhetoric is once again aimed at the sovereignty of parliament, with the barbed end-note that as things progress this sovereignty becomes less important because power is already drifting away. What is needed is a decisive shift away from parliament: 'Somebody has to wrest power from its reluctant hands and would that the deed could be seen as it is. Not a surrender of sovereignty - but a moment of liberation'[65].

The reordering of familiar structures of power entails a process of ideological reorientation from Atlanticism and the hegemony of the USA, to Europeanism. Marquand argues that the new European settlement will have a distinctly German feel, as it is Germany that is the economic power-house of Europe and for many, especially in the eastern block, the model of a successful political-economy. For the extant UK state-regime all this poses severe problems, and Marquand notes the options: 'We can be an increasingly junior partner to a decreasingly hegemonic United States. We can be a rather shop-soiled island Sweden. Or we can be part of an evolving European Union'[66]. The Thatcher epoch is seen as largely escapism, a return to 'Churchillian grandeurs', and her fall restates the fundamental question of UK identity. In sum: 'Our European debate has so far focused on institutions and procedures. The real question is cultural. Can we make the psychological leap, not just from Atlanticism to Europeanism, but ... to a Europeanism made increasingly in a German image?'[67].

Implied changes in UK structures of production and received thinking

The appropriateness of a shift away from Anglo-American market-centred political ideologies can be taken to be underscored by the present changes within the global economic structures which embrace the UK economy. The detail of these reorientations is complex and in brief comprise: (i) movement on a global level with the tendency to the emergence of three major blocks, the USA/Latin America, Japan/Asia, and the EC/Europe, which of course impacts on the UK as its patterns of trade might be expected to shift further in the direction of one of the blocks; (ii) movement within the EC/Europe block as there is increasing coherence/convergence amongst what had long been national economies, in other words there is an emergent European economic space, and this increasingly embraces the UK economic space; (iii) and finally there is a cross-cutting movement towards a global economic system, most obviously in finance but also in services involving intellectual property and in trans-national company

---

64 ibid.

65 ibid.

66 D. Marquand in *The Guardian* 7 December 1990

67 ibid.

manufacturing[68]. The upshot of all these processes of structural adjustment is to shift the UK economic space away from the Atlantic sphere towards the European sphere.

Such patterns of change have been a central concern of European political leaders and the Brussels Commission, and indeed found expression in the Cecchini Report and the programme for the completion of the single market. However, there is some doubt as to the extent to which the UK state-regime has grasped the logic of these dynamics of change and Palmer has suggested that the UK has become marginalized as Paris and Bonn make all the running[69], and Hutton[70] too has argued that the UK government did not seem to realize that the drive for EMU, which pulls so much along behind it in terms of further unificatory moves, is more or less a settled matter between the French and the Germans. Just as the earlier incarnation of the EC revolved around the CAP, which balanced French agricultural and German industrial interests, the proposed euro-fed balances French interests in having a say in determining euro-economic policy (instead of leaving it to the Bundesbank) and German desires to fix euro-stability in institutional forms. Hutton noted: 'Bonn and Paris are combining to create a watershed in British history ... [and] the Government does not even understand what is happening ... [or if it does] judges it expedient to keep it well hidden'[71].

There is a wider economic-cultural aspect to all this, and can be summed as the shift from Anglo-Saxon 'markets' to European 'social markets'. In brief the line of argument suggests that the way in which the business of economic activity, and thereafter the proper role of the state, is construed within the Anglo-Saxon tradition is quite different to the way these matters are set-up and dealt with in the traditions of the mainland. The nub of the matter is that whereas the Anglo-Saxons take the market to be a reality sui generis and amenable only to rule-maintaining protective intervention by the state, the mainlanders lodge economies within societies and construe the community-serving role of the state in more active terms. These are of course matters close to the core line of the arguments of Marquand, and it must be said that the balance of intellectual opinion in respect of theorizing the market lies with the proponents of 'economies-as-lodged-within-societies'[72]. This debate reappeared when the UK government entered the ERM. Hutton[73] celebrated the decision to enter, noting that membership implied a convergence of UK economic patterns with those of mainland

68 See L. Sklair *The Sociology of the Global System*, London, Harvester, 1991

69 J. Palmer in *The Guardian* 12 December 1990

70 W. Hutton in *The Guardian* 12 December 1990

71 ibid.

72 See R. Dilley ed. *Contesting Markets*, Edinburgh, Edinburgh University Press, 1992

73 W. Hutton in *The Guardian* 6 October 1990

Europe[74]. Further, as economies are embedded in political-economies and cultures, the changes implied in UK patterns of life were extensive.

The whole business of the reorientation of structures of production, and the way in which agent groups have read these structures is extremely problematic for the UK state-regime. In brief the drift of events looks as though it will force them to shift the focus of their theorizing from the market to the community. In the run-up to the December 1991 Maastricht Summit, which was concerned with European economic and political union, all the above noted anxieties of the UK political class came into sharp relief. Both major parties engaged in a ritual posturing in regard to protecting 'Britain's interests' whilst the reality was of continuing movement towards a federal goal. Peter Luff, director of the European Movement, arguing that it was time that the UK government stopped dragging behind change and shifted instead to whole-hearted commitment, noted that 'It seems, at times, as if the idea of European political union fills the British with the uneasy feeling that the revolution they have avoided since 1789 is finally blowing ... Perhaps they're right'[75].

In the final months running-up to the Maastricht Summit there was considerable public manoeuvering in regard to the details of the agreement: with the French and German governments pressing for more federalist solutions and the British government arguing a minimalist case. Matters reported in the press covered the range of EMU/political union issues: currency, labour law, European army, European parliament, institutional and procedural reform of the EC machinery, and what came to be dubbed 'the F word', which was only deleted late in the process of negotiation. The consistent ploy of the UK government was to play down the importance of Maastricht, to deny that anything very dramatic was happening, and to affirm a conceit of British pragmatism calming excitable continentals. However White argued that Maastricht was a major development in European history, perhaps 'the decisive turning point ... because all of the attributes of sovereignty [were] on the inter-twined negotiating tables for economic and political union'[76]. In the final days before the meeting Hutton summarized the achievements of the EC, noting that the EC's 'managed capitalism' had been a success in contrast to the competitive situation of the inter-war period, and whilst it had thus far proceded under US auspices it had now to move forward under EC direction. The drive for further integration was structural, a matter not of ideologies or utopias but of patterns of global structural power. Yet the UK government's response to these issues was 'an attempt to reinvent the nineteenth century concept of Europe ... an attempt to export Anglo-Saxon marketism to the mainland'[77].

---

[74] Subsequently Hutton became a sharp critic of the way in which the ERM was being run, seeing it deployed wrongly as an anti-inflation weapon.

[75] P. Luff in *The Observer* 22 September 1991

[76] M. White in *The Guardian* 20 November 1991

[77] W. Hutton in *The Guardian* 9 December 1991

In the event monetary and political union were agreed at the summit and represented clear steps towards federal union. The UK government insisted on two opt-out clauses, one in regard to finally joining EMU and the other the social chapter of the treaty: both are in line with the post-Thatcher strategy of 'dilute and delay', advertised in the UK press as 'victory', and in the end they are irrelevant to the ongoing dynamics of economic and political union, with Keegan characterizing Major's performance derisively as a 'hollow triumph'[78].

The 1992 Danish referendum result re-ignited debate within the UK and notwithstanding John Major's spring election victory he was apparently unable to prevent what seemed to be open schisms within his party. An active group of some forty MPs, along with sympathizers outside parliament, began a very public campaign to block ratification of the Maastrict treaty. Through the autumn months of 1992 in the run-up to the December Edinburgh European Council a series of political disasters befell the Major government with the consequence that he arrived in Edinburgh with the political obituarists preparing not only for the end of John Major but also the Maastricht treaty. In the event the assembled EC leaders drew back from the brink and matters were for the time-being put in order. However one thing now became clear, and it was that the business of the post-Maastricht development of the community would be fraught with difficulties as each European country looked to translate general theory into a particular practice which favoured its own set of political-cultural expectations and interests. Overall, the business of structural change and agent response, lodged on the agendas of European political leaders by the events of 1989-92, looked set to run over the decade of the 1990s as the optimism of the December 1991 meeting in Maastricht gently faded away.

Implied changes in cultural structures, and familiar lines of understanding

It is clear that the increasing interpenetration of European nationstates as they are subsumed within a wider European Union will have far reaching effects on the ways in which citizens of the various countries read their relationship to the polities of which they are members: broadly, a matter of reorientation from national unit to some sort of European entity. In the case of the political culture of the UK this will entail a broad switch from membership of the free west to membership of Europe, and within the frame of this general revision one might anticipate local-level reorientations: from British identity to a European-Scottish, European-Welsh, or European-English identity. Paradoxically one might suppose that the English will have the most problems with all this as Britishness has often been taken to be coterminous with Englishness. The Scottish and Welsh in comparison have not usually confused their national identity with

---

[78] W. Keegan in *The Observer* 15 December 1991

Britishness. One thing the various inhabitants of the UK will have in common is the switch from being subjects of the crown-in-parliament to being citizens of a European union: a first experience of citizenship. One might envision the creation over a longer period of time of a new European identity (new ideas of what it is to be 'European') and the rather more rapid production of a new European history (new ideas of how we came to be 'European'). And, of course, one would expect all these matters to be buttressed in an accumulation of informal knowledge and experience: new European travel and new European living (both matters of practice rather than ideas).

In regard to the response of UK political agents to these implied changes it is quite clear that the Conservative Party are both wrong-footed by recent acceleration of moves towards EC unification, and that they are internally split on how to respond (whatever the basis of this split). For the Conservative Party down-playing the EC is an obvious move. But it does not seem to many commentators to be an obvious move for the Labour Party. Europe is one issue where the centre/left in the UK could move ahead. Marquand argues precisely this point: without an affirmation of the EC Labour's claim to have renewed itself as a European social democratic type party will founder. 'In today's world, European social democrats are federalists or nothing'[79]. All of which may be true, but the extent to which labourism needs to be overhauled in order to address the problems of UK industrial, social and political renewal cannot be underestimated. Paul Hirst[80] has addressed this matter and, noting present debates on the centre/left, he argues for a corporatist polity centred on a national development strategy which would include reform of parliament to make it more representative, reform of labour relations to make them centrally cooperative, and the reform of industrial strategy to encourage flexible specialization. Hirst returns to the theme of the extensive changes needed in the UK in a latter piece, and he states quite directly that membership of an integrated Europe is not a panacea: 'Make no mistake, joining an integrated Europe may accelerate our decline - if we fail to make the social changes that membership requires'[81]. And he adds: 'A programme of major institutional reforms, and a big change in popular attitudes, are required if we are to be able to compete in Europe'[82]. Most Britains he notes have no idea how affluent people in Germany and France are, or how much work is needed to achieve these levels of success. In sum, it is a matter of catching-up and joining-in: 'Only by adopting the objective of matching European

---

[79] D. Marquand in *New Statesman and Society* 2 November 1990

[80] P. Hirst *After Thatcher*, London, Collins, 1989

[81] P. Hirst in *New Statesman and Society* 16 November 1990

[82] ibid.

performance does a national economic policy acquire a clear rationale. The British need to decide to become properly European, and fast'[83].

The stifling of wider debates

The upshot of this situation is a virtual absence in the UK of discussion on the dynamics of change in Europe. A routinely non-discursive polity is here resoundingly silent. The mainstream is dominated by the national, economistic, and unreflexive non-debate of Conservative and Labour. The parliamentary-electoral system has the effect on this issue of blocking the effective articulation of alternative, that is pro-European views. Two such debates can be noted here: the first is the matter of political-institutional forms, in particular federalism; and the second concerns the reanimation of the classic modernist project.

In a piece published early in 1990 Marquand notes:

> The order within which Europe has lived since the Marshall Plan is visibly disintegrating. Jaques Delor's speech to the European Parliament arguing that the EC should respond to the changes in eastern Europe by moving more decisively towards radical union should be seen against that background[84].

Marquand goes on to point out that the post-Second World War settlement with its divided continent was neither particularly just nor had it been sought by the Europeans, it had in fact been imposed as a settlement to a long drawn out quasi-civil war. Marquand congratulates Delors on having understood three things: that the best solution to nationalist xenophobia is to make the nationstate irrelevant; that a supranational system must be just that and not some further mix of national units; and relatedly, that a supranational Europe, including East and West, will finally solve the problem of Germany.

In terms of the political self-understandings current within the UK the events since early 1989 have been quite dramatic, and overall they seem to add up to the possibility of reanimating the old modernist project of the pursuit of formal and substantive democracy. J.K. Galbraith[85] remarks that what has been lost sight of in all the brouhaha in respect of the failure of socialism is that the conservative ideology of the 1980s has also failed. Offering a variant of the well worn themes of convergence and the overturning of conventional wisdoms by events, Galbraith urges that it is not merely orthodox command economy socialism that has failed the translation to a sophisticated consumer/knowledge political-economy but also the 1980s Anglo-Saxon celebrations of the power of the market place. Galbraith argues that ideology has been derailed by events in both parts of

---

83 ibid.
84 D. Marquand in *New Statesman and Society* 26 January 1990
85 J. K. Galbraith in *The Guardian* 16 December 1990

the world and in place of slogans theorists and politicians will just have to try thought instead; and the implication is that this will require a return to received traditions of sceptical thinking. The idea that the eclipse of the post-war block system, with its associated ideologies, might open-up the possibility of new thinking has been picked up by the centre/left. Regarding this matter narrowly, I have already noted that commentators have seen change in the EC as a great opportunity, largely going begging, for the Labour Party. But it is probably the more radically democratic left that has the greater opportunities, precisely because the conventional block-ideology has gone.

Stuart Hall[86] argues that the collapse of the cold war plus east block socialism provides an opportunity for the left. Forty years of imposed straight-jacketed thinking is now gone, and the left can argue their case all the better. In the same vein Ernesto Laclau[87], in a sister piece to Hall's, goes on to argue that the left must rethink four themes: the issue of state control versus markets; the nature of the proletariat as the agent of history must be reworked; the nationstate focus has to be revised to encompass both localism and supranationalism; and the debate on revolution versus reform is definitively settled in favour of the latter.

As regards the opposition between markets and social control, a move in favour of some sort of mixed system is advocated:

> the project of the left has to abandon the utopian world of social control and be redefined in terms of radical and plural democracy. In the same way ... the notion of 'the market' can be redefined in such a way that it loses its necessary links with the ideas of self-regulatory mechanisms and unlimited profit maximization[88].

In other words, in place of debate predicated on the familiar received idea of the market, the notion can be critically re-appropriated for social science. In which case markets are social constructs and what is at issue is not freedom versus control but actual patterns of institutionalized economic practices. Similarly, in the matter of agency the left must revise its views and move away from specified unitary agents of history towards an acknowledgement of actually existing diversity in regard to identities affirmed within society. Says Laclau:

> this plurality and fragmentation opens the possibility of a more radical and democratic politics than in the past, given that the project of the Left has to consist of a painful effort to bring together many demands and identities through political dialogue and negotiation[89].

---

[86] S. Hall in *Marxism Today* March 1990

[87] E .Laclau in *Marxism Today* March 1990

[88] ibid.

[89] ibid.

Further, Laclau thinks the old theoretical idea of the relationship of base and superstructure must also be given up. Again simple models have obscured complexities of reality, and just as patterns of economic activity are diverse so too are the ways in which political-economic structures are read by participants. Culture and politics cannot be straightforwardly read-off economy. The upshot is that the 'political spaces in which the left operates are changing substantially'[90]. The traditional point of reference of debate was the nationstate but new patterns are emerging which are both local and supranational. Finally, the matter of whether the left should pursue revolution or reform has in Laclau's view been definitively settled in favour of reform, yet cautious social-democratic reformism has also been found wanting, leading to statism and bureaucracy. A new politics concerned with enabling people is needed, a revolutionary reformism, and aimed at 'radical and plural democracy'[91].

More broadly, there is the matter of the relationship of received notions of socialism to the modernist project itself, and the matter of how to read the idea of postmodernity. Zygmunt Bauman[92] characterizes the modernist project, the scientific and industrial society of capitalism, and identifies socialism's role as that of counter-culture, always pointing to how the modernist project could be fully realized. Thus where the modernist project pointed to the pursuit of liberty, equality and fraternity, the socialist counter-culture both applauded the project and pointed to the limited way in which these goals were acheived in present capitalist society: thus liberty was reduced to the freedom to make money, and became a vehicle for social division; equality was confined to formal equality before the law and actual massive practical inequalities were ignored; and finally, fraternity rather disappeared altogether to be parodied as loyalty and patriotism. In sum, there was nothing wrong with the project, but a lot wrong with the execution. As regards the present 'crisis of socialism' this is rather more than the collapse of the eastern block variant of that project, which Bauman[93] characterizes elsewhere as the realm of state sponsored welfarism, for the real crisis of socialism parallels the crisis of modernity. Bauman goes on to note that postmodernism offers a critique of the modernist project, as unrelexive, solidary, and hubristic: simple confidence in the modernist project, as it has been enunciated by intellectuals and pursued by political groups, has evaporated. In place is an appreciation of both the complexity of the goal and the difficulties and ambiguities of approaching the goal. Bauman sees this as modernity becoming self-aware, and thus, in Habermasian terms, seeking to work on 'the unfinished project of modernity'. The postmodern critique points to a revised trio of goals: to

---

90 ibid.
91 ibid.
92 Z. Bauman in *Marxism Today* February 1990
93 Z. Bauman *Freedom*,Milton Keynes, Open University Press, 1988

liberty, diversity and tolerance. Looking to the new postmodernist forms of industrial and scientific capitalism we find claims to diversity and tolerance, but when this is examined it rather boils down to further instances of market-indifference to the needs of the collectivity. A socialist critique is needed but it is one that must learn the lessons of postmodernism and not just seek to do a better job of managing capitalism. Against the siren calls of those who would reduce political life to the deployment of putatively technical competences the newly articulated counter-culture of postmodernity must affirm the role of the political, the ethics of democracy, and the ideal of citizenship. Says Bauman:

> Post-modernity is not the end of politics, as it is not the end of history. On the contrary, whatever may be attractive in its promise calls for more politics, more political engagement, more political effectivity of individual and communal action. The call is stifled, though, by the hubbub of consumer bustle ... And so it remains the task of the socialist counter-culture to make the call audible[94].

Overall, in sum one might say that UK public discourse has been narrowly national, economistic, and unreflexive. A broader reading of present patterns of complex change indicates that radical shifts in UK structures-discourses are inevitable. For the political right all this poses considerable problems, thus far evaded rather than confronted, whilst for the centre/left this seems to be an opportunity to re-animate the classical modernist project of the pursuit of formal and substantive democracy.

Responses to change in eastern Europe

The events of 1989-91 in eastern Europe clearly took political leaders in Europe by suprise. The late 1980s reforms which had been intiated by Gorbachev turned into an overwhelming flood of change and the final equilibrium point of the emergent system is presently most unclear. The issue for this text is the way these changes call into question the comfortable political certainties and official ideologies of the post-Second World War period. There are two responses in the UK: New Right triumphalism and centre/left embarassment, and it seems to me that neither is appropriate.

Problems of ongoing structural change

The second major occasion of new thinking in respect of Europe has been the dramatic reform movements in the old eastern block. Starting with the democratization and liberalization moves within the USSR/CIS, initiated by the Gorbachev government in the 1980s, patterns of change within the old eastern block have become very extensive. Following the dramatic

------

94 Z. Bauman in *Marxism Today* February 1990

upheavals of 1989-91 reform continues within the USSR/CIS itself, and now the depth of the problems facing the new leadership is clearer, as are the apparent difficulties of securing desired change. Turning to the old eastern block territories of Europe the situation is at once clearer in some respects whilst in others earlier clarity has given way to deeper confusion. In the case of political reforms the generally peaceful shifts from block-given Stalinist style command political-economies to a mix of variants on the western model was completed with elections throughout 1990. However, it has become clear that many tensions within these countries will have to be resolved before they begin to look stable, the reappearance of nationalism being one such problem, and quite how these countries are going to look when a new position of relative stability is reached is at present anybody's guess. In regard to matters economic the situation is more obscure, and an initial enthusiasm for raw models of laissez-faire capitalism is giving way to a dawning appreciation of the difficulties of securing economic reform and of the problematical nature of the pure market schemes advocated both by intellectual groups within eastern Europe and by western experts in the guise of the IMF/World Bank.

Throughout this text I have argued that the dynamic of change evident within the EC had implications for the political-economy and culture of the UK which were likely to be significantly non-negotiable, that is they were likely to require changes within the UK. It seems to me that the events in eastern Europe have both underscored this observation and rendered the business of fashioning a coherent intellectual response yet more urgent. In terms of our received political-cultural understandings of the position of the UK the world changed underneath our feet in the autumn of 1989 and the extent of change was made clear in December 1991.

These changes have been claimed by the Anglo-American New Right and commentators have spoken of the West having 'won the cold war' with the consequence that further development within the global system would necessarily follow the western model. However this position is implausible and we can make a series of comments. Most obviously, that it was Gorbachev who engineered the reform of the bi-polar system. Thereafter, it was the people of eastern Europe who made their revolution and it was a revolution lead by intellectuals, unionists, church groups and artists, and not by the New Right. The final resting point of these upheavals is yet to be established and their politics are in flux. Remaking the political-economic and political-cultural structures of eastern European countries will take time, and the business of the post-December 1991 reconstruction of the USSR/CIS will take years. Whether affirmations of New Right ideas (for example, the Polish-experiment) are fixed commitments, or just the deployment of 'the available recipe' will become clear over time. It has been suggested that the crucial distinction in respect of eastern European politics will be between backward looking nationalists, and European-modernists. For the present in this text the key point is the most obvious one, that the post-Second World War settlement is now overthrown and that matters hitherto decided are once again in question.

If we look at the business of engineering reform in ways of understanding the crucial actions were those of the USSR and in particular the reconstruction of its foreign policy thinking. This was discussed in a pre-autumn 1989 text by Neil Malcolm[95] who made it clear that after the accession to power of Gorbachev moves were initiated to adopt a posture of constructive engagement with the EC. Malcolm argued that the Soviet view of the EC had been through a series of phases: (i) in the 1950s the EEC was seen as a US sponsored project to weaken socialism; (ii) in the 1960s a role as defending Europe against the US began to be seen; (iii) in the late 1970s Atlantic interdependence was again stressed; and (iv) in the early 1980s the USA was seen to be reasserting its hegemony.

Moving on to consider the Soviet handling of matters in phase four Malcolm began by detailing the Soviet tradition of international relations thinking, which followed Lenin and saw the imperialist powers both cooperating and in conflict, and this language allowed Soviet commentators talk about international exchanges in much the same way as Western commentators. Overall since 1985 there was increasing concern for a long present theme, that of global interdependence, and a reliance on autarchy was no longer seen as a plausible strategy. Both the role of regional groupings, like the EC, and the global system became more central in Soviet thinking, and internationalization came 'to be treated by the majority of academic foreign affairs experts in the Soviet Union as something which is both irresistible and beneficial'[96]. In this new thinking the EC figured quite centrally. Soviet analyses of the institutional mechanisms and achievements of the EC were, reported Malcolm, both realistic and positive, and so were estimations of EC foreign policy. The industrial record of the EC was not seen as being so successful, and on defence Europe was taken to have remained a US protectorate. More broadly, evaluations of the relationship of USA to EC varied significantly and Malcolm distinguished between moderate Europeanists, who saw increasing global integration and urged the USSR to join in, obviously with the EC and with the USA, and strong Europeanists, who looked to increasing integration, multi-polarity, and regional conflict, and who urged the USSR to join in with the EC (implicitly against the USA). Malcolm identified three phases in the 1980s through which Soviet thinking has gone, all the time becoming more realistic: (i) at the time of the Reagan administration the Soviets expected European independent mindedness and were surprised when Europe fell in line behind rearmament programmes; (ii) an acknowledgement that European fears of Soviet armed force was real, coupled to view of Europeans as a moderating influence on USA; (iii) finally, realization that

---

95 N. Malcolm *Soviet Policy Perspectives on Western Europe*, London, Pinter, 1989
96 ibid. p.18

improved USSR/USA relationships might well turn Europe into a much more independent player.

The upshot of all this was Gorbachev's opening to the west. Malcolm commented that 'acceptance of greater unity in the West has been expressed as part of a new vision of interdependence ... in which the European Community is invited to play a part in forwarding continent-wide European cooperation'[97]. In turn this fed into the notion of a 'common European home' which Malcolm, writing before the autumn 1989 reforms in eastern Europe, found vague, anti-American, and unlikely to be of much interest. Malcolm thus tells us much about Soviet thinking in the Gorbachev period, and about the background to the Soviet moves to withdraw from the cold war system; he also tells us much about the slowness with which the British political classes recognised what was going on. This failure to recognise the pace of change in eastern Europe and the way in which these changes reinforced dynamics for change in the EC did not last long: in the immediate wake of the reforms of autumn 1989 there was a very sharp reaction on the part of the UK political establishment, and it took the form of denial.

Recipe-ism I: the triumph of the free world

It is clear that laying claim to the events of eastern Europe is a New Right tactic, it continues their hitherto domestic ideology of the free west by imputing this idea-system to the eastern Europe whose peoples are seen to have spoken decisively for 'freedom'. An overt celebration of the ideological reading of the right was given by Hugo Young who began by noting that these events dwarfed the domestic business of political life, and added that the events would have a large impact on our thinking: 'The very scale of the earthquake leaves its residue on our politics ... and the consequences of it is not entirely clear'[98]. However, the broad outline of what had happened was perfectly clear: 'We won, of course. That is what happened'[99]. Thereafter he looked to the downside of this celebration: that notwithstanding the victory, the West neither had much to do with making it, the people in the eastern Europe did that, and nor if one looks to the UK did western Europe look like much of a model to emulate.

The latter comments were well made, but unfortunately it is the former celebrations that best capture the views of the UK political classes in these matters, and speaking of victory is just plain childish. Of course, this has been widespread in the media. John Pilger noted that 'With honourable exceptions, the coverage of Europe's upheaval has been so beset by jingoism ... that the nature of change, and the emerging hopes and alternatives, have

---

[97] ibid. p.67
[98] H. Young in *The Guardian* 29 December 1989
[99] ibid.

been obscured'[100]. Other commentators took this view, and Figes[101] argued that it was a mistake for the New Right to lay claim to the revolutions in the eastern Europe and that they would not under any conceivable circumstance inherit the post-revolutionary phase. Of the right Figes noted their 'aim is to use the East Europeans as a living, historical proof of the 'common sense' (and cliched) truths of free-market Western capitalism'[102]. Against this strategy of analysis, looking through 'blue-tinted spectacles', Figes urged that what 'is actually happening there is the collapse of the state, around which the old system was based. This is inevitably followed by a period of chaos and social breakdown'[103]. Figes went on to argue that during the transitional phase eastern block governments would have to continue with high levels of welfare spending as their populations both needed and expected it, and the natural resting point for an eastern European politics was thus social-democratic. More generally: 'This augurs well for the centre-left in Europe, as a whole, which must now think very hard about the principles of post-Marxian socialism'[104].

Nonetheless, Figes notes that if social-democracy did not succeed in eastern Europe then the alternative was not some sort of relatively mild mannered UK style toryism, but rather the extremes of racist and nationalist movements. And commenting in a similar way Marquand[105] was less sanguine about the future as the notions of capitalism being bandied about by eastern block thinkers, and it seemed being translated into policy practice by new governments, were those of the Anglo-American right. Marquand following Susan Strange[106] calls this 'casino capitalism', the political-economic system of quick profit. In this model the fate of eastern Europe would not be to join in a sophisticated European social-democratic system but instead the area would become Europe's Third World.

If anything, subsequent events have tended in the direction of a 'new Third World'. The early optimism in eastern Europe for marketism has faded as IMF and World Bank austerity-adjustment has gone ahead, and with the December 1991 dissolution of the USSR in favour of the seemingly politically inchoate and economically damaged CIS all the conditions for 'third worldization' are in place.

One aspect of the New Right's response to events in eastern Europe has been to affirm the triumph of liberal-democracy. Francis Fukuyama[107], reaching back to the beginning of the modern period to re-read the history of the West in terms redolent of 1950s notions of industrialism,

---

[100] J. Pilger in *The Guardian* 12 February 1989

[101] O. Figes in *The Guardian* 17 February 1990

[102] ibid.

[103] ibid.

[104] ibid.

[105] D. Marquand in *The Guardian* 9 November 1990

[106] S. Strange *Casino Capitalism*, Oxford, Blackwell, 1986

[107] F. Fukuyama *The End of History and the Last Man*, London, Hamish Hamilton, 1992

convergence, modernization, and the end-of-ideology, offers a celebration of westernization as the ethico-political 'end of history'[108]. Setting aside all this nonsense we can cite local, and more intellectually discreet, theorists who nonetheless work the same vein. One such commentator has been Timothy Garton-Ash who has both interpreted the realm of eastern Europe before the revolutions and has gone on to offer marvellous exercises in reportage of those revolutions-in-progress[109]. However Garton-Ash apparently thinks that there are no lessons for the West in all this, merely confirmation of the value of long held liberal-democratic patterns. Anthony Barnett[110] tackles Garton-Ash on this matter and, noting that Garton-Ash's book *We the people* had reviewed events in eastern Europe and concluded that they had nothing fundamentally new to teach us, comments that this is evidence of 'staggering complacency' and asserts that the reverse is the case. Thus in eastern Europe, with the mass rallies and so on that made the revolutions, there was a rediscovery of a direct and practical/ethical driven democracy that has degenerated in the West, and certainly in the UK, to a cynical periodic plebiscitary affirmation of this or that political class group. Michael Ignatieff[111] has made the same point, that in eastern Europe masses of people reasserted their rights, and in the West we see politics as a game for professional politicians. Ignatieff is not at all sure that we have lessons to teach them about democracy. In brief, the claims of the New Right to be the legatees of the democratic revolutions in eastern Europe must be denied. To defeat this propaganda manoeuvre we must distinguish between the idea of democracy, the idea of liberalism, what the now discredited central-plan socialists did achieve, and finally what could be asserted as a presently relevant affirmation of modernism (thus, after Bauman, decentralization, libertarianism, citizenship).

Overall it seems to me that the real battle in all this is not about which model of development eastern Europe should adopt but is much wider; it is about the shape of an emergent Europe as political and economic reforms continue in CIS/USSR, and as the EC which is disengaging from the US sphere moves towards some sort of unity. The New Right's attempt to annex to its position the events in eastern Europe is essentially a defensive manoeuvre within a broader game. The right cling to the idea of a 'New Atlanticism', and looking to the UK situation directly their desperation to

---

108 Astonishingly, and one suspects ironically, Fukuyama cites his intellectual mentor Alexandre Kojeve as giving up 'teaching in the latter part of his life to work as a bureaucrat for the European Community. The end of history, he believed, meant the end not only of large political struggles and conflicts, but the end of philosophy as well; the European Community was therefore an appropriate institutional embodiment of the end of history' p.67

109 T. Garton-Ash *The Uses of Adversity*, Cambridge, Granta, 1989; T Garton-Ash *We the People*, Cambridge, Granta, 1990

110 A. Barnett in *New Statesman and Society* 6 April 1990

111 M. Ignatieff in *The Observer* 6 April 1990

deny that broad structural change is underway, in this case by a totally spurious reading of events in eastern Europe, is quite understandable.

Recipe-ism II: the triumph of the market

One of the more notable displays of confidence on the part of the political right in respect of the changes in eastern Europe has centred on the celebration of the possibility of exporting technical expert economic recipes to the eastern block. That those who have failed so comprehensively in their policy advice in the West should feel confident about recycling the material in the East would be astonishing were it not for the extent of the available hubris of the marketeers. On this Keegan commented:

> East European governments seeking financial and economic advice from the west should beware. They are prey to all manner of evangelising from economists and bankers ... Quick fix 'monetary' solutions will be no good until the 'real' economy underneath is producing the goods[112].

Once the familiar claims to technical expertise of the IMF, World Bank and the other massed ranks of recipe-mongers are denied, then they are revealed as at best misguided and at worst as agents of what Noam Chomsky[113] has dubbed the Latin Americanization of eastern Europe. Against the New Right, the notions of privatization and marketization must be addressed, and as broad theoretical issues[114]. All this would seem to imply that the matter of the making of markets in the old eastern block systems is going to be not merely a fraught and difficult business in practice, but is also going to be a realm of ideological experiment for the presently powerful right, and thereafter of obfuscatory apologies in the light of the failures that must on general social scientific grounds be regarded as inevitable. The attempts of the New Right and other market-recipe celebrants will end in ambiguous failure: the business of scholarly commentary must be with recording accurately the details, at least in the first instance.

All of this would seem to involve the following: (i) the general business of market-making (for there are no spontaneously given market systems); (ii) the issue of what New Right marketism has done to extant political-economic systems - in the UK, USA, and so on; and (iii) what could happen in eastern Europe, and here we must separate out ideological recipes and claims from the slow patterns of political-economic reform which will emerge. The nature of the overall shift in prospect for the old eastern block political-economies is quite novel, and on this Portes comments: 'These

---

112 W. Keegan in *The Observer* 11 February 1990

113 N. Chomsky *BBC Radio 4 Analysis* 28 February 1990

114 See Dilley *Contesting Markets*; and W. Keegan *The Spectre of Capitalism*, London, Radius, 1992

countries will be moving from a bureaucratic centralized socialism towards a more market-centred economy. But to assume that there is only one capitalist model is facile'[115].

Similarly Traynor[116] notes that as Christian-democracy, under various labels and with many quirks, comes back to power, they face many problems of economics, politics, social reform and so on which are likely to prove at least in the short term overwhelming. Patterns of local reassertion of long suppressed, or distorted, traditions are being conditioned by the general economic-political environment of the collapse of communist central planning, the withdrawal of the USSR's subsidies and markets, and the relentless promulgation by imported western experts of market-ism. Panic takes a similar line and comments that 'it is precisely in the key area of economic performance that things have gone from bad to worse virtually everywhere in Eastern Europe'[117]. Continuing, he notes that the causes are complex, but there is 'a real danger that East European countries are rushing to replace one unworkable economic system (central planning) with another (unregulated free market) which has, historically, been proved to be an even greater failure'[118].

And finally, more broadly, Misha Glenny[119] reviews the situation of the eastern block countries as they move to reassert local political-economic and cultural models in the wake of the abrupt ending of bloc-imposed conformity, and whilst problems are legion, two are cited: the resurgence of nationalism; and the severe problems of economic system adjustment in the face of a legacy of problems, debts, and western market-nonsense coupled to practical indifference (for example, no debt relief). Having reviewed the situation in the east block countries Glenny offers a series of conclusions: (i) the political-cultural framework of block-time, ideas of socialism, comecom, talk of 'middle Europe', are all now disregarded or of no help; (ii) relatedly there are ambiguous new cultural idea-sets being drawn down upon, in particular varieties of nationalism; and (iii) the most often cited new political-cultural notion is that of a 'return to Europe', where this is neither left nor right and counts as some sort of 'coming home'. By way of response to all these events Glenny offers two thoughts, echoed in many of the commentaries noted earlier: the first is that the resurgence of nationalism is a danger; and the second is that it is precisely the indifference of the West, illustrated in their thoughtless market recipe-ism, that is most likely to trigger political and social upheavals in the eastern block as they flounder under their received economic problems[120].

---

115 R. Portes in *The Times Higher Education Supplement* 9 February 1990
116 I Traynor in *The Guardian* 11 April 1990
117 M. Panic in *The Guardian* 1 October 1990
118 ibid.
119 M. Glenny *The Rebirth of History*, Harmondsworth, Penguin, 1990
120 See B. Denitch *The End of the Cold War*, London, Verso, 1990

Reanimating the modernist project

Broadly it is the case that much centre/left politics whilst dominated intellectually by the social-democratic tradition, and this is certainly the case over the post-Second World War period, has had an ambiguous relationship to the intellectual and practical tradition of marxism. What we have is a mix of intellectual-political tensions within the centre/left made the more problematic by the arguments of the right to the effect that any 'socialist' position was tainted by association with the USSR. As Perry Anderson[121] has noted, the main vehicle of reform politics in northwestern Europe has been social-democracy, which was successful until the economic dislocations of the early 1970s when it proved unable to deal with either the contemporary crises or the resurgent opportunism of the New Right. In southern Europe, by contrast, the social-democratic parties came to power only in the wake of dictatorships and whilst they have not repeated the economic-social success of their northern sister parties they have secured broadly liberal-democratic political systems. The upshot of the collapse of the USSR, and the reduced relevance in the EC countries of nineteenth century style mass working class movements, is that to a significant degree the political centre/left is bereft of obvious direction. In many northwest European countries minority parties, of left and right, are gaining support at the expense of familiar centre/right groupings.

The theme of epoches of history coming to an end has been widespread amongst the UK left; thus Eric Hobsbawm[122] speaks of the whole tradition inaugurated by the October Revolution as having come to an end. That particular recourse to a specific country and specific events and their use as a model probably has come to an end. In reviewing the history of the post-October period it is clear that the model of the USSR was initially positive, and that it is only in the post-Second World War period that the USSR has ceased to be any sort of exemplar[123]. And in this period we have seen the economic and military competition of the cold war; a competition that has also undermined the US economy. It seems to me to be much better to regard the ending of the cold war, the collapse of the antagonistic block system, and the undermining of the political-cultural certainties that went along with it (and which were so convenient to western ruling groups which had so assiduously fostered them) as a good thing: the matter now at hand for the European left is the re-animation of the modernist project[124].

Overall, in sum the matter of complex change in eastern Europe has thus far been little considered in UK public political discourse. The mould may

---

[121] Anderson *English Questions* chapter 6
[122] E. Hobsbawm in *The Guardian* 26 January 1990
[123] A. Callinicos *The Revenge of History*, Cambridge, Polity, 1991
[124] See *Marxism Today* January 1990

have been broken but as yet little thought seems to have been given to what might usefully happen next. The New Right have fatuously laid claim to these revolutions and the Labour Party, and the wider left it seems, has stayed rather quiet.

Responses to changes in Germany

One of the most dramatic consequences of the collapse of the eastern block system in the autumn of 1989 was the subsequent re-unification of Germany, which not only marked the definitive end of the western post-Second World War settlement but also placed a nation of some eighty millions at the heart of Europe. The events of 1989-90 added a new cultural and political influence to existing political-economic strength. Here I will take note of the initial public reaction of the UK political classes and then look to those who would affirm Germany as a model for the developing European Community.

The re-emergence of Germany

Out of moves towards EC integration, discussion of re-armament proposals within NATO, and latterly reform in eastern Europe which spilled over into an unexpected and precipitate reunification of the two Germanys, a new issue has arisen: the matter of Germany its place in Europe. Around this complex issue a simple polarization is identifiable within UK political culture: at one end of the spectrum we find a backward looking English nationalism that verges on anti-Germanism, which was neatly revealed in the 1992 unveiling by the Queen Mother of a statue to 'Bomber Harris', a war-criminal on any account[125], whilst at the other end we find commentators like Hutton and Marquand explicitly taking Germany as a model for the UK. Here I take note of the sequence whereby the German Question re-entered UK political discourse.

Bloomfield[126], writing before the events of the autumn of 1989, detailed the emergence of German dissent on the matter of continued NATO re-armament when the issue of arms negotiation had been fixed in the public sphere by unilateral eastern block arms cuts. Bloomfield notes that the European public was in advance of the thinking of western politicians, with opinion surveys recording 'high levels of personal confidence in President Gorbachev'[127]. The German government favoured making a positive response to Gorbachev's overtures, however the UK government strongly opposed this position and insisted that a new generation of nuclear missiles

---

[125] See for example Max Hastings *Bomber Command*, London, Michael Joseph, 1979
[126] J. Bloomfield in *Marxism Today* July 1989
[127] ibid.

be based in Germany. The debate over short range rockets turned out to be very important because what began as a supposedly technical matter of weapons systems requisite to agreed strategy spiralled out of the politicians control into a general revision of accepted thinking about Nato. Bloomfield notes:

> The controversy came to a head on April 20. Kohl's coalition adopted a ... statement requesting postponement of any decision on the deployment of Lance and the 'speedy taking-up' of negotiations with the Warsaw Pact on short-range nuclear weapons ... By asserting itself in this way the German government signalled the end of an era[128].

At the meeting between George Bush and Helmut Kohl in May, in the German city of Mainz, the Americans deferred to the wishes of the Germans in this matter and at that point a significant shift in the order of precedence within the Atlantic Alliance had been acomplished[129]. As the months of 1989 passed, it quickly became apparent that this exchange had marked the beginning of the end of the entire post-Second World War settlement in western Europe.

This shift of power relationships within NATO directly threatened the UK's strategic/diplomatic role and thereafter deep-seated politico-cultural ideas in regard to the identity of the UK and its position in the world. In brief, as the cold war wound down the USA would no longer need a 'number one European ally', and the consequence of this would be a shift of political attention into Europe, and here the weakness of the UK economy would be fully exposed. The broader politico-cultural issues flowed from this quite automatically: if the role/identity as 'number one ally', with its Atlanticism, and the idea of a 'special relationship', were to be swept away, and with it the internal official ideological self-understanding of the UK as having moral stature by virtue of its role in World War Two, the issue would open up of how to fill the gap, and here the obvious place to look would be to the EC and the problem for the UK state-regime would then become that of resisting the democratization of the UK that would be implied by bringing the UK into political, social and economic line with the mainland.

For the UK state-regime matters subsequently became even more problematical. Over the summer months there had been a growing crisis in the GDR, occasioned by the blank refusal of the Honecker regime to respond to notions of perestroika, and triggered by the decision of the Hungarian authorites to allow the citizens of East Germany to transit to Austria. In the GDR itself there were massive demonstrations in favour of reform organised by New Forum, and the final collapse of the regime was signalled by the decision to open the inner-German border, and when in

---

[128] ibid.

[129] M. Walker in *The Guardian* 7 February 1990

early November 1989 the Berlin Wall was opened, given its politico-cultural and diplomatic significance, this event marked the definitive and very public end of the post-Second World War period. At the time Martin Woollacott noted: 'From the crisis over NATO modernization in March to the casting down of the Wall in November stretch an astonishing nine months in which Germans on both sides have reached out with increasing boldness and taken their destiny into their own hands'[130]. And more broadly he continued:

> The international landscape with which we began 1989 - the old, familiar structures of the two alliances, the Anglo-American special relationship, the European Community's halting progress toward greater unity, and the newer but also beginning to be familiar element of reform in the Soviet Union - is being transformed, and it is Germany which is leading that transformation[131].

In the subsequent days a clutch of received wisdoms saw their quietus: the role of NATO in defending the free west against the USSR, now utterly irrelevant; the role of NATO in defending Europe against a resurgent Germany, now utterly overtaken by events; the division of Europe into blocks, the free and the enslaved with the Berlin Wall as the symbol, now irrelevant (and with the symbol being literally demolished in front of the world's television cameras); the role of Germany as the dutiful, defeated, and deferential power of Europe, now evidently stood on its head; and the political role of the British, the guardians of Europe in 1939-45 and the 'number one ally' in the cold war against the Soviets, was now irrelevant. In brief, the period from spring through to autumn 1989 not only undermined the UK state-regimes political project of dual parasitism, but it also overthrew the post-Second World War political-cultural certainties of the UK public sphere.

The reunification of Germany has occasioned some extraordinary responses. In the UK in early 1990 Mrs Thatcher held a seminar in Downing Street which characterized the Germans in astonishingly childish terms (indifferent to others, fearful, pushy, having an inferiorty complex, and yet wanting to be loved[132]). In the summer of July 1990 a close adviser, Nicholas Ridley, went public with the view held by the Tory right and it turned out to be an almost comical anti-Germanism, with the EC as a 'racket' put together by 'uppity' Germans. Nonetheless, the extent to which the situation of post-war Germany was embedded within the wider post-war settlement is made clear by Renata Fritsch-Bournazel[133]. The opening of the Berlin Wall was problematical as Germany was located at the intersection of three systems: the European Community, the Atlantic Alliance, and the

---

130 M. Woollacott in *The Guardian* 11 November 1989
131 ibid.
132 Noted in Fritsch-Bournazel *German Unification*
133 ibid.

East-West blocks. In the wake of the Second World War the FRG was firmly lodged within the western block, and the GDR within the eastern, and whilst NATO had affirmed in 1967 a policy of deterrence and detente, and the SPD had established an Ostpolitik, there had been no expectations of rapid and total collapse of the block system. In western Europe expectations had been of slow rapprochement, and in eastern Europe such talk of reunification as there had been was typically cast in terms of the neutralization of Germany. Fritsch-Bournazel makes clear that the abrupt collapse of the GDR and subsequent German reunification reopens old issues of the place of Germany in Europe, and relatedly its national identity, an issue-complex neatly summed by the question of the capital of the newly reconstituted state, with Berlin being preferred to Bonn in a close ballot in the Bundestag. The reactions of Germany's EC neighbours to reunification was broadly positive and the accession of the eastern Lander to the EC was passed 'on the nod'. Nonetheless, the future role and identity of Germany within Europe is a matter of some unclarity, and Fritsch-Bournzel notes that whatever the answer it cannot simply be a continuation of the FRG, now somewhat larger[134].

Affirming the German model

In the UK the responses to the new-uncertainties were quick in coming, and on the one hand we find affirmations of a new German-centred EC, whilst on the other a variety of strategies of denial. The latter strategy was adopted apparently automatically by Thatcher and as noted earlier it eventually destroyed her government. The government of John Major has signalled a much more discreet line whereby opposition will be expressed via a strategy of dilution and delay in the process of gradual acquiescence in the inevitable. Similarly, the Labour Party, with its little-Englander nationalism, seems to be as bereft of enthusiasm as the Conservative Party, and consequently positive responses to the prospect of European unification have come from outside the main lines of party political thinking.

The reunification of Germany has major implications for the future development of Europe and the EC. The manner of reunification could hardly have been more dramatic, with the television pictures of people dancing on the Berlin Wall in front of the Brandenburg Gate summing up the whole episode. As regards the UK it is clear that the responses of the political ruling groups have revealed a great fear, an updated version of the old 'German Question'; but for the rest of us, looking at the economic prosperity and extensive and routine democracy, it might be more sensible to speak of 'the German Answer'.

---

134 ibid. See also B. Nelson ed. *The European Community in the 1990s: Economics, Politics, Defence*, London, Berg, 1992

Christopher Harvie[135] has offered an increasingly familiar unpacking of what such an answer might involve and he begins with a sketch of a plausible future for the UK, and the capitalist world more generally, and suggests that it is available in the form of 'super-industry', a kind of sustainable development for the advanced industrial countries, environmentally and socially concerned and ordered by discourse oriented to securing consensus. Harvie characterizes Germany as a decentralized consensus polity oriented to industrial society. In contrast the UK is class-ridden, suffused with conflict, and ordered by a rentier ruling class. Harvie suggests that the reasons for German success 'lie in three main factors: finance is committed to industry; workers are highly-trained and involved in the strategy of firms; and the culture is egalitarian and work rather than expenditure governed'[136]. Underlying the first two is a notion of social partnership, in effect industrial activity is rooted in the community, rather than understood as lodged in a competitive marketplace[137], and much of the reason for this community-embedding can be traced to a 'political order which promotes economic and fiscal stability, and decentralized decision making'[138]. It is a model of progressive regionalism that Europe can look to, and if it does have problems it is maybe in the present relative exhaustion of the parties, both SPD and CDU/CSU, the former unable to articulate effectively a socialist vision of a new Europe, thus Oskar Lafontaine was both the right sort of candidate and trounced in the all German elections of December 1990, and the latter unable to escape from the grip of its own very effective apparatchik Helmut Kohl. Harvie concludes that German regionalism is an ambiguous model for a Europe of the regions, it is simultaneously succesful and rather parochial[139].

Responses to Europe after the power-blocks

It was suggested immediately above that the events of the year 1989 had profound effects for the political strategy of the present UK state-regime and for the political culture of both the political classes and the public sphere. The occasions of the radical undermining of received certainties have been the rise of the EC, the reunification of Germany, and the revolutions in eastern Europe. I now turn to consider a related issue, one which is immediately implicated but which draws in the USA quite directly, that is the collapse of the post-war system of power blocks. It seems safe to say that UK public political discourse on this issue is even less developed

---

[135] C. Harvie *Cultural Weapons: Scotland and Survival in a New Europe*, Edinburgh, Polygon, 1992

[136] ibid. p.46

[137] ibid.

[138] ibid. p.47

[139] ibid. p.72

than debates on EC and eastern Europe, for the issue of the UK's role has been routinely addressed via obeisances to NATO, and debate has been in terms of 'strong defence': in other words for years it has been a mainstream non-debate, plus marginal critics in the 'Peace Movement'.

For the Conservative Party the problems of the new period of uncertainty are extensive: they lose a useful enemy and with it an international political role; relatedly they lose a useful internal propaganda reference, thus they lose a major way of interpreting themselves to the UK population - as defenders of freedom and so on; and they have to confront the issue of running down the very influential defence industry. And beyond these problems looms the dreadful 'good example' of mainland Europe. Relatedly, for the Labour Party analogous problems emerge because they can no longer rest content with supporting NATO, with the resultant comfortable nationalism/patriotism plus a little war-Keynesian job creation, instead they must both think about these issues and fashion a coherent position. In this section I will look at right triumphalism and some of the new problems that have to be addressed, and then at how the centre/left can respond.

Right triumphalism, and 'New Atlanticism'

In December 1989 the Atlantic-right moved to assert itself in the wake of the changes wrought by the autumn revolutions. Hella Pick reported that: 'NATO is poised to embrace the new US initiative aimed at remoulding the alliance into a political instrument equipped to handle the radical changes in East West relations'[140]. A recent speech of Mr Baker was noted which called for a new Atlanticism, a new more political role for NATO, out-of-area operations to be undertaken, and a close link of the USA to the EC. For the USA it is clear that existing NATO machineries are seen as a vehicle for retaining a measure of control of Europe. However this is an issue that is very complex: not merely the matter of US overlordship in European military matters, but also the fact of the alliance being a key institutional link between the Europeans and the Americans. Generations of bureaucrats on both side of the Atlantic, have seen their professional lives shaped by NATO. Disentangling these institutions and at the same time finding some new machineries to ensure security within Europe will take some considerable time. It is not too difficult to see a clear US interest in maintaining NATO for without it US influence in Europe would wane, and given the UK governments position it too can be expected to maintain support, but an organisation that has just lost its overt and publicly celebrated role cannot survive in the long term. The real question here is how the US protectorate will be wound down.

---

[140] H. Pick in *The Guardian* 14 December 1989

The broad triumphalist right vision, the optimistic hope that all could continue as before, only without a USSR inhibiting action, was neatly captured in the piece by Young noted earlier in which he voiced the opinion that 'we' had 'won'[141]. And this theme was also picked out by Sarah Benton[142] who noted that the New Right claimed the revolutions in eastern Europe as their own, and as evidence of their general success. Rightist triumphalism is thus not unexpected but it is a reaction of denial. It is an assertion, politically brave and quite empty, that things will go on as before. That the revolutions which have cut the core ideological ground from under their feet with the loss of their enemy, and in the case of the UK destroyed their political project, are of no direct account, rather they are further celebrations of 'our victory'. For the right it is to be business as usual: hence Baker's new Atlanticism.

A systematic reply to this stance was given by Edward Thompson who, having characterized the triumphalist position, pointed out that the posture of NATO did not hasten these changes, rather 'the cold war aggro delayed all these events. Nothing is more obvious than that these changes were long overdue ... Brezhnev and his clique derived their only legitimacy precisely from the western "threat"'[143]. Thompson went on to remark that he was 'perplexed by the smug notion that over there they are adopting 'our values' ... In fact, the 'free west' has had rather little influence'[144]. In brief, there was 'a ludicrous notion that the whole of eastern and central Europe is now intent upon hurling itself helter-skelter into a 'market economy', the restoration of capitalism in a Thatcherite form'[145]. Thompson noted that the alternatives presented by triumphalists, of liberalism or Stalinism, are absurd, and said 'we must watch and listen before predicting the outcome. And the outcome may well be different in different nations'[146].

As regards the great unexpectedness of all these events, Thompson suggests that it should be noted that END has been working for these ends for the last decade, and what is now needed given that disarmament is seemingly secured is a revision of western attitudes to the eastern block. It seems to me that Thompson's response to the right's triumphalist conceit is broadly correct. That there is a political battle to be fought with the US and their European-Atlanticist allies in regard to their withdrawal from overlordship seems to be clear. The rhetoric of triumph is a part of this process.

---

[141] H. Young in *The Guardian* 29 December 1989

[142] S. Benton in *New Statesman and Society* 20 October 1989

[143] E. P. Thompson in *New Statesman and Society* 12 January 1990, see also E. P. Thompson in *New Statesman and Society* 26 February 1990

[144] ibid.

[145] ibid.

[146] ibid.

Centre/Left responses

A specific and original response to the European revolutions has been published by Enzensberger[147]: he argues that the western block nations have yet to find their hero-of-deconstruction. It is true that through the long period of European history we have had a steady supply of necessary heroes, assorted victors, often to be found adorning town squares as equestrian statues. But times have changed, and in 'the past few decades, a more significant protagonist has stepped forward; a hero of a new kind, representing not victory, conquest and triumph, but renunciation, reduction and dismantling'[148]. And he adds: 'We have every reason to concern ourselves with these specialists in denial, for our continent depends on them if it is to survive'[149]. A series of instances are given: from Kruschev, through Janos Kadar, Adolfo Suarez and General Jaruzelski, to Mikhail Gorbachev. All have it in common that they seek to secure far reaching reforms to the systems which they ruled, reforms which would ensure both their unpopularity and their eventual supersession; they act in order to move history on. Of Gorbachev, Enzensberger argued:

> [he] is the initiator of a process with which others, willingly or unwillingly, can only struggle to keep up ... He is attempting to dismantle the second to last remaining monolithic empire of the twentieth century without the use of force, without panic, in peace[150].

As regards the implications for the West, Enzensberger noted them in terms of the possibility of bringing under control two contemporary wars: of debt against the Third World, and of industrial life against the biosphere. These are two lines of withdrawal that will take much imagination and effort:

> But instead our political leadership senses victory, indulging in ridiculous posturing and self satisfied lies. It gloats and it stonewalls, thinking it can master the future by sitting it out. It hasn't the slightest idea about the moral imperative of sacrifice. It knows nothing of the politics of retreat. It has a lot to learn[151].

I will come back to this business of a creative response to the revolutions at the end of this chapter, for the moment however I conclude this section by taking note of the implications in respect of UK political-cultural resources of an early specimen of triumphalist right post-Cold War action.

---

[147] H. M. Enzensberger in *The Guardian* 19 February 1990
[148] ibid.
[149] ibid.
[150] ibid.
[151] ibid.

Bush's Gulf War, the martial 'Brits', and the New World Order

The withdrawal of the USSR from cold war competition evoked mixed responses on the part of the Atlantic right generally and the US right in particular. In line with the general strategy of denial of change has gone a particular line of affirmation of old certainties, and into the present global system interegnum the US has projected its celebrations of 'the American way'. Wallace has addressed the question of the implications of the Gulf War for the post-cold war era. The diagnosis is complex as matters are unclear and in flux. Looking at the matter very broadly Wallace speculates that we may be on the verge of a 'world divided into three camps on a basis rather different from those which we have grown used to over the past 40 years'[152]. Wallace suggests that:

> The new "first world" will additionally include most of those countries which under the cold war paradigm belonged to the second ... The Middle East will constitute a loose "second world", with claims to share an alternative ideology and culture, posing a perceived threat to the security and way of life of "first world" countries ... The "third world" will consist of those countries left behind by rapid technological change and held back by explosive population growth, poor government, and insufficient resources of food and energy[153].

Looking at the internal structures of the new First World one thing is clear thinks Wallace: it is that the 'United States has the desire to provide 'global leadership' without the resources to succeed. The West Europeans and the Japanese have the resources without the desire ... American leadership has thus been reasserted on an unsustainable basis'[154]. The consequences are clear both in terms of likely instability and tensions within this new First World, and in terms of a clear need to establish new international institutional structures to promote 'collective action in an intensely interdependent world'[155]. Walker picks up this matter of the internal conflicts within the new First World seeing the USA seizing a brief window of opportunity, with the USSR in retreat, and the Germans, Japanese and Europeans otherwise preoccupied, to achieve by military means a position from which to confront the nascent tripolar world, and he argues that we 'are witnessing the birth of the Bush Doctrine, a strategy to minimize the implications of American economic and social decline through vigorous exploitation of the leverage available to the world's unique superpower'[156]. Recalling Enzensberger's commentary one might say that Bush's Gulf War definitively established his un-heroic status.

---

152 W. Wallace in *Marxism Today* October 1990
153 ibid.
154 ibid.
155 ibid.
156 M. Walker in *Marxism Today* October 1990

However I now turn to the UK aspects of this tension within the new First World. Out of the commentary presented in the UK press it is possible to pick out a series of quite distinct though inevitably overlapping themes, and I will take note of some of them here, in particular those lines of commentary that throw some light on received UK political culture.

Many commentators called attention to the enthusiasm with which the British joined in the Gulf War: both in direct terms with the dispatch of a UK contingent, which made up 5.59% of the total coalition troops[157], and with the adoption of all the rhetoric of wartime in the UK itself. The government and media all acted in line with evidently deeply lodged cultural interpretive responses to create, against dissenting voices utterly marginal to the political mainstream, a general cultural posture of 'wartime'. Stephen wrote: 'Visting Britain for a couple of days last week, I very much felt that my country was going through a kind of national psychosis: a collective madness and self-delusion over the Gulf War that seems quite unreal to a semi-outsider'[158]. Noting that the economy was in recession, services breaking down, the BBC censoring its output in case anything 'unsuitable' went out, the government forming a 'War Cabinet', and Radio 4 running a continuous commentary on the progress of the war, Stephen asked: 'So what on earth is happening? It seems to me, on reflection, to be a kind of vicarious imperialism'[159]. No one, he noted, seems to be advancing the view that the war was unnecessary, or that the consequences in the Middle East were likely to be almost uniformly bad. The imperial delusion continues and the UK now seems happy to have found a role, that of 'obedient poodle of the United States'[160]. In similar vein Edward Pearce[161] commented that the British seemed to need the therapy of war and speculated that the enthusiasm flowed from nostalgia for the martial greatness of earlier years, moral childishness, and present economic weakness. All themes picked up by Ascherson who, noting that European friends are astonished at the ease with which the British inaugurate "wartime": a sober yet total mobilisation'[162], points out that the UK experience of actual wartime has been quite different to that of the mainland: for the UK wars have been useful instruments deployed overseas whereas for the mainland wars have been periods of disaster. Beyond that the British have a folk memory of war, as a time of sacrifice, equality, community, as a time when the British showed the best side of their character. Moreover, echoing Nairn[163], Ascherson points to the construction of the ideology of British-ness as a late nineteenth century empire ideology,

157 M. Stephen in *The Observer* 17 February 1991
158 ibid.
159 ibid.
160 ibid.
161 E. Pearce in *The Guardian* 5 October 1990
162 N. Ascherson in *Independent on Sunday* 24 February 1991
163 Nairn *Enchanted Glass*

and Linda Colley[164] has made it clear that the notion of 'Britain' has an historically necessary rather than contingent relation to war. Returning to this theme later, Pearce runs together economic failure, cultural impoverishment and dependence on the USA in one remarkable and eloquent statement of resigned dismay in respect of the British:

> What suppressed sense of inferiority about trade deficits, institutionalised and rising unemployment, and an over-valued currency make war so attractive to them? Why are they such swaggering bullies; why are they emotionally dependent on American smiles; why do they want so badly to re-live their past? Britain, with its pack mentality, its power worship and ache for violence, its habit of sucking up and spitting down, is not these days a country you can like much, still less respect[165].

The reaction of the UK political classes as expressed in the media towards the mainland Europeans was hostile. The European Community was condemned for failing to fall in line behind the American led war, and enthusiastic right wingers offered an untearful farewell to dreams of European unity. The response to Germany in particular was extraordinary: as Ian Aitken[166] pointed out the jingoistic British castigated the Europeans generally for not quickly joining in and the Germans who a few short weeks ago had been charged with wanting to dominate Europe were now accused of being feeble stay-at-homes. Similarly, the relationship of the UK political classes with Europe was at the centre of Marquand's analysis which began by mordantly noting: 'As so often, all of Europe is out of step except our Johnny. Having succumbed yet again to the umbilical pull of the special relationship, the British political class cannot understand why other European Community countries do not share its enthusiasm for the United States policy in the Gulf'[167]. Unpacking this response Marquand goes back to DeGaulle whom he finds to have been right in his fundamental insight that the interests of Europe were not coterminous with those of the United States, yet whilst the faltering steps towards unity taken by the European Community have reflected a lack of clarity of vision on the part of the Europeans, the Gulf War might just have given the mainlanders the political push necessary to solidify established relationships into a definite union. Marquand based this thought on the observation that European vacillation, as the Brits would have it, is maybe a sign that De Gaulle's insight is now widely granted: 'that the American view of the world does not necessarily coincide with Europe's and Europe therefore cannot trust the US with control of its destiny'[168]. And Marquand took the implications for the British ruling classes to be serious, as the matter of their relationship with

---

164 Linda Colley *Britons: The Forging the Nation*, London, Yale University Press, 1992, chapter one where she argues that constructing this identity relied on wars

165 E. Pearce in *The Guardian* 6 February 1991

166 I. Aitken in *The Guardian* 28 January 1991

167 D. Marquand in *The Guardian* 1 February 1991

168 ibid.

the mainland, a question put-off for the whole of the post-war period, might finally have to be confronted directly.

Finally, picking up the theme with which I began this section, the responses of the USA to the collapse of the old bi-polar world, we can note that one strong theme of commentary on the Gulf War was in regard to the notion of US-sponsored New World Order. Reaction was strongly negative. Hutton[169] noted that historians would come to look at the early months of 1991 as having seen serious errors of political judgement being made: failure on the part of the West to offer aid to the USSR, and the prosecution of the war in the gulf. The money wasted on the latter could have been spent on the former. But the anxieties of many commentators ran far beyond lost opportunities for constructive engagements with the post-block world, and most are fearful for the unipolar system with the economically weak USA at the centre. Richard Gott[170] argued that the American actions in the Gulf were best seen as a high-tech version of a nineeenth century colonial war of pacification with control of resources as the goal. As regards the victims, as ever in colonial war the aggressors become deaf to their cries[171]. On this, finally, Theo Sommer[172] has argued that Bush's New World Order is an untenable fantasy in a world system moving from a military-national articulation of cultural power to an economic-technological articulation. The relative decline of the USA is taken as inevitable: the task for Europeans is to complete the business of unification, a political, economic and cultural project of some magnitude and subsequent broad implication. There is much scope for optimism in such a position with its crucial reaffirmation of the idea of progress[173].

In sum, overall, after the power blocks we have something of an ideological vacuum. The USA's New World Order is both appalling and untenable. The unification of the EC coupled to the reaffirmation of the modernist project offers a route to the future.

---

[169] W. Hutton in *The Guardian* 4 February 1991

[170] R. Gott in *The Guardian* 29 January 1991

[171] J. Berger in *The Guardian* 2 March 1991

[172] T. Sommer in *The Guardian* 13 April 1991

[173] It is also clear that the route to the European future is not going to be straightforward. The disintegration of Jugoslavia has seen the return of a violent nationalism which one suspects the majority of western Europeans had taken to belong to the past. The Jugoslavian war has been a catastrophe not merely for its unfortunate population but also, less acutely of course, for proponents of European union. In this case the role of the UK state-regime has been as might have been expected, and has drawn from critics references back to the appeasement strategies of the 1930s.

Conclusion

UK public political discourse has for a long period been tightly controlled by the UK political classes. Effectively they have demobilized the UK population. The elite has thus remained in power and has pursued its several projects as the global system changed. However, present changes in the EC, Europe and the global system are of a very far reaching kind. There must be some doubt that the ruling class will be able to contain present pressures for change within the UK. Public political discourse on these matters has thus far involved a strategy of denial. Active denial by Conservative Party and a muted denial-cum-opportunistic affirmation by the Labour Party. Considered and prospective political discourse has been marginalized. However, for the future, it is impossible to believe that UK political structures/discourses will not have change impressed upon them.

8 Analysing complex change in Europe

Introduction

This text has discussed the political-cultural structures of the UK with particular reference to the responses made by major political groups to the business of complex change in Europe, and in particular to the pressure for European Community union[1]. The position taken in the text is that structural pressures for change within the system in which the UK is embedded are likely to prove overwhelming and occasion far reaching changes within the UK itself[2]. Such reflections imply new agendas of research and action in regard to the UK's embedding within these shifting patterns. By way of a preliminary attempt to unpack such matters I will look at the business of analysing complex change in Europe[3].

---

[1] See J. Pinder *European Community: The Building of a Union*, Oxford, Oxford University Press, 1991

[2] See W. Wallace *The Transformation of Western Europe*, London, Pinter 1990

[3] I should note that this chapter is simply a rather speculative sketch of how this analytic approach might look - it attempts to outline the business of analysing the emergent European Community political-economic and cultural space.

Analysing complex change in Europe

It has become clear since 1989 that Europe is experiencing a period of change[4]. If we review the events of 1989 we find that a series of longer term process came to a climax: the slow relative decline of the USA in regard to Europe; the process of the decline of the command system in the eastern block; the slow reworking of patterns of power within the global economy with the rise of Japan; and the hesitant moves within western Europe towards some sort of unified system.

All these patterns came to a head in 1989 in a series of crucial events. First, there was the May visit of President Bush to Chancellor Kohl in Mainz when the Americans gave way to the Germans in respect of the business of a new short range nuclear weapon for NATO. The Americans thus acknowledged the economic power of Germany within Europe. Then, second, there was the June visit of President Gorbachev to Germany when he was treated as a hero and the small scale steps which had been taken towards military detente in western Europe received strong popular backing. Finally we had the autumn revolutions in the old eastern block when a series of citizen-protest groups formed and took to the streets. In East Germany this lead to the opening of the Berlin Wall in November 1989. This pattern was repeated in Czechoslovakia, Hungary, Bulgaria, and finally Romania.

At this point the old post-Second World War settlement was overthrown: the block system, the cold war, and the dominance of West by the USA. Received discourses were rendered irrelevant. At the same time, in western Europe moves which had begun independently to reanimate the project of European union, the single market programme, received a strong fillip: the project of a united Europe was available to fill the void left by the collapse of the post-Second World War settlement[5]. At the present time this drive to construct new structures and discourses continues. However the end-point of this activity is as yet very unclear. Broadly, it seems safe to say that Europe now faces a period of reworking established economic, social, political, and cultural structures.

---

[4] In early 1989 this was all still a matter for specialists, see *Marxism Today*, April 1989

[5] One of the reasons why the business of reading complex change in Europe is such an interesting matter is that the whole episode seemed to take place on television, and along with the changes we had the clear sight of the bafflement of UK politicians and mainstream commentators. In a short period of time received patterns of understanding simply became irrelevant - and manifestly so.

Classical social theory and the analysis complex change in Europe

Within the core tradition of European social theorizing there is a long
established concern with analysing complex change[6]. By complex change we
can understand those periods when inter-related change takes place in the
economy, society, polity and culture of a people. Such periods are often
somewhat traumatic as clarity in regard to sequences and endpoints is not
readily available to those caught up in the processes. The classical tradition
of European social theory (where this encompasses the work of sociology,
political-science, economics, and history) concerned itself with trying to
grasp the dynamics of the shift from traditional agrarian-feudal society to
modern industrial-democratic society. We have recently been reminded of
the nature of such work in the efforts of development theorists to grasp the
business of complex change in Third World countries as they have pursued
programmes of development[7]. The lessons of such work are that such
theorizing is very difficult and the derivation of concrete policy proposals
equally awkward, with the business of development planning seen as the
out-turn of complicated political interactions[8]. Relatedly, it is clear that in
addressing the business of analysing complex change social theorists need to
be aware of the influence of received metaphors upon their thinking. A.D.
Smith[9] discusses this under a series of points: the decision to intellectually
prioritize change or stability; whether change is read as actively caused or
passively experienced; whether change is seen as temporally discontinuous
or continuous; whether change is seen as morally beneficial or pernicious.
It is clear that how theorists regard change, in terms of such underlying
metaphors, will shape any resultant substantive analysis.

Ernest Gellner has addressed this problem of theorizing the modern world
by looking to established social scientific work in order to fashion his own
theory of analysing change[10]. He begins by arguing that any society needs a
legitimating ideology (which explains what sort of society it is, and why it
is legitimate), and notes that at the present time any society must be
industrial (or industrializing) and national (have a sense of itself as a
coherent community). Reviewing episodic theories of change (one shift
from a bad state of affairs to a good state) and evolutionary theories (of
continual pervasive change), Gellner opts for a neo-episodic theory of

---

[6] This idea owes much to my reading development theory in the light of Gellner, see E. Gellner
Thought and Change, London, Weidenfeld, 1964

[7] See P.W. Preston *Theories of Development*, London, Routledge, 1982

[8] See Norman Long *Battlefields of Knowledge*, London, Routledge, 1992; P.W.Preston *Rethinking
Development*, London, Routledge, 1987; J. Toye *Dilemmas of Development*, Oxford, Blackwell,
1987

[9] A.D. Smith *Social Change: Social Theory and Historical Processes*, London, Routledge, 1976

[10] Gellner *Thought and Change*, see also E. Gellner *Plough, Sword and Book*, London, Palladin,
1988

industrialism which presents the transition to the modern world as one presently continuing episode of pervasive change, where we have a rough idea of its end-point (that is, it will be industrial rather than say agricultural), and which we needs must analyse from the inside using the sceptical techniques of classical sociology (the heir to classical political philosophy). The task for social science is to elucidate the continuing dynamics of the developing industrial system. Thus, if we follow Gellner's approach,we have an idea of how we can approach the analysis of change in Europe: it is an episode of complex change to received structures and discourses which we can attempt to elucidate by deploying the methods of classical social science in the expectation that we have a rough idea of its endpoint; that is, some sort of EC unification.

As I have argued earlier in this text, the analytical core of the received classical tradition comprises the political-economic analysis of structures and the culture-critical elucidation of patterns of meaning. The work of Susan Strange on international political-economy offers a simple way of approaching the analysis of structures[11]. Strange argues that the global political-economy must be thought of as a network of structures of power within which agents (usually states, or some other political authority) manoeuvre for position. Strange distinguishes between structural power (which sets the broad agendas within which agents operate), relational power (which focuses on specific exchanges between agents), and bargains (which are the compromises agents make within a given situation). The received structures shape the actions of agents, and in turn the actions of agents modify structures: it is a dialectic of structure and agency. Strange identifies four key structures of power in the global system: the security structure (which embraces matters relating to the deployment of force, plus attendant bi-lateral and multi-lateral regulatory linkages); the productive structure (which embraces matters relating to extent to which any country is effective in the production of goods and services); the financial structure (which embraces matters relating to the ability of countries or other organisations to obtain or create credit, the necessary condition of development); and the knowledge structure (which indicates where new ideas and technologies are generated, and this is important as Gellner has remarked that 'science is the mode of cognition of industrial societies'[12]). It is with reference to these four basic power structures that agent groups manoeuvre as they endeavour to assert their interests in exchanges with other groups acting similarly. The practical out-turn of such manoeuverings thereafter modifies the received structures. What is of particular interest in the case of Europe is that the pattern of inter-group relations constructed with reference to these structures over the post-Second World War period is now changing rapidly. New configurations of these structures are being

---

11 S. Strange *States and Markets*, London, Pinter, 1988
12 Gellner *Thought and Change*

made. New relationships of agent groups are being made. New patterns of understanding might thereafter be expected to emerge.

As I have argued above, it seems to me that in respect of these real world changes there are three spheres, interacting, but distinct: (i) moves within western Europe towards some sort of federal EC; (ii) related international shifts in relations of economic and political power as the EC joins the USA and Japan as a further major world economic force; and (iii) the dramatic reform processes in the eastern block and the USSR/CIS. An initial analysis of complex change in Europe could centre on the classical social theoretic concerns for power, production, and knowledge.

Structural change in power/state

We can think of the state as a membrane which acts to control linkages of internal and external systems. It filters incoming messages and directs those outgoing. Strange[13] takes a similar line by stressing the trans-national systems of political, productive, financial, and cultural power as the appropriate frame within which the actions of states could be read. This position entails a complete break with the idea of state-as-bounded-unit interacting with other similar units in favour of seeing state-machines as concentration-points within wider systems. In the case of the EC it seems clear that the present pattern of states is in process of dissolution.

A.G. Frank[14], writing in 1983, argued that the post-Second World War Atlanticist settlement had been under pressure since the early 1970s. He noted the following: conflicts over economic policy for the Western block, with accusations of self-interest made; conflicts over international trade regulation, again with accusations of self-interest; conflicts over North/South trade as this becomes an area of competition for resources; conflicts over trade with the eastern European block, with the USA attempting to restrict the Europeans; and conflicts within NATO as to the future of the organisation. Frank was sanguine about the outcome of these conflicts, seeing the possibility of a pan-European space within which post-cold war politics of cooperation could be pursued. Later in 1988, we find John Palmer[15] offering a similar analysis of the structural dynamics surrounding American-European relationships. The pattern of exchanges over the post-Second World War period is shifting and Palmer offers four possible lines of development: (i) Atlantic reformism, where the Atlantic area would continue as a loose area of economic and political cooperation with the USA as a diminished key state; (ii) European reformism, which essentially affirms a new system on the basis of the EC, and movement is

---

13 Strange *States and Markets*

14 A.G. Frank *The European Challenge*, Nottingham, Spokesman, 1983

15 J. Palmer *Europe without America*, Oxford, Oxford University Press, 1988

made towards a federal Europe; (iii) European 'Gaullism', which could come about in reaction to failures of market integration, with an authoritarian nationalistic European unity; and (iv) a socialist Europe, a reaffirmation on the European stage of the received modernist project, and this is the optimistic red/green view. Of these, the Atlantic ruling class[16] will clearly look to an Atlantic reformist line (already announced in Washington as the notion of a New Atlanticism). With the recent reforms in both Central Europe and the USSR/CIS it is difficult to see how such a position could be sold to the populations of Europe generally, or Germany in particular. And European Gaullism, with its nationalism and authoritarianism, looks implausible precisely because of these traits. The future thus looks in outline to be federal. In Palmer's terms, lines (ii) and (iv) have been the ones that have developed, and line (ii) arguably found expression at Maastricht. We will have to address what David Marquand has called state deregulation coupled to supra-state and regional level reregulation of socio-economic formations[17]. It may be that complete layer in the structure of political authority is to be remade and left with a much diminished role.

This broad expectation of change readily generates a further set of questions: (i) how will the reform of extant political structures be accomplished, and what precisely are the crucial sets of institutionally embodied powers/authorities which will have to be relocated at the European level; (ii) what will be the distribution of institutionally embodied powers/authorities in the new system, at European level, old-state level, and regional level; (iii) to what extent will old-state law be replaced by European level law, both in terms of the production of new law and the codification of extant law, where this process might, as with the UK, imply system changes; (iv) how will the old-state relationships with the world system generally be re-integrated at a European level (alliances, trade links etcetera); and (v) how will emergent structures of power be legitimated in terms of electoral and parliamentary mechanisms at the regional, old-state, and European level?

These issues have ever been a part of ongoing debate in respect of the development of the European Community. The Treaty of Rome established a trans-national organisation, and this implied a transfer of power to the new centre. This was confirmed and advanced by the SEA (in particular with qualified majority voting in regard to a spread of economic issues). Further transfers of power to the centre were affirmed at the Maastrict Summit. The overall trend of EC institutional and political development is towards some sort of federalism; it is driven by present patterns of change within the global system. The matter of ordering these institutional centre/periphery relationships has recently been approached via the notion

---

[16] Kees van der Pijl *The Making of an Atlantic Ruling Class*, London, Verso, 1984

[17] D. Marquand in *Marxism Today* April 1989, and *New Statesman and Society* 20 January 1989

of subsidiarity, affirmed at Maastricht, which requires that decisions be taken at the lowest possible level in the formal political-administrative system. Read functionally, as the mainland/Brussels apparently does, this means a hierarchy of regional, state, and European levels of authority. Read politically, as the UK state-regime apparently does, it means nationstate and a minimum EC level of authority.

The detail of the evolving pattern of reforms of the EC are discussed by Juliet Lodge[18], and a series of points are dealt with. Firstly, institutional perspectives where Lodge notes that the machinery of the EC has developed slowly over many years. It is only in recent years that national governments have regarded the EC machine as anything other than marginal. Now there is much manoeuvering in the process of reform and advance. A major problem is that of the 'democratic deficit'. The existing EC is essentially an inter-governmental arrangement and the extent of direct democratic input is low. Secondly, internal perspectives where, around the business of the completion of the single market, Lodge takes note of the extensive implications in various fields of policy. Power is shifting towards the centre. Rule-setting is increasingly European in orientation as the single market implies, rather than merely inter-governmentally aggregative. Thirdly, external perspectives recall that the EC has not until very recently acted on the international stage as a unity. However, the EC is a member of many international organisations and is increasingly important as a player. Finally Lodge concludes that the EC is changing fast, and that the changes are very dramatic for the political elites. The EC is increasingly important for national level governments/politics, at the European level, and also in the international sphere. It may be the case that no one is too clear what the EC is, or where precisely it is going, but debates in regard to the futures of European countries are increasingly conducted with reference to the EC.

Government involvement in the market

The nature of patterns of political-economic power in Europe has been long discussed, and there are two main available areas of analysis, those which focus on the role of the state and those, looked at later, which speak of the role of the market. In regard to the former, picking up from Strange's discussions of the relationships of structures and agents we can look at the idea of corporatism. This has been one of the UK New Right's pejorative terms for post-Second World War Keynesian welfare state consensus building (elite ordered growth and welfare) yet the term designates a broader discussion which encompasses forms of political-economic life on the mainland, what Marquand[19] has tagged 'developmental states'. On Leo Panitch's analysis the essence of the notion is that in the modern world it is

---

18 J. Lodge ed. *The European Community and the Challenge of the Future*, London, Pinter, 1989

19 D. Marquand *The Unprincipled Society*, London, Fontana, 1988

to the advantage of all parties to come together to secure a minimum agreement about the ordering of economy and society[20]. The theory of corporatism points to mechanisms to secure such state-level agreements between the major players in the economy and society. Typically in western Europe the major players, in this context, have been the government, the employers federations, and the trade unions. Decisions are made at this level which both plot a direction for the development of the economy and society in general, and bind the members of the relevant groups.

The notion of corporatism has a history reaching back to the late nineteenth century when it was presented as an alternative to laissez-faire capitalism and socialism. The idea that economy and society constituted an organic unity was stressed. In the 1930s the notion of corporatism became associated with European fascism. However recent usage of the idea has dismissed the general theories of society and focused on the idea of expressing and resolving the interests of groups in society. Katzenstein[21] offers a review of the recent experience of the West, and identifies three state strategies of responding to global change: the liberal strategies of the USA and UK (which stress market solutions whilst using protection to secure a 'breathing space' for threatened industrial sectors); the statist strategies of France and Japan (which stress state-led planning to adjust to global system demands, and which again have recourse to protection); the corporatist strategies of the smaller European states of Sweden, Norway, Denmark, the Netherlands, Belgium, Austria and Switzerland, (which seek to cooperatively adjust to demands flowing through the global system).

Katzenstein characterizes democratic corporatism as follows: an ideology of social partnership expressed at national level; a relatively centralized and concentrated system of interest groups; and voluntary coordination of conflicting objectives through continuous political bargaining between interest groups, state bureaucracies, and political parties. Katzenstein offers a summary statement which identifies two variants of democratic corporatism, the Austrian and the Swiss models. The first is liberal corporatism (Swiss), and has a strong internationally focused business class with weak decentralized unions, and political compromise is effected privately. It has a relatively less centralized decision making system, but it is stable and effective. It addresses broad questions (excluding investment and employment), and bargains in a bi-lateral way with trade-offs left implicit. Political inequalities between actors are narrowed. In contrast the second is social corporatism (Austrian), which has a weak national focused business class with stronger centralized unions, and political compromise is effected publicly. It has a relatively more centralized decision making system, but it is stable and effective. It addresses narrower questions (including investment and employment), and bargains in a tri-lateral way

[20] L. Panitch 'Recent theorizations of corporatism' in *British Journal of Sociology* 31, 1980
[21] P. Katzenstein *Small States in World Markets*, London, Cornell, 1985

with trade-offs explicit. Political inequalities between actors are narrowed. The situations in Sweden, Norway, Denmark tend to social corporatism; and the situations in the Netherlands and Belgium tend to liberal corporatism. Katzenstein is quite clear that the corporatist states have been more successful in adjusting to the pressures for change transmitted through the power structures of the global system. The governments of these corporatist states have pursued policies of cooperative and consensual flexible adjustment to the demands of the global system.

The German variant of corporatism has been called 'the social market': a notion often heard in the UK during the phase of the decline of Thatcherism. Charles Leadbeater[22] offers a useful overview, and one which stresses the differences between this idea and familiar ideas of corporatism: not elite ordered top-down consensus building but rather a diffuse network of linkages between groups through all levels of society. Leadbeater is quite clear that the notion of the social market admits of various readings, including neo-liberal and Fabian left, and that neither of those versions are accurate or will be helpful to the UK. The notion, as Leadbeater reads it, entails an acceptance that production is social, and that a polity must affirm notions of common interests (social justice). In the German case these broad commitments find expression in a dense network of duties and obligations accepted by groups within society. All in sharp contrast to the UK's divisive and unsuccesful liberalism. However Marquand, who would surely grant much of Leadbeater's case, rejects the social market as wedded in the end to a notion of individualism. The idea of the social market, comments Marquand, attempts to 'squeeze communitarian conclusions out of individualistic premises'[23]; the future lies via a politics of educative dialogue, and for the UK Marquand sees this as implying extensive institutional and cultural change. Yet in regard to Germany, setting aside debates about ideologies, Christopher Harvie, echoing both commentators, stresses the presence of a dense network of duties and obligations and notes that the social market involves a 'mixture of state-sponsored technological innovation, long-term indicative planning and social corporatism'[24]. Harvie argues that there are three main reasons for success: 'finance is committed to industry; workers are highly-trained and involved in the strategy of firms; and the culture is egalitarian and work - rather than expenditure - governed. Underlying the first two is the key notion of social partnership'[25]. Finally, the economy rests within a polity which stresses stability and decentralization: 'The key to it ... lies in the mix between civil

---

[22] C. Leadbeater in *Marxism Today* July 1991

[23] Marquand *Unprincipled Society* p.226

[24] C. Harvie *Cultural Weapons*, Edinburgh, Polygon, 1992 p.45

[25] ibid. p.46

society and the state'[26]. In Germany with its decentralized system, the local-state is close to the citizens, and powerful.

Changes in patterns of power/nation

One feature of the rise of the modern world has been the invention of nationhood. On Benedict Anderson's[27] analysis an episode taking place in phases and stretching over some two hundred years, with the USA as the first specimen of a modern nationstate. Ever an ambiguous political-cultural construct the nation is now, so far as EC Europe is concerned, in relative eclipse, and within the EC ideas of nationalism are now in process of sharp reformulation. In the wake of the Second World War, which was rooted in part in nineteenth century-style nationalism, and the subsequent long period of US hegemony, the idea of nationalism was already in decline in the EC countries. It was neither a central element of state level political activity, and nor was it as important as it had been in constituting the identity of individuals-as-citizens. With the growing movement towards EC union such long established trends, notwithstanding noticeable exceptions such as the Conservative Party in the UK, are accelerating. Thus on both systemic and historical grounds, both centring albeit for different reasons on the notion of interdependence, nationalism is flowing out of the routine experience of western Europeans. And in contrast, of course, it is flowing strongly back into, again ambiguously, the experience of eastern Europeans.

In regard to this often discussed matter a series of issues can be identified. We can ask how nationalism has figured in Europe in the modern period including in particular the phase of its final catastrophe in the 1930s and 1940s: if states make nations, how did the various nineteenth and twentieth century European states go about making nations? In more detail we could ask how nationalism was used both internally and externally: in brief, which groups used which nationalisms in order to advance their structurally conditioned political programmes? In the post-Second World War period it has been suggested that there has been a decline in European nationalist sentiment and this had been evidenced in fewer nationalist flags, parades and anthems. It has been suggested that more non-national popular imagery has been made generally available. Here it might be that the role of the media-given cultural example of the USA was important initially, and subsequently what is now dubbed consumerism. Personal identity becomes bound up with freedom to consume, life-style and so on. All now theorized under the fashionable heading of postmodernism. Relatedly, in the light of the expectation of some sort of shift to a united Europe we can look to the ways in which nationalism might finally disappear, when in conjunction

---

[26] ibid. p.48
[27] B Anderson *Imagined Communities*, London, Verso, 1983

with the private sphere of consumer identities replacements for nationalisms in the public sphere come to be advanced: already Europe has its anthem and flag! More broadly, it might be possible to envision a new notion of 'European-ness' emerging along with supra-national political structures, and within this overarching frame it is possible to envision regional particularisms developing. Gwyn Williams, for example, has argued that the emergence of a supra-national Europe would constitute a last chance for some of Europe's regions, thus the Welsh for example could be rescued by Europe from decline-by-assimilation into the UK[28]. Other groups might take their chance to establish autonomous units, thus the Scottish National Party's slogan of 'independence in Europe', a thoroughly plausible case let us note[29]. And, finally, there is the possibility of reaction from disappointed nationalists and/or marginal groups: thus Thatcher's fraction of the UK ruling-class is appalled at recent events in Europe, and there are small right wing reactionary nationalist groups in other western European countries.

Such issues of securing stable political and cultural situations have figured prominently within the literature of Third World development. It is clear that nationalism, and its relative, ethnicity, can be created and used by elite groups to secure their political programme goals. In the case of Singapore, for example, regional and trans-regional networks of political and productive power have been controlled by presenting official definitions of nationality and ethnicity, and unwanted ideas have been read-out. As the idea of 'Europe' comes to challenge 'nation' we might expect a lengthy period of establishing new identities, new 'contested compromises'. In the case of the UK, for example, in this situation what Tom Nairn[30] has characterized as the monarchy-centred nationalism of 'Britishness' which buttresses the extant political status quo is under threat by emergent supra-national structures, and the particular political-programme stance of successive governments of Atlanticism is similarly overthrown by moves to a post-block system. Recent trans-system changes thus generate challenges at the level of the legitimating ideas of the state-level structure: one commentator noted, apropos moves towards German unification, that the Bush-Kohl meeting at Mainz in May 1989, 'was the moment when the whole cause of German re-unification was given its new legitimacy, when an appalled Mrs Thatcher and an ecstatic Chancellor Kohl realized how much the map of Europe was changing'[31]. Official ideologies, with their approved nationalisms and ethnicities, are deeply implicated in given patterns of internal state arrangements. When the trans-state system changes so as to occasion internal state changes, then established contested

---

28 G. Williams in *Marxism Today* April 1989

29 Harvie *Cultural Weapons*, argues that Scotland's tradition of civic humanism is both closer to the culture of the mainland than that of Britain, and that it offers something of a model for the future development of Europe.

30 T. Nairn *Enchanted Glass*, London, Radius, 1988

31 M. Walker in *The Guardian* 7 February 1990

compromises are radically disturbed and the process of reestablishing such compromises is likely to be a difficult and lengthy process.

Structural change in production/market

There has been something of a consensus during most of the post-Second World War period in respect of the nature of state and society, and this position may roughly be characterized as reformist social-democracy. There have been differences amongst countries in respect of this compromise, and conflict within countries: it has been, as might be expected in class divided systems, a contested compromise. In recent years this compromise has broken down. Recalling the outline of the presently eclipsed orthodoxy within the broad spread of social sciences we find theorems of industrialism which, as Anthony Giddens[32] has shown, committed themselves to the naturalistically conceived structural-functionalist analysis of industrial societies; this being the core of an ideological package comprising the elements of industrialism, convergence, modernization, and ideas of the end of ideology. The influence of this intellectual-political package was closely bound up with the post-Second World War industrial, military and political preeminence of the USA. Putting the matter very generally, and setting aside the complexities flowing from the circumstance of contestedness, this intellectual-political package has taken the position that social scientific enquiry could provide the knowledge necessary for the planned alleviation of social deprivations and the securing of economic growth and welfare. It has been, in brief, the ideological counterpart to the post-Second World War 'long boom' and, relatedly, the vehicle whereby the post-war settlement between capital and labour was expressed and ordered. Through the late 1960s there were increasing signs that the boom was coming to an end, and whilst how one dates such an event is a matter for economic historians, it is enough to note here that the oil crisis of 1973 did put an end to the period of economic growth. As the period of growth drew to a close the intellectual-political and institutional vehicles of the compromise that sustained that growth also fell into decline. There were two major intellectual-political responses to this decline: the formal and substantive democratic response, and the reactionary New Right position.

One response to the failure of what he would take to be the reformist-technocratic approach to the politics of the present day has been advanced by Jurgen Habermas[33] and the gist of his position being that what is needed is not more technocratic planning, and certainly no attempted return to

[32] A. Giddens *Central Problems in Social Theory*, London, Macmillan, 1979

[33] Habermas's work is usefully reviewed by R.C. Holub *Jurgen Habermas: Critic in the Public Sphere*, London, Routledge, 1991

situations of less planning, but instead more democracy. The present of monopoly capitalism has seen the increasing rationalization of the human life world: we have become ever more subject to the pronouncements of purported experts of one sort or another, whose cumulative impact is to withdraw control of the social world from the citizenry and lodge it in the technocratic-management systems of the present day capitalist system. On this view the arguments of the New Right are designed to further restrict the power of citizens in favour of the various apparatuses of monopoly capitalism.

The second line of response to the comparative decline of the post war reformist social-democratic package has been the reaffirmation of conservative ideologies of the free markets; roughly, the New Right package. Key relevant names here would be: Milton Friedman, Friedrich Hayek, Karl Popper, Peter Bauer, and Bela Belassa. The free marketeers advance a series of claims. Taking their efforts as delimited-formal ideology, we can note these core aspects: economically, the claim is that free markets are optimally efficient, thus we have claims to maximize material welfare; socially the claim is that as action and responsibility for action reside with the person of the individual then social or moral worth is maximized in non-state centred, free market, systems, thus we have a claim to maximize human moral values; politically the related claim is that liberalism best expresses and protects the interests of individuals, thus we have a claim to maximize political freedom; and epistemologically we have a claim to genuine positive scientific status, thus knowledge is maximized. Quite how the practical episode of right wing government will come to be judged must be in some doubt: the actions of Reagan and Thatcher have been as much opportunistic as ideological. Paradoxically however, at the time New Rightism enters eclipse in the UK and USA the simplistic slogans affirming the power of the market are being repeated, as William Keegan[34] noted, across eastern Europe. The post-Gorbachev patterns of reform and disintegration have, in part, been theorized and legitimized in terms of a classic economic liberalism.

In general what can be noted here is how the ideology of the New Right centres on a celebration of the purported power of the market place: their social philosophy is liberal, and their economics reach back to neo-classical work. Yet, in a recent text Geoffrey Hodgson remarks that whilst the 'study of market behaviour is a major theme, if not the major theme, of economic science as we know it ... definitions of the market in the economic literature are not easy to find'[35]. He goes on to say that 'For too long 'the market' has been taken for granted'[36]. Further reflection in the history and theory of economics, where the variety of economics and their relationships to the

---

[34]W. Keegan in *The Observer* 7 February 1990

[35] G. Hodgson *Economics and Institutions*, Cambridge, Cambridge University Press, 1978 p.172

[36] ibid. p.173

intellectual-political world must be noted[37], strongly suggests that the sphere of the economic, exemplified in enquiry by the received notion of the market, has to be reappropriated for social science against the ideologues, knowing and unknowing, of laissez faire capitalism[38]. I would argue that the matter of the social scientific analysis of the sphere of 'human economic activity' must be recovered from the grasp of orthodox neo-classicism and recast in terms which reach back to the core traditions of political-economic analysis, or relatedly, the institutionalist tradition.

It seems to me that the importance of these observations have been heavily underscored by events in Europe. There is the movement towards EC unity, which at present is conceived in terms of an initial move to complete the internal market, thus the Cecchini Report[39] is cast in conventional business-economic terms such as 'removal of barriers', 'freeing the market', and so on. Relatedly, there are the East block reform programmes whereby centrally-planned one party systems are in process of shifting to political pluralist systems coupled to de-centralized or market economic structures. There is also the business of dismantling the post-Second World War system of power-blocks, which has been presented by the political right as a victory for liberal-democracy over socialism, and by the centre/left in terms of the USSR's unilateral withdrawal from the cold war system established with the Atlantic right in the driving seat in the late 1940s. Any consideration of economic structural change in Europe, east and west, will have to be sensitive to the very heavy ideological load carried by discussions in this area. Within social science the recipes are typically disguised as neutral technical-analytical machineries, and against this strategy we have to counterpose the political-economic elucidation of structures and processes.

It would seem that as we shift from thinking in terms of national economic trajectories to operating in terms of a European economic trajectory we might ask after the particular concern of an holistic and engaged treatment of matters economic in contrast to orthodox type work. Surely, it might be said, we do not want to repeat the work of the technical-information managers of the extant system. If we take the view that social theorizing comprises a diversity of loosely related essentially practical modes of engagement with the social world, then it is clear that what is needed in respect of the scholarly apprehension of complex change in Europe is an essentially structural and dynamic analysis. Such analyses will have to look to identify relevant economic structures at a European level, and this might include: (i) patterns of industrial location (where are the key centres and thereafter peripheries); (ii) patterns of industrial culture (how do attitudes

[37] See for example, P. Deane *The Evolution of Economic Ideas*, Cambridge, Cambridge University Press, 1978

[38] See R. Dilley ed. *Contesting Markets*, Edinburgh, Edinburgh University Press, 1992

[39] P. Cecchini *1992 The European Challenge*, London, Wildwood, 1988

to workplace activities vary across Europe); (iii) patterns of social welfare provision (levels/types of provision); (iv) patterns of industry linkages to local political structures (types and industry-effectivity of linkages); (v) patterns of economic linkage to local social/cultural structures (types of links); (vi) the identification of European-level patterns (thus internal European multi-site industrial production, and similarly finance industry patterns); (vii) the identification of European-level articulations of industry, society, and political institutions; and so on. Thereafter, if we cast these matters in more familiar general policy analytic terms, then the sorts of agendas of issues generated include a familiar spread of matters. In respect of the EC patterns of change the following structural changes were specified by Cecchini and Delors. In the first case from Cecchini we have the completion of the single market: removal of trade barriers; removal of government protections; removal of divergent specifications and standards; removal of blocks to trans-border activity; plus competitions policy, to encourage it; plus regional policy, to upgrade regional economies; plus European level economic management policy; and all these supply side improvements will improve government revenues. In the second case, from Delors, we have: the establishment of economic and monetary union, a phased movement to supra-national economic policy regulation, including a common currency and central bank; and the establishment of a programme of political unification to support the integrated economic space. All of these reforms are designed to shift extant nationstate systems which are already extensively integrated via long established linkages towards a unitary system. The detail of the specified changes is large, practical problems equally large, and progress has until recently been slow, and is likely to be intermittent and uneven.

The EC economic space

The EC is one of three major economic groupings within the global industrial capitalist system. The USA has a population of some 250 million with a 1990 GNP per capita of US$21,790; Japan a population of 123.5 million with a 1990 GNP per capita of US$25,430; and the EC twelve a population of approximately 353 million with a 1990 GNP per capita ranging from US$4,900 in Portugal, to US$22,320 in Germany[40]. A general table of wealth in Europe is offered by Franklin and with an EC index of 100, Switzerland scores 182, Denmark 138, Germany 123, France 114, Italy 102, Britain 98, Ireland 60, and Portugal 31[41]. Within the local context of the European area the EC is economically dominant. The countries of eastern Europe together with the USSR/CIS have a numerically marginally larger population but are economically very much weaker.

---

[40] Data from World Bank *World Development Report 1992*, Oxford, Oxford University Press
[41] Data from M. Franklin *Britains Future in Europe*, London, Pinter, 1990 p.20

Indeed, to the extent that one can rely on World Bank data, the eastern areas of the continent approach Third World levels of living.

The Cecchini Report was produced for the European Commission and looked at the likely benefits from the removal of all remaining tariff and non-tariff barriers to free trade within the EC. The report operated within the intellectual frame of orthodox business-economics and perhaps not surprisingly came to the conclusion that free trade within the EC would enhance the material welfare of all citizens. This report formed the basis of the programme for the completion of the single market in 1992, subsequently supplemented by the Maastricht agreement. The treaties now involve ideas of economic and monetary union, a social dimension to the EC, plus finally political union. In other words the SEA has turned out to be the occasion for a much broader reaffirmation of the original Rome treaty hopes for a federal Europe.

In regard to the single market and the optimism of Cecchini we can note that there are dissenting voices. Cutler et al.[42] begin from a position of doubting that arguments from neo-classical premises are of much real interest. They prefer an institutional/political-economy line. The upshot of their analyses is the claim that the present policy posture of the EC will lead to the further concentration in Germany of European manufacturing industry to the detriment of all other areas of the EC. They are deeply unimpressed by claims that a regional policy will help peripheral areas. Drawing a distinction between liberal market and liberal collectivist (or 'social market') philosophies they argue that less of the former is needed, and much more of the latter if regional disparities are not to be deepened.

Cultural change in knowledges and ideologies

The foregoing material has dealt primarily with the structural aspects of complex change. I turn now to the matter of agency, not so much in terms of institutional forms and active groups, some of which was touched upon in respect of state/market, but rather in terms of those sets of ideas which groups, individuals, and institutions will draw on to order their activities.

Confronted with the demanding business of grasping the nature of complex change those concerned will draw automatically on stocks of available ideas. Geoffrey Hawthorn[43] has pointed out that there are distinct national variations amongst social scientific traditions, and such variations in concern for general theory in particular flowed from the differential relationships between national intelligentsias and their states. It seems appropriate therefore to raise the matter of differences of intellectual-cultural tradition within Europe insofar as these might be taken to bear

---

[42] T. Cutler et al. *1992 The Struggle for Europe*, Oxford, Berg, 1989
[43] G. Hawthorn *Enlightenment and Despair*, Cambridge, Cambridge University Press, 1976

upon theorizing, lay or professional. Thus for example: nationalisms; regional particularisms; ethnicities; religious traditions; and informal traditions of class. If these can be taken as possible occasions for reading the world differently, then, following Hawthorn, what will thereafter shape these ideas will be their institutional possibilities of expression. Hawthorn's work looked mainly at western Europe and considered fairly directly the relationship of specific intelligentsias and specific states. These are familiar themes: German idealism as flowing from fragmented polity and independent professoriat; English evolutionary gradualism as flowing from de-mobilizing absorption into the broad mechanism of government; French theoretical strengths as shaped by republican and rationalist traditions, and so on. Against recipe-exporters, a condition of process-centred interpretation is a grasp of the detail of particular histories as these condition theorizing.

In respect of formal knowledge claims this might involve rediscovering cultural resources already available, and reaffirming them. This could include noting that Europe has a rich common history and that this will have to be read out of power block dominated national frameworks and read into a common history. A part of such a common history would be the affirmation of the world-historical role of post-Renaissance Europe, both as world power (only recently eclipsed by USA in the wake of two world wars) and as originators/inventors of the modernist project.

Such interpretive constructs will be used by various groups in the formal political struggle surrounding change in Europe, and here is the matter of delimited-formal ideology: crucial debates will involve federation in respect of the EC, and the creation of new patterns of exchange within the old eastern block and new linkages to the EC. In all, debates about the shape and character of an emergent new Europe. This is, in a way, familiar territory: party statements, political writing, newspaper and media debates. Formal organisations will join in: employers groupings, labour organisations, the myriad research groups within Europe, the existing institutional centres (state, para-state, and supra-national), and so on. Explicit programmatic statements in regard to Community development have been made, indeed they have a distinguished history. Brugmans[44], the first Rector of the College of Europe in Brugges, attempted to remind Europeans in the early 1980s period of EC drift just what thoughts had animated those, like Monet, who had argued for a united Europe. Arguing that a federal system was needed both to address global-system level problems and to overcome residual nationalism, Brugmans went on to specify four basic questions in regard to the project of building a united Europe: the matter of identity; the problem of defence/security; the social dimension of welfare; and the political issue of democracy. Thereafter, in a marvellous overview, Brugmans rehearses the outline of a series of specific

---

[44] H. Brugmans *Europe: A Leap in the Dark*, Stoke on Trent, Trentham, 1985

debates, concluding broadly that a federal Europe is the route to a reaffirmation of Europe's place in the developing global system. Wistrich[45] echoes these arguments in a 1991 text, underscoring the message by pointing to the upheavals in eastern Europe and the USSR/CIS, and commenting that the UK cannot afford to stand aside whilst the process of securing union continues. So too does Jacques Delors who, whilst addressing the people of France, points out that in the modern world the national community cannot reliably secure economic and social harmony, adding that the 'consequences of globalization would be much more severe without the construction of Europe'[46].

All this business of reading the shift towards European unity will have a common-sense level version, the sphere of pervasive-informal ideology. The present pattern of complex change is not a matter solely for elite inspection, broad citizen responses will constrain formal political programmes, and extant thinking is itself shaped by political struggles, that is, hegemonic and counter-hegemonic idea-sets. Thus we can ask how common sense has variously regarded the project of EC unity, and how it might read the emergent EC unified system with its seemingly dominant role for Germany. All this might turn out to be a crucial area of political struggle, and a fascinating issue for social scientists. Attempts to read these changes are of course now being made, and picking-up from the explicit remarks about federalism, with its core idea of the dispersal of power, quite unexpected celebrations of available traditions of democracy and diversity can be found.

Christopher Harvie considers the situation of Scotland in relations to contemporary history. Noting that Ukania is slowly modulating into Europe, Harvie suggests that its inhabitants must acknowledge their fellow Europeans and the various legacies they can draw upon. In the case of the Scots there is the tradition of the Scottish Enlightenment, with figures such as Smith, Ferguson, and Hume. In all Harvie diagnoses a legacy of 'civic humanism', an appreciation of the 'small knowable polis existing within loose structures'[47], which resembles the eastern European civic forum notions of discourse. It is a tradition that is quite distinct from Anglo-Saxon marketism, with its economic liberalism and minimum state, and more closely approximates the model of the Germany's Lander system where power is regionalized. Harvie is confident both that Scotland, thus understood, could contribute to a new notion of Europe, and that to secure this future for Scotland requires the removal of the centralizing hand of London, in other words, independence.

Jacques Darras offers a similarly unexpectedly sourced celebration of diversity, linking it closely to the notion of democracy. Darras looks to an

---

[45] E. Wistrich *After 1992: The United States of Europe*, London, Routledge, 1989

[46] J. Delors *Our Europe*, London, Verso, 1992

[47] Harvie *Cultural Weapons* p.19

overcoming of nationalism and its attendant boundary-making, and a supercession of materialist notions of progress attatched thereto, suggesting that the future could be a mix of the local and the transnational:

> perhaps we should talk of the emergence of a number of overlapping sub-cultures that between them provide the warp and weft of the Europe of the future: the young athletes and musicians who criss-cross the continent, a rapidly expanding business network, long-distance lorry drivers who meet for a demi or a pint along the motorways of Europe; and, of course, writers and academics such as myself, at home wherever their learning and their linguistic skills take them...few now think in the narrow national terms of their forebears. Their frame of reference is at once smaller and larger that the nation state. It is smaller in that it is often limited to people rather like themselves ... But these links very often stretch far beyond traditional national boundaries ... across old animosities often almost ignoring the national capitals which try to keep them under control[48].

Darras suggests that the process of European unification will entail the rewriting of old national histories, as they are suffused with a now redundant nationalism. The model he affirms of the emergent Europe comprises a concrete exemplification, the Market Square of Brussels with its jostling symbols of princely, religious, merchant, and civil power, and an historical precedent in the rich and diverse trading centre of medieval Burgundy.

UK responses, new readings of Europe

In the period since mid-1989 it has become clear beyond doubt that the UK is bound-up in a pattern of complex political-economic and cultural change that is remaking Europe. In western Europe the response to change has taken the central form of a re-affirmation of the ideal of European unity which animated the founding of the European Community. The need for new thinking within the UK body-politic is now acute. The current phase of the development of the UK can be illuminated after the fashion of Ferdinand Braudel[49]. We can identify a series of relevant time-scales: (i) long term relative decline of the UK (late nineteenth century onwards); (ii) post-Second World War absorption within the Atlantic sphere (that is, US hegemony); (iii) post-1973 collapse of Keynesianism and rise of the New Right.

The hey-day of UK industry was the mid-nineteenth century. Thereafter the industrial bourgeoisie were slowly absorbed by the ethos of the aristocracy, and decline sets in from the mid-nineteenth century as the industrial bourgeoisie fail to become dominant. The response to increasing international competition was empire, a sideways expansion, not reform.

---

[48] J. Darras and D. Snowman *Beyond the Tunnel of History*, London, Macmillan, 1990 pp.60-61

[49] A line I take from H. Overbeek *Global Capitalism and National Decline*, London, Allen and Unwin, 1990

The working class were absorbed with empire-patriotism and the Labour Party quickly accommodated to the establishment. Marquand[50] looks to this period as having fixed in essentials UK political structures, ideas, institutions, groupings, and patterns of debate. Marquand notes that many tried to fashion reform; from the social imperialism of Joseph Chamberlain, the proto-Keynesianism of Lloyd George and Oswald Mosley, to post-war Keynesianism. None of them succeeded in establishing a developmental state, and nor did the subsequent attempts of Wilson or Heath.

The inter-war period is important overall as it marks the point at which economic problems ceased to be soluble inside the UK economic space. As the global system shifted towards the mass production of 'fordism' the UK, within the context of empire-block protection, did not fully internalize this production mode. The period of the Second World War ended the UK's economic policy autonomy, and henceforth the UK acted within the ambit of the US sphere. It was the era of the Keynesian welfare state at home and the Pax Americana abroad. The UK attempted to situate itself, with Ernest Bevin's 'Churchill option', between USA, empire, and Europe. As the empire/commonwealth declined into a generalized outward-directedness, and as Atlanticism strongly predominated over Europe (indeed the UK refused to join early EC), the City plus outward looking industries came to the fore. The UK economic space was internationalized with the City predominant and increasingly detached from UK markets[51]. The system lasted until 1971-73 when a combination of Nixon ending the Bretton Woods system plus the oil shock, occasioned a crisis which presented three alternatives to the UK government: (i) do nothing and hope for rescue by the EC (Heath) or the revival of the world economy (Wilson/Callaghan); (ii) institute a national-economic-space recovery programme, this was the Alternative Economic Strategy of the Labour left; and (iii) free-up the economy and open-up the market system, the strategy of the New Right[52].

From the Heath years on the New Right organised. In government James Callaghan accepted proto-monetarism in 1976 with the IMF visit, and the late 1970s saw intellectual-political collapse of Keynesianism in the face of emergent monetarism/New Rightism. The present UK state-regime has pursued a coherent neo-liberal accumulation strategy; presented through the eighties in the familiar guise of Thatcherism. The actions and arguments of the Thatcher governments can be understood within this system-context framework. A key strategy revolved around policies designed to advance the priority of the 'market sector' within the political-economy by reducing the extent and depth of democratic institutions and mechanisms. Local government has been brought under central government control. Para-statal

---

[50] Marquand *Unprincipled Society*
[51] ibid. and Overbeek *Global Capitalism*
[52] ibid.

advisory and regulatory bodies have been attacked and replaced by organisations subject to direct central regulation, or market sector regulation, or no regulation at all. Professional groupings have been attacked: the law, medicine, and the universities. The independent media has been subject to routine attack. Relatedly political power has been further centralized in the Whitehall-Downing Street machine. The UK executive has been powerful and unconstrained in contrast to the other modern states ever since it was constructed in the period of the English Revolution. However, under the UK New Right long established centralizing tendencies have been massively reinforced. In the sphere of economic activity a key area of attack has been upon the assumptions, institutions, and established patterns of activity of the post-Second World War contested compromise of Keynesian growth and welfare: hence the commitment to privatization; the deregulation of the City; the preference for market-led industrial recovery; plus systematic attacks upon the Trades Union movement. To break up the Keynesian welfare consensus which was built in part on ideals of universalistic provision the New Right stressed particular provision, and thus were old solidarities broken down.

Overall, the UK economy has been opened up and groups linked to City and UK based transnational capitalism have prospered. But there is no sign of a widespread industrial recovery. Nor are service industries looking as if they will replace declining manufactures. Prosperity is geographically concentrated. It is also class concentrated and Bob Jessop[53] speaks of a two-nations hegemonic project, those with jobs in new flexible high skill post-fordist industries, and the disadvantaged unskilled rest. In terms of global system context it is a strategy of dual-parasitism: politically on the USA, and economically on the markets of the EC. Yet the strategy is now clearly under threat as the global system reconstructs itself. The political-dependency was weakening as USA turned to Germany in May 1989, but with Nato now irrelevant, and in process of collapse, the role of political-dependent is no longer possible as the USA does not need a 'Number One Ally' in Europe to confront communism. The particular role which the UK ruling class had fashioned for itself, in the wake of the loss of empire, is thus irrelevant to the new situation. And the strategy of economic-dependency is similarly overthrown by events. When the inner-German border was opened in November 1989, followed by the ripple of revolutions throughout the old eastern block, the UK state-regime's economic strategy of international finance/trading capital plus home MNC assembly work via deregulation and cheap labour, simply collapsed. On the one hand the opening up of eastern Europe, coupled to the US turn to Germany, gave a wholly unanticipated boost to moves to EC unification, and on the other, eastern Europe looked even more deregulated and cheaper

53 B. Jessop et al. *Thatcherism: A Tale of Two Nations*, Cambridge, Polity, 1988

than the UK, and moreover closer to the new emergent centre of Europe as the Atlanticist era came to a close.

The end of the cold war, the reunification of Germany, the revolutions in eastern Europe and the related end of the block-system, plus the drive to EC integration all point to the collapse of the UK New Right's strategy of dual-parasitism, and to the overarching official ideology of the free world that went with it. Confronted with this catastrophe the New Right have responded with furious denial. The problem for the UK right is that present changes in Europe, and the programme for a united European Community threaten directly their political grip on the UK, and thus their externally-focused economic interests. The only available strategy, the one that seems post-Thatcher to have been adopted, is to dilute and delay moves towards a federal Europe in the hope of arriving at what in effect would be merely a free-trade area. In the case of the Labour Party, if we understand them to have been effectively coopted years ago by the established power holders agreeing to modest programmes of ameliorist welfare, then the problem is precisely that of suddenly having to deal with the possibility of reaffirming that modernist project to which their late nineteenth century style mass manual working class socialism nominally commits them. Overall, in regard to the UK political classes we can insist that a new reading of Europe is now obligatory, for the old certainties are overthrown by events.

Post-Maastricht tensions

I have argued throughout this text that over the period of the 1980s the UK state-regime ran a strategy of dual parasitism in respect of the wider global structures within which it moved: politically on the USA via the notion of the special relationship, and economically on the EC which they affected to understood as a loose free-trade area. However, it seems to me that this strategy was fatally undermined by the upheavals of 1989-91 and it is only after an interregnum of uncertainty when the state-regime followed behind events that a new posture in respect of the emergent crucial sphere of the EC has been adopted: this may be tagged a strategy of 'dilute and delay'. One might take this strategy to have been articulated in a preliminary form at Maastricht, when John Major struck-out the overt references to federalism and reduced the relevant elements of democratic reform in favour of an arrangement which stressed inter-governmentalism.

More broadly it became clear over the difficult period from Maastricht to Edinburgh, as the European Community's economy slid towards general recession and as social and political problems mounted, that the post-Maastricht phase of European development was going to be much more problematic than the heady optimism of December 1991 might have led commentators to believe. It now seems important to take note of the likely spread of tensions which will shape how the treaty, or any replacement in the event of an unresolvable breakdown[54], is translated into practice: we can posit a process whereby diverse national understandings of ostensibly agreed theory and its relation to practice will be mutually negotiated over a long-drawn out period. In other words, the final shape of the post-Maastricht European Community is a matter of ongoing political exchange and will only become clear over time.

A speculative outline of these interactive dynamics can be offered at a general analytic level in terms of a series of 'scenarios', which in line with the central expectations of this text in regard to the inevitability of some sort of union I will construct around a 'rational model' of the out-turn of these dynamics, namely a post-Maastricht republican democratic federal system. Such speculations about the way in which theory will come to be translated into practice can be optimistic, the whole matter being taken to be likely to continue, or pessimistic, where ideas of breakdown are entertained.

The optimistic 'rational model' affirms the goal of a federal Europe and this is clearly a matter of some considerable concern to the UK New Right. It is not difficult to see why this should be so, it presents the 'threat' of the democratization of the UK. Any movement along a developmental line towards securing the rational model would present the UK right with all the problems which I have noted in this text. However, there must be some doubt as to the likelihood of this model being generally affirmed at a European level, and to the extent that it is, one might anticipate a much less emphatic dynamic. It might be thought that a more likely route to securing the rational model, particularly after the shock of the Danish referendum, which in part was an affirmation of local-level democracy against the developing intergovernmental elitism of the community, would entail more 'bottom-up' citizen involvement to supplement the existing 'top-down' style. This would imply decentralization and wide citizen involvement and debate in respect of the development of the community would, arguably, shift from recipes to processes. One variant of this sort of route-to-the-future has been characterized in terms of an uneven and multi-tracked style of development, where the community continues to move towards some sort of union but continues to be political-institutionally sui generis[55]. However, for the UK state-regime the problem remains of the developmental dynamic of the community leading strongly away from UK-style oligarchic pre-democratic rule towards a late-twentieth century cashing of the old modernist project of formal and substantive democracy.

---

[54] A replacement could be expected as, to recall, and against UK public discourse which disingenuously presents these matters in voluntaristic terms, the move to EC unification has a global structural occasion. A point again acknowledged in the EC's response to the ERM's summer 1993 problems when the Maastricht package was re-affirmed.

[55] C. Crouch and D. Marquand 'Introduction' in C. Crouch and D. Marquand eds. *Towards a Greater Europe*, Oxford, Blackwell, 1992

There are other ways of imagining the future of the community and these revolve around notions of breakdown, either de jure or merely de facto, and the reassertion of nationalism. In the UK a collapse of the Maastrich project would be regarded as a victory by both the vocal nationalist right wing (Brugges Group et al) and by the less vocal labourist nationalists. In the former case it would be seen as a victory for a Europe-of-the-nations operating via inter-governmental machineries, and the rational model EC project would come to an end with the present arrangements used merely as a customs union/common market. For the latter group it would be seen as a victory for the possibility of a national economic recovery plan, an echo of the AES of the 1970s and 1980s, plus a familiar national politics. In both these cases it would represent an appeal to the status quo ante. One might comment that if ever this un-holy alliance were to take the lead in formulating UK responses, thus affirming or running with the wider reinvention of nationalism in Europe, then there would be clear lines of implication, we could expect certain sorts of things to happen in the UK and Europe. A withdrawal into nationalism implies that Europe's economic, political and cultural futures would be primarily shaped by the Americans, the Japanese and the Germans. In particular, Germany would in fairly short order come to dominate Europe. In the longer term such an outcome would also imply the indefinite postponement of political-economic and cultural reform inside the UK.

Another possibility is of an economic nationalism as competition between extant states becomes the order of the day in place of present EC-vehicled cooperation. Economic nationalists would leave each agent, that is state, to read and react to global structural pressure as it saw fit[56]. In this eventuality we might expect to see existing institutions continuing, the familiar fora of debate (EC, IMF, G7 etcetera), but with the expectation of the continuing harmonization of EC responses removed. In the UK the persistence of established centres of debate might encourage the familiar UK ruling-class strategy of pretending that nothing had happened and waiting for something to turn-up[57]. In this case one might expect the political centre plus political establishment to proceed on an ad hoc basis. Given that this could be a way of characterizing the entire post-Second World War period prior to the grudging affirmation of the EC project made in recent years, this implies a continuation of familiar patterns of political argument and action. Exchanges with the continuing EC institutions (no longer seen as the vehicle for unification) would be dominated by economistic, national, and unreflexive thinking. In practical terms this could be taken to entail continuing relative decline, both economic and political. All projects for Europeanization and democratization would be where they are now, visible,

---

56 See W. Hutton on the great ERM disaster: *The Guardian* 30 November 1992; 1 December 1992; and 2 December 1992

57 See N.Ascherson on 'the quiet after defeat' in *The Independent on Sunday* 11 October 1992

desirable, and probably out of reach. In terms of global structures the Americans, Japanese, and Germans would increase in importance.

Those associated with the project for a unified federal Europe, for example the commentator John Palmer, have spoken of a 'variable-geometry' EC with a core group going ahead with EMU/PU and a periphery of weaker economies or politically uncommitted countries forming a second tier. The likely core would include Germany, the Benelux countries and France. The periphery could include Italy, Spain, Portugal and Ireland, which might be expected to join with the core as soon as their economies permitted, with Greece left in its present position. The detached periphery would then be the UK and maybe Denmark. Of course this schematic pattern might alter with the accession of some of the EFTA countries. A key issue would be the extent to which 'variable-geometry' turned out to be the same in practice as a 'two-speed' Europe. It is clear that for the political agents in the UK any 'two-speed' version of a 'variable-geometry' development of the EC in the wake of an unrecoverable breakdown of the process envisioned at Maastricht would pose the clearest challenge: for whilst both the above noted 'pessimistic alternatives' could be taken as, and certainly by participants read as, continuity of a sort with what had gone before, in a 'two-speed' case the claim to continuity could not plausibly be made. The formation of a two-speed Europe would imply that the UK was marginalized politically, economically, and culturally and it is difficult to imagine how this would not figure as a severe problem in UK political discourse. It might be that the formation of a two-speed Europe would be the way to maximize the impact on UK domestic politics of EC unification. A developing core EC would be an everpresent 'good example' for UK political agents. For the UK ruling-class their strategy of dilute and delay in pursuit of a loose free trade area would be overthrown, as they would not have the necessary influence to pursue what can only be an insider's strategy, and there would not seem to be any other obvious state-regime projects. The compromise fudge achieved at Maastricht and apparently reaffirmed at Edinburgh would be gone, leaving the ruling-class to re-run its internally damaging arguments about how to respond to changing global structural circumstances in general and the development of the EC in particular. As for the centre/left opposition it would seem to imply more of the established and muted argument, maybe a little hightened. Sections of the centre/left are wedded to the idea of EC unification and for them the presence of the good example would sustain the repeated presentation of arguments in favour of joining-in and catching-up. Centre/left opponents of the Maastricht process would have to take up some sort of position in regard to lines to the future, and a reactionary labourist conservatism is going to look even more implausible than before, thus any presence of a good example could only sharpen debate in the UK.

Clearly when one comes to speculate about how the post-Maastricht pursuit of EC unification might work out in practice one can easily make these 'scenarios'. However whilst they are of some utility in sketching ranges of broad possibility they are unlikely to be an effective substitute for the attention to the detail of the relevant economic, political, and cultural processes. One of the clearest lessons of the post-Second World War career of Third World development studies, concerned precisely with the attempt to authoritatively characterize complex dynamics of change, is that the pursuit of recipes in regard to change must be eschewed in favour of the sceptical deployment of the received classical core of European social theory: we can elucidate dynamics of change, and maybe thereafter run arguments in favour of particular restricted lines of change, but we cannot decipher or govern authoritatively the whole complex process.

Conclusion

At the present time a series of structural tensions have unexpectedly run together, and the upshot is that there is now in process a phase of complex change. As we try to decipher those processes which enfold us we can identify some broad key elements of this structural reconstruction: change in the EC towards a more unified system; change in eastern Europe and the USSR/CIS towards economic and political reform; and change in the European block-system, and broader world-system patterns. A clue to deciphering this pattern of complex change is given by the overall line of change, which would seem to be towards some sort of unification of the European Community. Relatedly, for the community of scholars, reading the matter after the approach of Gellner[58], the present phase of change can be addressed using the resources of the core European tradition of social theory, which is concerned precisely with the analysis of complex change.

---

58 Gellner *Thought and Change*

9 Europe, democracy and the dissolution of Britain

Introduction

I have been concerned in this essay to discuss the political-cultural structures of the UK with reference to the responses made by major political groups to the business of complex change in Europe, and in particular the pressure for some sort of European Community union. The position taken in the text has been that the drive to European union is a coherent and rational response to structural changes within the global-system, and that these broad dynamics will necessarily occasion a response within the UK. Such patterns of change might prove to be very extensive as the UK political-economy and polity is drawn inexorably towards the model of mainland Europe. It is possible to anticipate change in economic, political, social and cultural received structures and discourses. Overall, the pattern of changes which might reasonably be anticipated could be such as to fatally disturb the extant UK political-economic and political-cultural configuration, and the possibility thus emerges of the UK joining the European political and cultural mainstream. In this chapter I will offer a simple review of the main line of argument which I have presented.

The approach taken in the text

A fundamental assumption of the argument of this text is that any holistic-type analysis of patterns of change within a nationstate must attend to the wider sets of structures within which any nationstate unit will be lodged. This particular line of approach is familiar within development theory, and has recently been represented within academic discourse as 'international political-economy'. In brief, this approach insists that it is necessary to look at trans-national flows of productive, political, and cultural power when analysing the actions of any particular agent group. It is all a matter of structures and agents. The task of the analyst is the elucidation of the detail of the sets of circumstances within which specified agent-groups manoeuvre. Such exercises in elucidation will deploy two broad strategies: the political-economic description/explanation of structures (itself an exercise informed by the analyst's own culture), coupled to the culture-critical unpacking of the sets of available intellectual resources with reference to which agent-groups will fashion their courses of action (again an exercise informed by the analyst's own culture). The implications of using this strategy for the analysis of the political-economy and culture of the UK are quite clear: the general structural circumstances of the UK must be spelled-out with reference to the way in which the unit is lodged within global trans-national networks (economic, political and cultural); and the political-cultural resources available within the unit to the various players must be spelled out as these are the necessary bases of articulated responses, and in particular the behaviour of one key agent-group, the state-regime.

The occasion of the preparation of the text

Over the period May 1989 through to December 1991 the structures and associated discourse which had shaped the European experience of the post-Second World War period were abruptly overthrown. With the end of the system of blocks in Europe, and the associated patterns of state alliances and popular ideologies, agent-groups were faced with the task of reading and reacting to new (and developing) circumstances. In the European Community this took the form of a re-emphasis of the drive towards union which had animated the founding fathers of the organisation, and which had found recent partial expression in the 1985 SEA.

In the UK the reaction of the state-regime was one of horror as their very convenient enemy, and with it their sense of their role in the world, and their domestic legitimating ideology, disappeared. After an interregnum which lasted through to December 1991, during which period the UK state-regime clearly had no idea how to react, a new posture began to be discerned and at Maastrict it arguably found its first formulation, essentially a strategy of 'dilute and delay', for whilst the programme of European Community union is clearly a coherent and rational response to structural change it is one which threatens quite directly the grip on power of the UK ruling groups who would be faced with democratizing their essentially pre-democratic oligarchic polity.

The questions which this text has endeavoured to answer relate, firstly, to the occasion of this strategy of reply in terms of the political-economic projects pursued by the UK state-regime and the ways in which it is understood by them in terms informed by UK received political-culture, and, secondly, to the matter of fashioning a coherent agenda of research and action in respect of the dynamics of change in Europe.

Political-economic and political-cultural structures

The manuscript has sketched the political-economy of the UK as a backdrop to the central concern for political culture. The analysis of UK political culture was accomplished via three steps, each of which grew out of, and to some extent narrowed down, the preceding discussions.

It was with reference to the marvellous work of Tom Nairn, in particular, that I sketched the outline of the UK political culture in terms of a sequence of historical episodes each of which lodged in place certain cultural resources: the seventeenth century English Revolution established the importance of liberal political philosophies informed by the model of natural science; the late eighteenth and early nineteenth century saw the invention of the official nationalism of Britain in response to the demands of republican democracy; and then finally the late nineteenth and early twentieth century period of high Victorianism/Edwardianism saw the establishment of patterns which have existed, modified, down to the present day in the form of the broad character of institutional arrangements, the present spread of political parties, and familiar styles and topics of argument within the public sphere.

The key structures of contemporary UK political life were detailed: an official ideology of representative democracy with a sovereign parliament subject to the nominal authority of the monarch; the routine pervasive-informal ideology of liberal-individualism; and an acquiescent little tradition centring on notions of civility and individualism. This set of institutions and ideas, which are accepted by the main political parties, is quite distinctive. Alasdair MacIntyre has analysed the idea-set and diagnosed an impoverished moral emotivism, a deep childishness. In a similar vein David Marquand traces the root of the inability of the UK state-regime to ameliorate long term decline to the pervasive influence of possessive individualism: in place of a community with common concerns and problems, the familiar political culture of the UK construes matters in terms of atomistic individuals freely entering into contracts to secure their autonomously arising needs and wants. On the mainland, notes Marquand, states order their economies so as to secure the general good - and they have been successful. In contrast to extant UK political culture, and drawing on the lines of criticism made by our commentators, a different set of ideas which could inform political life were introduced: citizenship, civil society, the public sphere, and the Aristotelian scheme of practical wisdom - in sum, an ethic of formal and substantive democracy.

An important element of the political culture of the UK is the ideology of liberal-individualism, and it was suggested in the text that it is with this set of ideas that we find the informal extension of the great tradition ideas which carry the official ideology of parliamentary democracy. The idea-set of liberal-individualism finds extensive expression throughout the UK polity: it is a strategy of understanding that is routinely deployed. The idea-set can be traced back to the legacy of the English Revolution of the seventeenth century, and is thus deeply sedimented in UK culture. Drawing on the work of C.B.Macpherson it was noted that an essentially liberal ethic and social ontology is affirmed which prioritizes the autonomous individual. In this scheme the realm of society appears only as a mixture of naturally given family relationships, freely contracted institutional regularities outside this sphere, with all other persons understood as an apriori inchoate grouping, the mass. All persons construe themselves as individuals and all other individuals are taken as either opponents or possible allies in the overall matter of the pursuit of private satisfactions.

The ways in which this ideology operates in routine practice were considered and it was argued that the effects of this ideology are, in total, destructive: the UK has no notion of citizenship, and consequently no citizens; the social ontology affirms the existence of individuals but does so in a fashion which denies the notion of society, and if there is no society then, as Marquand points out, it cannot need ordering by the state on behalf of the collectivity and thus policy-making is less effective than it might be. The upshot of all this is an impoverished political community, what Germaine Greer dubbed an 'infantilized polity'. Against this the text cites a model of discourse-politics. This has been sketched by Jurgen Habermas in terms of political decentralization, citizen participation, and an affirmation of the role of the public sphere; again a reaching back to Aristotelian-derived schemes of practical wisdom. Overall, Habermas offers a way of cashing the classic modernist project in the context of the late twentieth century.

It is the case that the work of Habermas, and those whom I called the theorists of democracy, whilst influential in intellectual circles, has not been so strongly evidenced within the general public sphere. Indeed over the period of the 1980s in the UK we have had a reaffirmation of economic liberalism coupled to a distinctive social authoritarianism: in brief, we have had the narrow ideological efforts of the New Right, and more broadly, and much more interestingly, the theories of postmodernity.

Postmodernism celebrates consumption in the marketplace as a sphere of individual freedom within a system ever in flux. Individual actors choose from the proffered array of consumption goods and from them they construct a package, a life-style. The formal expositions of postmodern theory celebrate the transient, the decorative, the superficial. Ideas typical of modernity and modernism, progress and clarity of design, are ridiculed as aspects of a meta-discourse which has been overtaken by events. In a political-economy which is now very productive individuals relate to the collectivity via marketplace consumption rather than workplace production, and 'seduction' replaces 'control'. In place of overarching schemes of societal development, meta-discourses, postmodernists rest content with the gestural non-discourse of non-progress. After Zygmunt Bauman, this text has argued that much of the material of postmodernism is expressive of the disappointed consciousness of disheartened intellectuals over the 1980s period of New Right political-institutional dominance. Notwithstanding that many of the particular ideas advanced are thoroughly interesting, the material overall is nonsense. In particular the analyses they would offer in respect of the contemporary UK polity are deeply implausible: in brief, one could ask these theorists why, if consumer seduction is so powerful, is there so much evident demobilzation and repression? Against the postmodern reading of contemporary society, with its stress on fluidity and novelty, I would argue that it is better to look at how the UK population is politically demobilized in a system that stays essentially the same: thus the futile politics of deference and protest; the retreat into private consumption and the associated celebration of individualism; and the obverse of the consumption coin, state-policed welfarism; plus of course, and against the postmodernist prioritization of the marketplace, the routine deployment by the ruling groups of strategies of demobilization (secrecy, manipulation, the routine equation of dissent with disloyalty).

Overall, the UK polity is pre-democratic, and this institutional state of affairs is buttressed by a quite distinctive national ideology which finds both formal expression in an official ideology and informal extension via notion of liberal-individualism. It seems to me that this polity, and its associated ideological machineries, effectively demobilizes the bulk of the population. It is this structure and discourse which has been disturbed by the events of 1989-1991 and which is directly threatened by the rational project of European Community union because it cannot accommodate mainland European political-institutional arrangements and political-cultural forms.

Political agents

It is within the frame of the political-economic and political-cultural structures noted above that the major political agent groups within the UK have pursued their several projects.

The 1980s saw the right offering an emphatic celebration of the liberal market system. An analysis of the UK New Right restricted to the domestic sphere reveals both a series of structural economic changes which have opened the economy to global system forces, and the presence of continuing deep-seated problems when the UK economy is compared with the mainland. At the same time we find a political-cultural strategy of demobilizing the UK public, with centres of possible independent thought and action routinely attacked, and with the whole enterprise held together by the ideological package of economic liberalism and social authoritarianism. In all, the 1980s project of the UK right could be characterized as an authoritarian, intolerant, substantively anti-democratic, failed attempt to adjust to continuing relative decline within the global system by adopting a project of 'dual parasitism', politically on the USA via the special relationship, and economically on the European Community conceived as a loose free trade area.

The reasons for the political ascendancy of the right in the UK have much to do with the parlous state of the centre/left. This matter was addressed, in the company of Nairn and Marquand. It was argued that the Labour Party offers a specific reading of the modernist project rooted in the late nineteenth century expectations of elite led mass working class action, and that the track record of the Labour Party must be judged an historical failure (thus the UK Conservative Party is the most successful right party in Europe). Relatedly the Labour Party effectively blocks any contribution to political discourse and action from the non-Labour centre/left. In the text it has been argued that the UK needs electoral reform so as to break the present political log-jam. However it is clear that change will only be forced upon the political classes from the outside.

New structures, new discourses

It seems clear that the present dynamics of change in Europe will have a major impact on the UK polity, however public discussion is remarkably muted. The sequence of events from spring 1989 through to winter 1991 has undermined the UK ruling political classes view of itself and its role in the world. The construction of a new political discourse in the UK as it is absorbed into the European Community is now inevitable. In the text this issue has been pursued under a number of headings. First, in regard to the dynamic of European Community integration it was suggested that UK discourse has been limited in character, that is, national, economistic and unreflexively short-term. It seems to be the case that prospective dialogue is confined to the political margins. In regard, secondly, to the dynamics of change in eastern Europe and the CIS we find an unhelpful mix of ideological posturing from the right who lay claim to the revolutions, recipe-mongering from the same quarter in respect of the necessity of eastern Europe and the CIS adopting liberal-market systems, and embarrassed silences from the UK left. In regard, thirdly, to German reunification we find a curious amalgam of atavistic anxiety, present fear in regard to the country's economic power, and in the wake of the Gulf embroglio an incoherent set of demands that the country take up a more active political role in the world. Finally, there is the matter of the broader global system, with its emerging trio of groupings, Japan/Asia, USA/Latin America, and Europe, and again the reactions of the UK ruling groups have been limited and defensive.

Building on the analyses presented here it is possible, finally, to sketch out a plausible agenda of research work informed by the broad European tradition of social theorizing. The familiar political-economic and political-cultural structures of the post-Second World War are now overthrown by the events of 1989-91 and a crucial task for social scientists, whatever their particular interests might be, is the elucidation of these ongoing dynamics of change. This is a matter of spelling-out patterns of change in trans-national political, economic, and knowledge structures as the global system undergoes extensive reconfiguration. These trans-national system flows of power not only run-through the territory of the European Community, and as noted are the occasion of the rational project of EC union, but they also flow-through the territory of the UK. In the case of the UK the matter at hand for social scientists is the structural remaking of the UK. As the global and regional system within which the UK is embedded reconfigures the particular expression of these structural forces, what we have understood as a 'nationstate', will inevitably be remade. As the structural forces which flow-through the UK reconfigure the state-regime will endeavour to read and react to these developing patterns and ordinarily a new state-regime project might be expected, however the pressures for change are now so strong that it is difficult to see how the extant ruling group can retain any significant measure of continuity and control. As the system changes, and as the familiar state-regime and its familiar official ideology is carried along, then so too will the familiar discourses whereby we understand our polity and ourselves be remade. The final outcome, or new position of relative stability, of the present episode of complex change will take many years to achieve.

Bibliography

Abrams, P., *The Origins of British Sociology*, Chicago, Chicago University Press,1968

Addison, P., *The Road to 1945*, London, Jonathan Cape, 1977

Aglietta, M., *A Theory of Capitalist Regulation*, London, Verso, 1979

Albrow, M., *Bureaucracy*, London, Macmillan, 1970

Allen, J., and Massey, D., (eds), *The Economy in Question*,London, Sage,1989

Anderson, B., *Imagined Communities*,London, Verso, 1983

Anderson, P., *English Questions*, London, Verso, 1992

Arendt, H., *The Human Condition*, Chicago, Chicago University Press, 1958

Aron, R., *The Imperial Republic*, London, Weidenfeld, 1973

Ascherson, N., *Games with Shadows*, London, Hutchinson Radius, 1988

Baruma, I., *Gods Dust:A Modern Asian Journey*,London, Jonathan Cape, 1989

Bauman, Z., *Socialism the Active Utopia*, London, Allen and Unwin, 1976

Bauman, Z., *Towards a Critical Sociology*, London, Routledge, 1976

Bauman, Z., *Legislators and Interpreters*, Cambridge, Polity, 1987

Bauman, Z., *Freedom*, Milton Keynes, Open University Press, 1988

Bauman, Z., *Modernity and the Holocaust*, Cambridge, Polity, 1989

Bauman, Z., *Modernity and Ambivalence*, Cambridge, Polity, 1991

Bauman, Z., *Intimations of Modernity*, London, Routledge, 1992

Bello, W., and Rosenfeld, S., *Dragons in Distress: Asia's Miracle Economies in Crisis*, San Francisco, Institute for Food and Development Policy, 1990

Bennington, G., *Lyotard Writing the Event*, Manchester, Manchester University Press, 1988

Berger, P., and Luckman, T., *The Social Construction of Reality*, Harmondsworth, Penguin, 1976

Berlin, I., *Four Essays on Liberty*, Oxford, Oxford University Press, 1969

Bernstein, R., *The Restructuring of Social and Political Theory*, London, *Methuen, 1976*

Bernstein, R., *Beyond Objectivism and Relativism*, Oxford, Blackwell, 1983

Bernstein, R., *The New Constellation*, Cambridge, Polity, 1992

Brugmans, H., *Europe: A Leap in the Dark*, Stoke on Trent, Trentham, 1985

Callinicos, A., *Against Postmodernism*, Cambridge, Polity, 1989

Callinicos, A., *The Revenge of History*, Cambridge, Polity, 1991

Cecchini, P., *The European Challenge: 1992 the benefits of a single market* London, Wildwood House, 1988

Chesshyre, R., *The Return of the Native Reporter*, Harmondsworth, Penguin, 1988

Chomsky, N., *Deterring Democracy*, London, Vintage, 1992

Chomsky, N., *Analysis*, BBC Radio 4, 28 February 1990

Chua, B.H.,'Reopening ideological discussion in Singapore' in *Southeast Asian Journal of Social Science*, 1983

Chen, P., and Evers, H.D., (eds) *Studies in ASEAN Sociology*, Singapore, Chopmen, 1978

Coates, D., *The Labour Party and the Struggle for Socialism*, Cambridge, Cambridge University Press, 1975

Cohen, S., *Folk Devils and Moral Panics*, Oxford, Martin Robertson, 1972

Colley, L., *Britons: The Forging of The Nation*, London, Yale University Press, 1992

Collini, S., *Liberalism and Sociology: L T Hobhouse and Political Argument in England 1880-1914*, Cambridge, Cambridge University Press, 1979

Crouch, C., and Maraquand, D., (eds) *Towards a Greater Europe*, Oxford, Blackwell, 1992

Cutler, T., et al. *1992 Struggle for Europe*, London, Berg, 1989

Daiches, D., et al. (eds) *A Hotbed of Genius,* Edinburgh, Edinburgh University Press, 1986

Darrass, J.,and Snowman, D., *Beyond the Tunnel of History*, London, Macmillan, 1990

Dasgupta, A.K., *Epochs of Economic Theory*, Oxford, Blackwell, 1985

Deane, P., *The Evolution of Economic Ideas*, Cambridge, Cambridge Univerity Press, 1978

Denitch, B., *The End of the Cold War*, London, Verso, 1990

Delors, J., *Our Europe*, London, Verso, 1992

Dilley, R., (ed.) *Contesting Markets*, Edinburgh, Edinburgh University Press, 1992

Dobb, M., *Theories of Value and Distribution since Adam Smith*, Cambridge, Cambridge University Press, 1973

Dryzek, J.S., *Discursive Democracy*, Cambridge, CUP, 1990

Eagleton,T., *Ideology An Introduction*, London, Verso, 1991

Eco, U., *Travels in Hyper-reality*, London, Picador, 1987

Economist Publications, *The World in 1992* London, Economist Publications, 1991

Enzensberger, H.M., *Europe Europe*, London, Picador, 1990

Enzensberger, H.M., *Political Crumbs*, London, Verso, 1990

Enzensberger, H.M., *Mediocrity and Delusion*, London, Verso, 1992

Ewing, K.D., and Gearty, C.A., *Freedom under Thatcher*, Oxford, Oxford University Press, 1990

Fay, B., *Social Theory and Political Practice*, London, Allen and Unwin, 1975

Featherstone, M., *Consumer Capitalism and Postmodernism*, London, Sage, 1991

Feyerabend, P., *Science in a Free Society*, London, Verso, 1978

Flemming, D.F., *The Cold War and Its Origins*, New York, Doubleday, 1961

Frank, A.G., *The European Challenge*, Nottingham, Spokesman, 1983

Franklin, M., *Britain's Future in Europe*, London, Pinter, 1990

Friedman, M., *Essays in Positive Economics*, Chicago, Chicago University Press, 1953

Fristch-Bournazel, R., *Europe and German Unification*, London, Berg, 1992

Foot, P., *Ireland Why Britain Must Get Out*, London, Chatto, 1989

Fukuyama, F., *The End of History and the Last Man*, London, Hamish Hamilton, 1992

Galbraith, J.K., *The Affluent Society*, London, Hamish Hamilton, 1958

Galtung, J., *Europe the New Superpower*, London, Allen and Unwin, 1973

Gamble, A., *Britain in Decline: Economic Policy, Political Strategy and the British State*, London, Macmillan, 1990

Garton-Ash, T., *The Uses of Adversity*, Cambridge, Granta, 1989

Garton-Ash, T., *We the People*, Cambridge, Granta, 1990

Giddens, A., *Capitalism and Modern Social Theory*, Cambridge, Cambridge University Press, 1971

Giddens, A., *Central Problems in Social Theory*, London, Macmillan, 1979

Giddens, A., *Profiles and Critiques in Social Theory*, London, Macmillan, 1982

Giddens, A., *Social Theory and Modern Sociology*, Cambridge, Polity, 1987

Gellner, E., *Thought and Change*, London, Weidenfeld, 1964
Gellner, E., *Nations and Nationalism,*Cambridge, Cambridge University Press, 1983
Gellner, E., *Plough, Sword, and Book*, London, Palladin, 1988
George, S., (ed.) *Britain and the European Community: The Politics of Semi-Detachment*, Oxford, Oxford University Press, 1992
Glenny, M., *The Rebirth of History*, Harmondsworth, Penguin, 1990
Gorz, A., *Critique of Economic Reason*, London, Verso, 1989
Habermas, J., *Towards a Rational Society*, London, Heineman, 1971
Habermas, J., *Knowledge and Human Interest,* Boston, Beacon Press, 1971
Habermas, J., *Theory and Practice*, London, Heineman, 1974
Habermas, J., *On the Logic of the Social Sciences*, Cambridge, Polity, 1988
Habermas, J., *The Structural Transformation of the Public Sphere*, Cambridge, Polity, 1989
Hall, S., and Jacques, M., (eds) *The Politics of Thatcherism*, London, Lawrence and Wishart, 1983
Hall, S., *The Hard Road to Renewal,* London, Verso, 1988
Halliday, F., *Cold War, Third World*, London, Hutchison Radius, 1989
Hamilton, C., 'Capitalist Industrialization in East Asia's Four Little Tigers' in *Journal of Contemporary Asia vol 13*, 1983
Hankins, T.L., *Science and the Enlightenment*, Cambridge, Cambridge University Press, 1985
Harvey, D., *The Condition of Postmodernity*, Oxford, Blackwell, 1989
Harvie, C., *Cultural Weapons: Scotland and survival in a new Europe,* Edinburgh, Polygon, 1992
Hawthorn, G., *Enlightenment and Despair*, Cambridge, Cambridge University Press, 1976
Held, D., *Models of Democracy*, Cambridge, Polity, 1987
Hennessy, P., *Never Again*, London, Jonathan Cape, 1992
Hirst, P., *After Thatcher*, London, Collins, 1989
Hitchens, C., *Blood, Class and Nostalgia*, London, Vintage, 1990
Hitchens, C., *The Monarchy: a critique of Britain's favourite fetish,* London, Chatto, 1990
Hodgson, G., *Economics and Institutions*, Cambridge, Polity, 1988
Hollis, M., and Nell, E.J., *Rational Economic Man*, Cambridge, Cambridge University Press, 1975
Holub, R.C., *Jurgen Habermas: Critic in the Public Sphere*, London, Routledge, 1991
Honderich, T., *Conservatism,* London, Hamish Hamilton, 1990
Huhne, C., *Real World Economics*, Harmondsworth, Penguin, 1990
Jackson, R.H., *Quasi-States: Sovereignty, International Relations and the Third World,* Cambridge, Cambridge University Press, 1990
Jameson, F., *Postmodernism, Or the Cultural Logic of Late Capitalism,* London, Verso, 1991
Jay, M., *The Dialectical Imagination*, Boston, Little Brown, 1973

Jennings, P., *The Living Village*, London, Hodder and Stoughton, 1968

Jessop, B., et al. *Thatcherism: A tale of two nations*, Cambridge, Polity, 1988

Jessop, B., *State Theory*, Cambridge, Polity, 1990

Kaye, H., *The British Marxist Historians*, Cambridge, Polity, 1984

Katzenstein, P., *Small States in World Markets*, London, Cornell University Press, 1985

Keane, J., *Democracy and Civil Society*, London, Verso, 1988

Kee, R.,*1939 The World We Left Behind*, London, Weidenfeld, 1984

Kolko, G., *The Politics of War*, New York, Vintage, 1968

Kornhauser, A., *The Politics of Mass Society*,London, Collier-Macmillan,1959

Krieger, J., *Reagan, Thatcher and the Politics of Decline*, Cambridge, Polity, 1986

Kuhn, T.S., *The Structure of Scientific Revolutions*, Chicago, Chicago University Press, 1970

Lakatos, I., and Musgrave, A., (eds) *Criticism and the Growth of Knowledge*, Cambridge, Cambridge University Press, 1970

Laslett, P., and Runciman, W.G., (eds.) *Politics,Philosophy and Society Series 2*, Oxford, Blackwell, 1962

Laudan, L., *Progress and its Problems*, London, Routledge, 1977

Leys, C., *Politics in Britain: From Labourism to Thatcherism*, London, Verso, 1989

Linklater, A., *Beyond Marxism and Realism: Critical Theory and International Relations*, London, Macmillan, 1990

Livingstone, K., *If Voting Changed Anything, They'd Abolish It*, London, Fontana, 1987

Lodge, J., (ed.) *The European Community and the Challenge of the Future*, London, Pinter, 1989

Long, N., (ed.) *Battlefields of Knowledge*, London, Routledge, 1992

Lyotard, F., *The Postmodern Condition*, Manchester, Manchester University Press, 1979

MacIntyre, A., *After Virtue*, London, Duckworth, 1981

MacIntyre, A., *Whose Justice, Which Rationality*, London, Duckworth, 1988

Macpherson, C.B., *The Political Theory of Possessive Individualism*, Oxford, Oxford University Press, 1962

Macpherson, C.B., *Democratic Theory: Essays in Retrieval*, Oxford, Oxford University Press, 1973

Marcuse, H., *One Dimensional Man*, Boston, Beacon Press, 1964

Marquand, D., *The Unprincipled Society*, London, Fontana, 1988

Marquand, D., *The Progressive Dilemma*, London, Heineman, 1991

Malcolm, N., *Soviet Policy Perspectives on Western Europe*, London, Pinter, 1989

Mayer, A., *The Persistence of the Old Regime,* New York, Croom Helm, 1981

Mayne, R., *Postwar: The Dawn of Todays Europe,* London, Thames and Hudson, 1983

Marx, K., *The Economic and Philosophical Manuscripts,* London, Lawrence and Wishart, 1957

Meiskins-Wood, E., *The Pristine Culture of Capitalism,* London, Verso, 1991

Middlemas, K., *The Politics of Industrial Society,* London, Andre Deutsche, 1979

Miliband, R., *Capitalist Democracy in Britain,* Oxford, Oxford University Press, 1982

Mitchie, J.,(ed.) *The Economic Legacy 1979-1992*, London, Academic Press, 1992

Mooers, C., *The Making of Bourgeois Europe,* London, Verso, 1991

Moore, B., *The Social Origins of Dictatorship and Democracy*, Boston, Beacon Press, 1966

Munk, O., *The Difficult Dialogue: Marxism and Nationalism,* London, Zed, 1986

Nairn, T., *The Break-Up of Britain*, London, New Left Books, 1977

Nairn, T., *The Enchanted Glass, London*, Hutchison Radius, 1988

Nelson, B., (ed.) *The European Community in the 1990s: Economics, Politics, Defence*, Oxford, Berg, 1992

Nelson, B., (ed.) *The Idea of Europe: Problems of National and Transnational Identity*, Oxford, Berg, 1992

Orwell, G., *The Road to Wigan Pier,* London, Victor Gollancz, 1937

Overbeek, H., *Global Capitalism and National Decline,* London, Allen and Unwin, 1990

Palmer, J., *Europe without America*, Oxford, Oxford University Press, 1987

Pandy, B.N., *South and Southeast Asia,* London, Macmillan, 1980

Panitch, L., 'Recent theorizations of corporatism' in *British Journal of Sociology 31*, 1980

Parkin, F., *Class Inequality and Political Order,* London, Palladin, 1972

Passmore, J., *The Perfectibility of Man,* London, Duckworth, 1971

Paxman, J., *Friends in High Places*, Harmondsworth, Penguin, 1990

Pheby, J., *Methodology and Economics: A Critical Introduction,* London, Macmillan, 1988

van der Pijl, K., *The Making of an Atlantic Ruling Class,* London, Verso, 1984

Pimlott, B., (ed.) *The Alternative: Politics for a Change,* London, W.H. Allen, 1990

Pollard, S., *The Idea of Progress,* Harmondsworth, Penguin, 1971

Pollard, S., *The Wasting of the British Economy*, London, Croom Helm, 1982

Ponting, C., *Secrecy in Britain*, Oxford, Blackwell, 1990

Popper, K., *Conjectures and Refutations*, London, Routledge, 1963

Preston, P.W., *New Trends in Development Theory*, London, Routledge, 1985

Preston, P.W., *Rethinking Development*, London, Routledge, 1987

Raban, J., *God and Mrs Thatcher*, London, Chatto, 1990

Reuschemeyer, D., Huber-Stevens, E., and Stevens, J.D., *Capitalist Development and Democracy*, Cambridge, Polity, 1991

Rosenberg, A., *Democracy and Socialism*, London, 1938

Ross, G., 'Confronting the New Europe' in *New Left Review 191*, 1992

Rude, G., *The Crowd in History*, London, Wiley ,1981

Ryder, J., and Silver, H., *Modern English Society*, London, Methuen, 1985

Saville, J., *The Labour Movement in Britain*, London, Faber, 1988

Scott, J.C., 'Protest and Profanation: Revolt and the Little Tradition' in *Theory and Society 4*, 1971

Scott, P., *Knowledge and Nation*, Edinburgh, Edinburgh University Press, 1990

Sked, A., *Britains Decline: Problems and Perspectives*, Oxford, Blackwell, 1987

Sklair, L., *The Sociology of the Global System*, London, Harvester, 1991

Smith, A., *The Geopolitics of Information*, London, Faber, 1980

Smith, A.D., *Social Change*, London, Routledge, 1976

Smith, D., *The Rise and Fall of Monetarism*, Harmondsworth, Penguin, 1987

Smith, D., *The Rise of Historical Sociology*, Cambridge, Polity, 1991

Smith, K., *The British Economic Crisis*, Harmondsworth, Penguin, 1984

Strange, S., *States and Markets*, London, Pinter, 1988

Strange, S., *Casino Capitalism*, Oxford, Blackwell, 1989

Swedberg, R., 'Economic Sociology Past and Present' in *Current Sociology*, 1987

Thompson, E.P.,*The Making of the English Working Class*, Harmondsworth, Penguin, 1972

Toye, J., *Dilemmas of Development*, Oxford, Blackwell, 1987

Turner, G., *British Cultural Studies*, London, Allen and Unwin, 1990

Wallace, W., *The Transformation of Western Europe*, London, Pinter, 1990

Winch, P., *The Idea of a Social Science and its Relation to Philosophy*, London, Routledge, 1958

Wistrich, E., *After 1992: The United States of Europe*, London, Routledge, 1989

Williams, B., *Morality*, Harmondsworth, Penguin, 1972

Williams, R., *The Long Revolution*, London, Chatto, 1961

Williams, R., 'Base and Superstructure in Marxist Cultural Theory' in *New Left Review 82*, 1972

Williams, R., *Keywords*, London, Fontana, 1976

Wolf, J., *The Social Production of Art*, London, Macmillan, 1981
Wright, P., *On Living in an Old Country*, London, Verso, 1985

Index